Scriptwriting
for the
Audio-Visual Media

Radio
Films
Television
Filmstrips
Slidefilms
Multimedia

Scriptwriting for the Audio-Visual Media

Robert Edmonds
Columbia College, Chicago

Second Edition

TEACHERS COLLEGE PRESS

Teachers College, Columbia University
New York and London

Published by Teachers College Press, 1234 Amsterdam Avenue,
New York, N.Y. 10027

Library of Congress Cataloging in Publication Data

Edmonds, Robert.
  Scriptwriting for the audio-visual media.

  Includes index.
  1. Broadcasting—Authorship. 2. Moving-picture authorship.
3. Audio-visual materials—Authorship. I. Title.
PN1990.9.A88E35 1984   808.2   83-24335

ISBN 0-8077-2753-9

Manufactured in the United States of America

89 88 87 86 85 84 1 2 3 4 5 6

This book is lovingly for my sons, Ellis and Barney, and my daughter-in-law, Julie, all of whom, it happens, are engaged in the production and utilization of audio-visuals.

Contents

Acknowledgments

While I must accept the responsibility of having written some of the examples of scripts appearing in the following pages, others have been written by writers whom I am fortunate to count among my friends. The first two film script excerpts, *The Man Who Died Twice* by Lillian Wilentz and the adaptation of *An Enemy of The People* by Lewis Jacobs, appeared in a little booklet prepared by Mr. Jacobs as long ago as 1934. It was called *Film Writing Forms* and was published by Gotham Book Mart in New York in that year. Lewis Jacobs is now internationally famous as a film historian, but in those days he was a screenwriter in Hollywood. I want to express my sincere thanks to him and to Lillian Wilentz for permission to reprint their work here.

A young man who was once my student went on to become a professional film-maker. As part of his earlier work he made a series of films about film-making for Wesley Greene, the President of International Film Bureau, Inc., of Chicago. Wesley Greene has been a valued friend for a great many years, ever since we both worked for John Grierson at the then-very-young National Film Board of Canada. He was lucky to have Henry Cheharbakhshi working for him, and Henry was fortunate to find an employer as soon as he graduated from my classes. I thank them both for permission to reprint the script for *A Film About Film Editing*. This will be useful for potential screenwriters because they can learn something about film editing while they read a fairly classic kind of pedagogic film script. Further, the film itself is available, for rent or for sale, from International Film Bureau, Inc., and thus it is possible to see the film while reading the script. This is a resource of inestimable value.

Tom Daly and I have been friends since we attended the same school. He is an Executive Producer at the National Film Board of Canada, and has been kind enough to grant permission on behalf of the Film Board for my inclusion of portions of the script of *Fighting Ships*, which I wrote during the Second World War in 1942. I wish to express my deep thanks to him. The film was produced and directed by the late Graham MacInnes, with whom I worked on a number of projects before and after this film.

A friend valued for a score of years is Ernest Lukas of Lukas Film Productions, Inc., of Chicago. We have been colleagues and have even directed on adjoining stages. Through his good offices I met Terry Baker, an affable, talented, busy art director who provided the storyboards.

My son Bernard has written three scripts from which I have reprinted excerpts. My sincere thanks to him for *Fifty-Seventh Street,* and to him and to Michael J. Enzer, President of Saxton Communications Group, Ltd., where Barney was Director of Audio-Visual Services, for *LASH: The Ships for All Cargoes* and for *It Happened on Long Island.*

Through my colleague, Phil Ruskin, I was led to two CBS scripts, and I want to express my deep gratitude to Loring Mandel for his moving teleplay *Do Not Go Gentle into That Good Night* and to Gary Rowe, the Church Federation of Greater Chicago and WBBM-TV (CBS, Chicago) for the script from *Different Drummers.* Finally my thanks go to Cathleen Inglehart, Brand Advertising, Inc:, and Plywood Minnesota for scripts for their commercials. Al Parker, who brought them to my attention, is also a colleague at my College.

My wife, Shirley, is always encouraging and supportive, always a perceptive and discerning critic, always patient even when I don't listen; and she had the fortitude to type this manuscript in its final form. To no one am I more grateful than I am to her.

Every program that is presented in any of the media discussed in this book is collectively made, and it is clear that this volume is also the result of collective capabilities. Its virtues lie in the materials written by others; whatever faults are to be found in the remainder I can only claim as my own.

When it was decided to prepare a second, revised edition of this book additional scripts had to be obtained. Several writers were more than kind in permitting the use of their scripts. The two radio documentary scripts were provided by Charles Potter, a well-known and greatly experienced and skilled writer. His two scripts were for productions sponsored by various organizations that are named in the closing credits in the scripts themselves. To Mr. Potter and the sponsoring organizations I give my sincere gratitude.

James Martin is my friend and colleague. He is the director of the Southeast Chicago Historical Project, a project made in conjunction with Columbia College, Chicago, and financed by the National Endowment for the Humanities. My thanks go to Jim, to Columbia College, and to the NEH for the four stages of the Southeast Chicago Historical Project script for the film *Wrapped in Steel.*

Jerry Blumenthal and Gordon Quinn of Kartemquin Films, Ltd., made the documentary *The Last Pullman Car* with Public Broadcasting as the sponsor. I am grateful to them and to Public Broadcasting for the use of their script material.

Once again I want to thank my son Bernard Edmonds for permitting the use of portions of his script for Eqvalan and Michael J. Enzer, President of Saxton Communications Group, Ltd., who undertook the script for Ron Sheward, Division of Marketing Communications for

MSD AGVET, a division of Merck & Co., Inc., to whom I also express my gratitude. My thanks go to Aaron Gordon and Paul Chapman of AGS&R Communications, as well as to their clients, for allowing me to use the scripts *Creativity . . . the Key to Life* and *Meeting To-morrow's Challenges Today.*

Columbia College, Chicago, through Albert Gall, the Administrative Dean, gave me permission to quote from a published conversation with Edward Adler, and for this I am most grateful.

The narration for *The River* was commissioned by the U.S. Farm Security Administration. As such, the narration is in public domain, but I extend my gratitude to Pare Lorentz for having written it.

Introduction

Every student who goes through the present school system emerges with the idea that a playscript is something to be read. After all, very few of them ever have the opportunity to see a real live theatrical production. Teachers and students discuss playscripts as literature, forgetting entirely—if the thought ever occurred to them—that they are not being involved in a theatrical experience in any way. They are studying literature.

Theatre is something different: it is a performance that takes place in front of an audience, usually, but not always, on a stage. When one is a member of the audience at a theatrical performance, one never gives thought to the script. One never analyses it as literature. One comments on the theatrical experience. But that is not so strange. How many music lovers who are not trained musicians can get a musical experience from reading a musical score? Why, then, should we expect to get a theatrical experience from reading a play?

In the same way, a script for radio or film or television is an element of a total radio or film or television production. This is not to say that a play or a script may not be treated as literature. On the contrary, if scripts have literary quality, who would not treat them as literature? We must only remember that they were not written for that purpose. Shakespeare wrote because he couldn't find any plays that he thought were good enough to present. That his plays have become perhaps the cornerstone of English literature is a bonus that to him would have been totally unexpected and perhaps even unthinkable. His knowledge and skill as a manager—which in those days also meant director—gave him the confidence to write better plays, but he never invented a story, as almost everyone knows. He relied on his knowledge of theatre to write better plays that would make better theatre. His knowledge of his audience and his ability to gauge their responses are indicated by the comment of a contemporary critic, Drummond of Hawthornden, who said that he "wrote to tickle the ears of the groundlings." He meant that Shakespeare wrote to catch the fancy of the ordinary, everyday theatre-goer. That he did not write to be read is demonstrated by the criticism of Ben Jonson who complained that Shakespeare had "little Latin and less Greek" and was, therefore, to be considered an illiterate.

For the purposes of this volume, then, a script, all scripts, will be treated as elements of production, documents to be read by trained production-type people in one or another of the media—radio, film, or television. If your script also becomes literature at some time in the future, it will be a gain for everyone, just as Shakespeare's plays benefited all the world after their use to him had ceased.

To state the matter more clearly, a script is a kind of rough blueprint for a production. It is the "thing," the essential "what" of a radio show, or a film, or a TV presentation. All the technical people, those who are trained in all the crafts of their medium, take this *what* and, using their skills and experience, wrap it in all the dressing, using sound, color, actors, light, and recording and presentational equipment. This "dressing" is *how* a production is presented. To repeat, the script is really the *what*, and the *how* is the manner in which the production is presented.

Obviously, if a writer of a script wants to give the trained technical people—including actors and director—the material for a rich or slick production, for a competent or skillful presentation, he or she ought to know something about the medium for which he or she is writing. This little book will deal with these aspects of the job; it will not address itself to story development or dramatic line, to characterization or structure. I take it for granted that the art of storytelling is not very different from one medium to the next. What is different is the medium itself. It is the differences between the media that will be our concern. We shall seek to find out how to make use of the potentials of each medium, while respecting its limits, so that the script, which is a kind of instruction book for the producer and the director and the skilled artistic technical people, will make it possible for all involved to make the most creative use of the medium and therefore the most attractive or persuasive or moving presentation.

There are many schools that offer instruction in these matters. The instruction is not necessarily similar in each institution, nor should it be. Too often, however, it is offered by people who have not had to write for a living. Their instruction, therefore, was also learned from schools or books. As a professor myself I am not downgrading the instructional process, but I am saying, "Beware the books and the instructors that appear to repeat each other's erroneous instructions." What you will find in this book was not learned in school nor from other instructors, mainly because when I was learning the crafts of these kinds of writing, there weren't any such schools nor were there any such books. Therefore, I shall be presenting to you what I have learned as a writer, director, producer, narrator, and announcer in radio, and as a writer, producer, director, cameraman, and film editor for films and TV. I have since taught the crafts of writing for these media in college, and I have thus had the opportunity of finding out why I wrote the way I did. I had to find out in order to tell students, and the telling also clarified a lot of things for me as well.

Just as my background in these *métiers* is professional, so I assume your interest is to become a professional as well. For me, the definition of a professional is "one who earns his living at it"—or, at least, continues to make a relatively consistent income from the practice of a craft. I shall, therefore, also discuss just how writing for any of these media can be sold, what basic markets remain fairly constant, and how to get jobs in the several industries. Just as in newspaper writing or magazine writing, there are some jobs that are filled by professionals, and it is good to know how people come to sit behind those desks.

In this regard, we must recognize that being professional doesn't necessarily mean being good at it, if you are rendering a judgment of artistic merit. Being professional simply means being able to make consistent sales of one's output. The "art-ness" of one's work comes *after* being professional. The great advantage of being professional—even when the stuff one sells isn't very good, or, for that matter, isn't what one might want to write—is the imposed discipline of *writing every day.* Unless your control of your tools and your materials is first class, you won't write any art works, anyway. When you do have complete control of your tools and your materials, you will be, perhaps, a virtuoso. Don't be frightened by that word; virtuosity is the minimum requirement demanded by the audience of any art work. Think about that. Virtuosity isn't a substitute for "art-ness," it is the means by which an art work maker brings it off!

1

Radio

Because radio seems to have gone out of fashion under the ubiquitous pressure of television, we tend to think that it is one of the older media. Actually, radio began to become a commercial success during the 1920s, a quarter of a century after movies began. Even though radio isn't historically older than films, I'll start our explorations here because radio uses only one tool—the broadcasting of sound. There is no light nor color nor pictures of any kind—only sound. This is the overriding consideration. Everything done in radio must be done with sound. It is the use of sound that can create excitement, dramatic emotion, reverie, nostalgia, or whatever other kind of response writers seek. The various kinds of sound are their tools. What are they? They are: voices, music, sound effects—and *silence*.

It is important to understand how sound works on listeners, because by understanding something of this phenomenon, you can use the medium a great deal better.

Words are symbols of things, actions, ideas, or feelings. They develop their meanings because many people agree on the generalities they denote. Since people's experiences of "table" cannot be identical because not all tables are identical, the word "table" is a generalization of all tables each of us has known. Since no two people can have identical experiences, even of the same things, the meanings of words are also consensuses of our mutual or several experiences. Because words are generalizations, as well as being consensuses, they are all approximations, every one of them. When we need to try to make a meaning more and more exact, more and more specific, we add further color or further distinction to the word by the use of modifiers—adjectives, adverbs, phrases, similes, and so on. Each of the modifiers, of course, is also a generalization and can only have meaning in terms of (reader or listener) personal experience. Writers are simply refining the approximation in a very real sense.

For example, the word "box" means something to each of us. It has more or less rigid sides and is hollow so that it can contain something. But we don't know its size, color, material, purpose, method of closure, degree of permanence, nor a host of other attributes. We refine our meaning by modifiers, such as large (but still an inexact measure), black (or some other color), metal (still inexact), can be locked (with a

1

key or a padlock?), lined (with plastic foam or with satin?), water-proofed (inside or externally?), and so on. The addition of each modifier makes the meaning more and more specific because each modifier reduces the approximation. The area that remains unreduced by modifiers is the area in which each of us finds special personal meaning and is part of the reason that each of us is able to come to our own estimation of the meaning of the work in which the word is used, an estimation that is probably different from anyone else's.

The method of obtaining meaning from words through their generating a recall of past experience is called *association*. The word "box" has meaning because of past experience with "box-ness"; the word "box" causes us to associate with past experience of "box-ness," to recall boxes we have known. The same process is prompted by the use of each modifier. Thus, the effect each word has arises out of the associations with our past experiences that the word generates within us.

If you recognize this process, then you have learned a great deal of the background necessary for what you must do when you write. You must use words that, from your experience, you know will most likely generate the kinds of associations in your audience that you want them to have.

Words have to be used with some considerable care for another reason also. In contrast with the printed word, where a sentence or a paragraph can be read over again if it is not understood, there is no such opportunity in radio. Whatever a writer causes to be said, has to be understood the first time it is heard. There is no chance for repetition, no opportunity to go over it again to make sure that the listener understood it clearly. This means that writers must use sentences of relatively simple construction because sentences that are complicated, that have many modifying clauses or conditional clauses, which may leave a certain open-endedness, just can't be retained in the mind long enough to be clearly understood. (The foregoing sentence was purposely written in a non-radio way. On the air it would be relatively incomprehensible, I fear.)

A further elaboration of the last point is this. Do not write for the eye but for the ear, or, if you prefer, the tongue. Write for the *sound* of what you want to be said. Write with somebody's *voice and speech pattern in your head as you write*. If what you write cannot be spoken easily within this speech pattern, the chances are that it cannot easily be understood by the listener. My own writing, even in this book for example, is such that I can read it aloud comfortably; not just with ease, not because I know what I mean to say, but *comfortably* because it is the way I would speak if I were talking it myself.

Spot Announcements

A spot announcement is an announcement that is broadcast at certain breaks in radio programs or in the periods between programs.

Periods between programs are called *station breaks* because at such times the broadcasting station must identify itself by announcing its *call letters*, that is, its identification, such as WQXR or WBBM. Just as in television, announcements are broadcast on radio to advertise products or services or for less commercial purposes such as public service announcements ("Support the college of your choice," "Stop smoking," "Drive safely," and all manner of announcements of church and community activities, to name just a portion of the possible potpourri).

To be most effective, radio spots incorporate the suggestions made earlier. However, since the duration of each spot is of considerable moment (a sponsor pays the station more to broadcast a one-minute spot than he does for a 20-second spot), remember that you can't write an equal number of words for all spots—unless they are to have equal duration or running-time. As a good rule of thumb, allow about 100 words for a minute of vocal delivery. If you are always writing for the same voices, you will be able to become more accurate in this kind of estimate by studying the modes of delivery of those who are reading your material. You may well find that one announcer can read 115 words in the same time it takes another announcer to read 88. This is simply a reflection of personal speaking styles, and you will do well to write differently for each such style.

What does a radio spot look like? Let's invent one.

ANNOUNCER: Christmas cakes are here at Windsor's, State and Main. Real Christmas cakes, fresh from England, filled with fruits and nuts. They're made with sugar and cinnamon, almonds and pecans, candied cherries, orange peel and pineapple, currants and raisins . . . all the good things of an old-fashioned Christmas. Each delicious Christmas cake is packed in a gaily decorated metal box that you'll want to keep to remember a happy holiday. In one pound, two pound, and three pound sizes, real imported English Christmas cakes just where you'd expect to find them . . . at Windsor's, State and Main. Get your Merry Christmas cakes at Windsor's.

Because it is not possible to cast one's eyes back over the advertisement, we must make sure that the audience hears what is important more than once. In this spot announcement Christmas cakes are mentioned four times, Christmas five times, and Windsor's three times, and Windsor's location is given twice. The rest of the spot is written to provide some kind of appetizing reason for the listener to come and buy.

If one were to reduce the length of the spot from one minute to 30 seconds, it might look like this:

ANNOUNCER: Christmas cakes are here at Windsor's, State and Main. Real English Christmas cakes, filled with luscious fruits and nuts and all the rich aromas that make us think of Christmas. In one pound, two pound, and three pound sizes, these delicious imported English Christmas cakes are now at Windsor's, State and Main.

In a time only half as long as the first spot, there cannot be as much repetition, of course, but the important bits of information have been repeated. Note, too, that, while the grammar isn't strictly correct in either spot, it does conform with a common, comfortable, expected way of speaking.

There is one further hidden repetition, and that is in the company's name. If Windsor's is a regular advertiser, the writer might want to make sure that he or she always, or almost always, refers to it as "Windsor's, State and Main." This kind of repetition, linking name and location, becomes a valuable mnemonic, a kind of subliminal stimulus to silent recall on the part of listeners.

The shortest spot is not more than 10 seconds in running time and because that allows for very little more than the use of the name of the advertiser, such a spot is often called an *I.D.*, that is, an identification. For many years the Bulova Watch Company used to buy time on almost every radio station in which the time of day could be announced, especially during morning and evening rush hours. "It is now 8:17 BULOVA watch time." "Bulova watch time" became the mnemonic phrase.

If the spots are written at the radio station, they will be written in what is called the continuity department. This may be a very tiny department consisting of only one person, or, perhaps just a part-time person, or it may be a large department consisting of a number of writers. Many spots, however, are not written in the radio station but are supplied by advertising agencies, where they are written in the copy department.

Continuity

Continuity includes a number of kinds of writing, not least important of which are those that introduce each program and each element within it, as well, probably, as commentary on the material as it is being broadcast. As in all writing, you cannot afford to lose sight of the audience for whom you are writing. The radio audience, except in very unusual circumstances, is NOT a mass audience, even though your broadcast may be heard by millions of listeners. This apparent paradox is simply explained. No matter how many thousands of people are listening, they are not congregated together. On the contrary, they are listening in very small groups indeed, little groups of people ranging in number from one to several. The audience is like a multicellular body, in which each cell may have three, four, or five members at most, and in which each cell is independent of, and isolated from, yet interrelated with, all the others. This means that the mass kinds of responsiveness that occur in audiences of vast numbers all in the same hall don't occur for radio. The socializing effect of many neighbors upon listeners' responses is absent.

This sets out certain basic parameters for the expression of the messages. Whatever those messages may be, it is clear that they must be stated in terms that would be appropriate for addressing an individual or a small group of individuals in the living room of an ordinary home. The approach ought not to be that which might be suitable for large public meetings, for neither the platform style nor the style of a master of ceremonies in a night club is suitable for this more intimate kind of audience. Even when a studio audience is present, the presentation of a show must be for the multitudes of listening groups, not for the few in the studio. It is, after all, those multitudes of groups for which a program is primarily produced.

In discussing a manner of presentation that would be appropriate for a small group of people in the living room of an ordinary home, I also must emphasize that the language must conform to the manner of presentation—it must neither be the kind that would be suitable only in the home of totally uneducated people nor the language one might expect to hear in an academic think-tank. It should avoid being so colloquial as to degenerate into the language of the street, just as it should avoid being so precise as to be pedantic.

When you are writing continuity of any kind, use language that a well-educated person of broad attitudes and views might be expected to use when addressing any sort of group. Don't use long words for the sake of displaying learning. Remember the problems of the listeners: they can't ask the speaker, "What did you say?" As a basic general rule, a short word is preferable to a long one. By the same token, don't use a foreign word if an English word will serve the purpose. (You might want to read William Wordsworth, even though he wrote long before radio was invented.) By extension, this also means that you should try to avoid using technical words, unless you are absolutely sure that your listeners will know their meaning. If you achieve simplicity and directness, you probably will never run the risk of offending either the highbrow or the low-brow.

Once again, remember to *write for the ear*, not for the eye. Read *aloud* everything you have written and reconsider your writing in the light of what you hear. Ask yourself some direct questions about what you have written and what you have read aloud. Are the word groups consistent with easy breathing for the reader? Do the word stresses fall conveniently and meaningfully? Are the rhythms comfortable?

Just a word about clichés and exaggerations. Continuity written for musical programs cannot make good programs, good music, or good performers better by *saying* they are better, any more than your continuity can turn bad programs, bad music, or bad performers into good ones. Remember, you can't make a silk purse from a sow's ear! You don't need to use words like genius, magnificent, superb or famous when you are writing about Beethoven, or Toscanini, or Horowitz. Such words are clearly unnecessary. You don't need to write, "The Minute Waltz—a brilliant piece of musical writing from the pen of Frederic

Chopin." All that needs to be said is, "The Minute Waltz by Frederic Chopin." Adoration as expressed in your writing will detract from, instead of add anything to, a dignified statement of plain fact.

Many announcers, especially those who are new to radio announcing (and you must remember that it will be announcers who read your continuity on the air—if anybody does) don't like to read, preferring instead to ad lib, that is, to make up what they say as they go along, to improvise. Inexperience opens the way to another pitfall, too, and it is a pitfall that can be disastrous for beginning writers. Habits of speech, strong patterns, often lead to repetitive use of cliché phrases and overwriting. Performers play an instrument or sing a song: they do not *render* it (one does that with a piece of fat!) nor do they *give a rendition*. They simply *sing* or *play*. In the same way, it is only in special circumstances, where the meaning is really appropriate, that you need to write that an artist *interprets* or *gives an interpretation*.

Redundancy is a very common fault. "We bring you *at this time*" is a florid way of speaking. If the nature of time is indeed important, you only need to say *now* or *next*. *Listen* is perfectly good language; you don't need to say *listen in*. You don't need to say that something was written *by the pen of* or came *from the pen of* so-and-so. One might equally say, "Music from the horn of Louis Armstrong" or, more awkwardly, "From the organ of E. Power Biggs." Keep it simple. Keep it short. Remember that continuity is almost never the star of the show. When it is, then you can take some liberties with the other performers and their relationship to the audience. Meanwhile, make sure that you stay out of the limelight. Don't draw attention to yourself by bad writing.

Talks

One of the easiest ways of breaking into radio, strangely enough, is with talks. Later on in chapter 8 I'll discuss the whole problem of how to get a job writing for the different broadcast media, or, if not a job, how to sell your writing. Right now, let's address ourselves to talks. Talks can frequently not only be written by you, but actually delivered by you as the talker, the broadcaster.

When speakers are talking on the radio, they have only sound to work with. All the things people are used to relying on to help them interpret a speaker's meaning when they are face to face are missing. They do not have the benefit of gestures or facial movements, so the writing must provide all the means for conveying meanings and feelings by words alone and the expression of those words. The dramatist knows how to write dialogue so that it sounds like what it is, speech between people. The short sentences, the colloquialisms, the various personal tricks of speech that typify everyday conversation are just as appropriate to the broadcast monologue. Too often talks writers frame their sentences as though they were to be read instead of to be spoken; they have the structure and the words that might conform to literary or scientific conventions. Unfortunately, these conventions govern writing that is meant for the eye. Almost always, the tongue simply can't master them.

Not only must the sequence of words be such that a speaker can say them comfortably and easily, but the writing must be sufficiently subjective so that evidences of the personality of the speaker lie within them. A speaker's own feelings, interests, anticipations, and attitudes must lie in the words themselves, so that he can take them off paper and broadcast them to an audience.

A good many years ago, Christopher V. Salmon of the Talks Department of the British Broadcasting Corporation in London, England, wrote the following: "I remember a story written for broadcasting which dealt with the revolution in Russia. It opened with a description of a pile of dead bodies which lay at the mouth of a bridge on which machine guns had played. The road was not perfectly alone with its dead. There was a stir in the heap of the dead and something alive, which the onlooker presently saw was a wounded man, was heaving itself out of the pile. This was a grim beginning but not necessarily, I told the author, unfit for broadcasting. It required, I told him, some relation to the mood of the onlooker. This the author resisted. There is only one way, he said, a simple description of the event, *chose vue* and leave it at that! Impressions, he said, would soften the scene disagreeably and turn something in black-and-white into a stinking corpse. For the eye he was right, of course, but for the ear he was wrong. The story was going to hang on the tones of a voice, and a voice that is neutral when it talks of immediate horrors sounds inhuman. Give me pity or revulsion or fear, I said, or even, if your onlooker belongs to the guns, satisfaction, but some feeling I must have if the story itself is not to horrify."[*]

Salmon continued: "The ear likes the give and take of as many dimensions as you can afford and an invitation held out to approach the speaker, as it were, as well as to listen to him. This concerns matter and mood and there's a lot to be said besides about surface form. Appeal to the eye, varying of course with the skill of the reader, envisages at once not only many words, but several lines running often to as much as half a page. The eye's focus of attention is a ring of words, not more, perhaps, than six or eight, but these have an entourage which includes, let us say, some fifty words, of which the eye is at least imperfectly aware as it pushes to its horizon backwards and forwards across the page. But the voice strings its words on a line singly, one after another, and the sound of each dies with the sound of another. The ear hears one at a time, retains a couple perhaps and expects two or three more. Curi-

[*]*Radiodiffusion*, May 1938.

ously enough, if it can anticipate more than two or three it goes to sleep, for the voice is then talking in clichés and may be presumed to have nothing to say. The skillful broadcaster can enlarge his canvas a little by subtle rhythms and patterns both of word and argument. But the finest skill here can only extend memory or expectation by a word or two, and compared with the scope of the eye, the speaker's is small. The more intricate his subject the harder his task! He must work deftly and always with economy. He must use short sentences, active verbs and a masculine style. He must present his arguments with the strongest possible definition and put forward his concepts *au pair,* that is to say, one to a word. The quicker the sentence and the barer the style the better. . . ."

The last couple of lines of that quotation emphasize one further point that has, perhaps, been taken for granted. It is simply this: no matter how good the style, no matter how much control of the techniques of the medium, you still have to *have something to say!*

Drama

In the United States, radio drama seemed to have disappeared for a number of years, submerged by the almost sudden ubiquity of television just after 1950. Nowadays it shows some small signs of coming again to the surface. The Columbia Broadcasting System has reintroduced a series of mystery plays (although the plays themselves are new and not just resuscitated). A number of FM radio stations appear to use radio dramas from the Canadian Broadcasting Corporation, which, like the British Broadcasting Corporation and the Australian Broadcasting Company, continues to broadcast radio dramas. Presumably the Canadian shows are selected because the accents are at less variance with American English than are the British and Australian, and because of geographic proximity, the elements of life that engage Canadians are probably not so dissimilar either.

Radio drama is not dead in most countries that enjoy government radio networks—and in the three countries mentioned, the government networks exist side by side with private networks and stations—as is evidenced by the plays that have been written for this medium. It is forgotten, if it ever had been generally known, that Archibald Mac-Leish's *J. B.* was originally written for B.B.C. radio. It later became a successful theatre play. Robert Bolt's *A Man for All Seasons* was also written originally for radio before its successes on the stage and screen.

During the nineteen thirties radio really came to its maturity in the United States, and there was a great deal of radio drama to be heard. Daytime radio drama provided several hours a day of serial programs, usually in fifteen-minute episodes. These were addressed to housewives as they did their chores and, since radio and now television in the

United States are funded by income from advertisers, each of these serials had its own advertiser, called sponsor. Because of the nature of the
audience, most frequently sponsors for these programs were laundry
and household soaps and detergents, and so these day-time serial
dramas became known as *soap operas*. (In motion pictures the multi-
plicity of simple, even simplistic, low-budget films dealing with cowboys
and Indians became known as horse operas. Republic Pictures obtained its financial stability from making a host of low-budget horse
operas.)

The nature of the soap opera, as might be expected, was determined
by its intended audience and their observed listening patterns. Mother-
housewife was doing her work, cleaning, washing dishes, ironing, rest-
ing after a busy morning or during a coffee break. Her radio was
turned on, and her attention was not undivided. When she heard the
sound of Debussy's "Clair de Lune," however, she knew that her program, "Oxydol's Own Ma Perkins," was about to come on the air. She
could focus more of her attention on what she was to listen to, at least
she could give it all the attention she didn't need for whatever chore she
was doing. After the introductory theme music, the announcer summarized the last several episodes, before introducing the day's bit of
action. The summary was necessary because it could not be expected
that mother-housekeeper could listen every single day, five days in a
row each week. Also if the story became totally unfamiliar because of
some necessary suspension of listening due to some other more pressing
duties, if she lost track of the story and became unfamiliar with it,
then the sponsor would probably lose a listener. If he lost a listener, she
would not listen each day to his advertising message; indeed, she might
find another program, sponsored by a competitor, more attractive. Not
only did the announcer summarize each day quite a bit of what had
happened before, but the action itself developed so slowly that there
could not possibly be any chance of missing anything important. I think
my memory serves me correctly when I recall that Big Sister (in the
show of the same name) was in labor for about six weeks—on the air,
you understand!

While superficially there appeared to be a good variety of stories, they
all seemed, on closer analysis, to stem from three basic ideas: *1)* Don't
worry! You, too, can find a lover at 40! *2)* You think you have troubles?
Just listen to this! *3)* You have a crazy mother-in-law? Just listen to this
one! (It is clear that type three is really a special form of type two!)

Each segment was 15 minutes in length and was broadcast five
days a week, endlessly. But, a 15-minute segment such as that of a soap
opera did not require 15 minutes of dramatic material. You must remember there was the opening summary and an opening commercial
announcement, then a middle commercial announcement, then a closing teaser announcement to whet the appetite for the next episode, and
the closing commercial. All this, within the length of a 15-minute segment, which is, in fact, only 14 minutes and 40 seconds (to allow time

for the station break) left about nine or nine and a half minutes of dramatic material to be heard. The same kind of abbreviation takes place in all radio and television programs because the only financial subsidy that is available to commercial stations comes from sponsors, and they need time for their messages. (Even in non-commercial broadcasting, there are announcements of acknowledgement of grants that have been made by corporations or foundations.)

Even if I describe soap operas with some degree of mock seriousness, the shows attracted multitudes of faithful listeners, and they employed stables of writers. Each of the authors whose names may have been given broadcast credit did, in fact, more often than not, provide only the plot outline. Each show had a stable of at least four or five other writers who wrote the daily episodes, for nobody could turn out all by himself the sheer volume that was needed. One of the unfortunate, although moderately well-paid, results of this practice was the total submergence of any individuality in the members of the stable. Each had to write dialogue that sounded just like the dialogue that was being written by colleagues.

Because of the meandering plot of the soap opera and because it could not leave its listeners behind, each episode was concerned with action that remained essentially unresolved. Thus it was a kind of cliff-hanger. But the lack of resolution was unlike the classic cliff-hanger in that what was unresolved was not necessarily a climactic conflict. It might easily be simply an unresolved anticipation or anxiety. The lack of resolution served as a teaser to further bind the audience to the show.

It must be emphasized that the actors in these old day-time serials were usually superb. They were picked for voice quality, of course. It was necessary that the quality of voice have within it some quality consonant with the character being portrayed. (Sometimes in a show that had unusual longevity, there was a succession of actors or actresses for a given role, some of whom might play the part for a year or two or three and then were followed by someone else.) But quality of voice was not enough: the performer had to be good. Scripts were never available much in advance. Actors received their scripts, most of the time, the same day as the performance; rehearsed the show perhaps three times without sound effects and once, at most twice, with sound effects; and then, ON THE AIR. I have directed such serials, and I can report the great pleasure it is to work with such real professionals. They needed little instruction and, when direction was given, were intelligent in its application or modification. They knew all the modes of using the microphone and in controlling voice volume and quality.

Writers, too, must have some knowledge of the use of the microphone if they are to be able to give any indication of stage directions to the director of the show. Let's see what they can know without being actors or directors themselves.

A writer's first job, of course, is to learn how to hear. If he can't hear, how can he make any suggestions concerning acoustic values? After all, microphones are simply electronic ears that can be made very selective. They can select not only what person or object they hear (for example a parabolic mike at a baseball game even when it is mounted on top of the grand stand can pick out the sound of the bat hitting the ball) but they can also be used to emphasize certain frequency ranges. (Frequency ranges are what radio people call the ranges of pitch. High pitched sounds are in high frequency ranges; low pitched notes are in the low frequencies.) Unless you can hear such differences, the choice of microphones can't possibly be of interest to you.

But writers should know at least a few things so they can indicate qualities they wish to be incorporated in their presentations. The normal way to speak into a microphone is to stand about eight inches away from it and to speak normally. Radio actors *do* stand; they almost never sit in front of a microphone unless they are disabled. Standing allows for free body movement akin to the body movement of a violinist. It doesn't improve the sound, but it does give a performer the opportunity of fuller kinesthetic participation.

When louder volume than normal is needed, actors lean back from the mike as they speak more loudly so that the mechanical impact of the air waves is reduced. The sense of loudness remains. For very intimate sounds, actors move very close to the mike and speak at a much lower volume level. It will sound as though they are speaking into your ear. Generally, a microphone will respond more emphatically to the lower frequencies of a voice if one talks *across* it instead of *into* it. If you are a couple of feet away—off mike—there will be a kind of hollow sound that does imply distance.

A room in which there is considerable resonance is said to be *live;* one in which there is no resonance is called a *dead* room. Wherever radio drama is important, studios are built so that both qualities are present in one room. They are called *live-end/dead-end studios*, and, as their name indicates, one end is live and the other is dead. The reason is that certain locales are best indicated by a change of acoustics. A bathroom, for example, is live; that's why some of us like to sing there. The resonance, the life, seems to improve the sound of our singing. A basement is even more resonant. The outdoors has no resonance for there are no walls to bounce any sound back to our ears. Occasionally, however, we use the wrong acoustic because it indicates a better feeling for what we want. If we are outdoors (in the story's locale, of course) on a very cold day, after a heavy snow, we might want to use a bright, live sound to give the feeling of the brittle quality of the cold, even though we know that a blanket of fresh snow will damp any possible resonance.

All these qualities can be indicated by writers if they have the capability of hearing them and discriminating them. As experience increases and familiarity with the broadcasting techniques themselves increases, they can call for other effects if they need them. The operator in the radio station can increase the reverberation by the use of an *echo chamber* or by electronic means. This can not only increase the degree of resonance but it can also control the time delay between the sound and its reverberation. The operator can also give an actor a *filter mike*, which makes the sound of the voice thin and reedy, like the old fashioned sound of voices on the telephone. This sound is still used for just such purposes, even though modern telephones don't distort the voice that much any more.

If a special kind of voice sound, or voice usage, will be essential to do what you want, then indicate it in your script. It is a kind of stage direction, and the more specific you are, the easier you make the director's job, and the closer your production will come to match your expectations.

In the old days of the 30s, sound effects were created live by specialists during the rehearsals and performances. Nowadays they are available already recorded, or if not available, they will be prepared and recorded for use during the presentation. You need not worry about sound effects so long as you can describe exactly what sound you want to be provided. There are vast libraries of sound effects, and most radio stations have a good collection even if, because of the temporary demise of radio drama, it may have been interred in the vaults somewhere.

Once again it must be emphasized that you have to have a good story, something to say. No amount of acoustic trickery or complicated sound effects can substitute for it. Nor can music, although if you have something to say, music, too, can very well help you to say it. Again, you must be specific about what kind of music you are hearing in your mind's ear for such-and-such a passage. If you do know a certain piece of music that you want, name it. If you don't know the name of a piece of music that would serve, but do know just what kind of quality that music should have, describe it carefully and clearly. But a word of vigorous caution is necessary. Unless you are relying on the specific association of a piece of music, such as "White Christmas" or "Jingle Bells," be careful of using any well-known piece of music. The musical *quality,* although it may be exactly what you are seeking, may be overcome by the general public association generated by it. It's better to find lesser known pieces.

On the assumption that you have found something to write about, how do you write a radio drama? Here is the opening of the first episode of a series of short radio dramas for children that I wrote some years ago. The series deals with stories told by musical instruments about great composers or performers they have known. The audience is clearly intended to be of elementary school age. After you've read it, I'll discuss certain aspects of it to draw attention to some of the more important things to take care of when you write a drama for radio.

I will NOT discuss how to develop a story. That, I believe, is the same whether it is told in novel or short story or radio or almost any other medium. The only modifiers are the medium itself and your familiarity with its potentialities and limitations.

The Music Shop

ANNOUNCER: Over on the other side of town, Mr. Diapason keeps his
music shop. In it are all kinds of musical instruments.
There you will find a piano, a violin, a saxophone, a guitar,
a clarinet, a cello . . . all kinds of musical instruments. Mr.
Diapason also has two children. There is Jack, who is eight   5
years old, and Jack's sister, Jill, who is six. One night, not
very long ago, when it was nearly midnight, Jack and Jill
quietly slipped out of their beds and quietly crept
downstairs to their father's shop. . . . (*The voice of the
narrator has slowly faded out*)

JACK: (*whispering*) Hssst . . . be quiet . . . don't make a noise. . . .   10

JILL: (*Her voice is trembling, also in a whisper*) I *am* being quiet
. . . (*pause*) . . . Jack . . . aren't you scared? . . . Isn't it . . .
awfully . . . dark on the stairs? . . . awfully dark!

JACK: (*Still in a whisper, but disdainfully*) You wouldn't expect
it to be light at midnight, would you, silly! . . . (*A foot   15
stumbles. Jill draws in her breath quickly*) Be careful, for
God's sake!!!!!

JILL: Jack . . . please! . . . don't swear . . . it's dangerous to
swear when it's so dark. . . . (*her voice trembles more and
more. . . .*)

JACK: (*He sounds like a protecting big brother*) What can hap-   20
pen to you when I am with you? . . . Here, give me your
hand. There. Take care . . . there are only three more steps.
. . . One . . . two . . . three! See? . . . We're there.

JILL: Can you find the door of the shop in the dark?

JACK: Sure. Here it is. (*The door squeaks . . . there is a very   25
short pause*)

JILL: The door squeaked! (*She is still whispering*)

JACK: (*Derisive*) I can't keep anything from you, can I? (*Pause*)

JILL: Especially if we don't want to wake Daddy! (*Pause*)

JACK: I don't hear anything moving. . . . That's good. . . . Let's go
in. . . . Be careful, the cello is just by the door! . . . Don't   30
trip over it! Now, let's hide behind the stove. (*A soft thud*)
Ouch!! I hit my head on that darned piano!!!

JILL: Don't you want to use your flashlight?

JACK: Are you crazy? Do you *really* think the instruments will
wake up and talk to each other if people are stupid enough   35
to turn lights on at midnight?

JILL: If you really want to know, I *never* heard that the instruments wake up and talk together, anyway!!!

JACK: Well, I told you, I dreamed it. Three times in a row. I
dreamed that the instruments woke up and told stories.   40
And if you dream something three times in a row . . . well,
it's bound to happen!

JILL: Well . . . you often dreamed that you got ten in spelling,
and what did you get? Four! So there!

JACK: You're mean. I never dreamed it three times in a row . . .   45
not in a row!

JILL: *(She snickers)* Sure . . . not when you got four the next day!

JACK: You really are mean. It isn't the same thing at all. Anyway, if you don't believe it, you can go upstairs and go back to bed.

JILL: Don't be angry. I believe you.
        (A soft sound in the background as if strings on a variety of instruments were vibrating in the wind.)

JILL: *(Whispering, timorous)* Did you hear that? That funny   5
        noise?

JACK: Yes, I heard it. . . . It's as though the tiles were shaking. . . .

JILL: Maybe it's the wind?

JACK: No . . . no . . . it isn't that . . . *(The strange sound continues. Jack speaks, overjoyed)* It's music!!!! It's beginning!

JILL: Jack . . . take my hand, please . . . I'm frightened. . . .   10
        (A clock begins to strike . . . slowly)

JACK: There! *(He counts the strokes.)* . . . three . . . four . . . five . . . remember . . . six . . . seven . . . after the last stroke . . . nine . . . ten . . . we must stay very quiet . . . *(in a very low voice)* . . . eleven . . . twelve.
        (The last stroke has sounded
            then
        there is a long sigh, as though from someone who is just waking up . . .
            then
        very gently, there are three ascending notes on the guitar, the last of which is sustained.
            then
        the voice of the guitar is heard yawning, but in descending notes. The guitar is awake.)

GUITAR: *(She speaks in a soft, slow voice)* Well, now . . . *(She*   15
        sneezes) Goodness, I must have caught cold last night. *(She sneezes again)* Oh, dear . . . my rheumatism! I always say, when you get to be two hundred and seventy-five years old, you begin to feel it! *(She sneezes again)* Is everybody still asleep? Am I the first to wake up? *(Another*   20
        sneeze).

PIANO: Bless you, Madame Guitar, bless you! But you are mistaken. I have been awake a long time already. I have heard the whole of your concert of sneezes.

GUITAR: *(chuckling)* You're making fun of me, aren't you, Master Piano! Wait until you get to be my age!   25

PIANO: Why, Madame Guitar. A lady so charming as you doesn't need to talk about her age. Look in the mirror! There isn't a young guitar anywhere who doesn't envy your looks and your marvellous voice.

GUITAR: *(laughing)* Dear Master Piano . . . you sound as if you are   30
        flirting with me!
        (A few sounds from the clarinet nearby)

There! Madame Clarinet is waking up now. She'll be jealous!

(Now the sounds of the saxophone, quietly, in a jazz rhythm).

PIANO: Listen . . . Mr. Saxophone is beginning to move about. The younger one is, the more one wants to sleep, I suppose. . . . *(A little louder)* Good morning, my young friend . . . I hope you slept well. 5

SAXOPHONE: *(His voice is energetic and happy)* Thank you very much, Mister Piano. Very well . . . as always. . . . And you? How are you?

PIANO: I don't really know. . . . I don't think I do feel very well, though . . . There is something that seems to weigh on my 10 stomach. We'll have to see what it is. . . .

(One hears an octave on the piano, but the seventh note is out of tune.)

Yes . . . there it is! *(The octave is repeated)* I must have indigestion!

SAXOPHONE: *(He breaks out laughing)* Hahahaha! . . . It's no wonder! . . . A piece of crayon is really indigestible for a piano! . . . Hahahah! 15

PIANO: *(Alarmed)* A piece of crayon, Mister Saxophone!!? Good heavens! Just imagine, a piece of crayon???? *(Three times in a row the bad note is repeated. The piano speaks while the notes are struck)* Oh, my poor stomach! . . .

SAXOPHONE: Yes, it's very clear. In your stomach there is the prettiest crayon you could imagine! *(laughing)* It's green . . . and 20 what's more, it's brand new!!!

PIANO: *(Sorrowfully)* But how do you know that?

SAXOPHONE: Because I saw with my own eyes that little devil Jack putting it inside you. *(He laughs again).*

JILL: *(In a low voice)* Jack . . . Your crayon! And you told me you 25 lost it!

JACK: Hush . . . Keep quiet!

PIANO: Jack? That doesn't seem likely. He's such a nice little boy. He wouldn't do a thing like that!

GUITAR: I'm sure he didn't do it on purpose. 30

JACK: *(In a low voice)* That's right! It might have slipped into the piano without my noticing it.

PIANO: It's frightening to think of that green horror lying in my stomach!

GUITAR: Don't get upset, my dear friend. When little Jack comes in tomorrow he'll notice that green crayon and relieve 35 you of it.

JACK: *(Whispering)* For sure!! *Poor piano!!* If I could, I'd take it out now!

JILL: Shhh! Don't move!

GUITAR: Tell me, my friends, do you know our new colleague, the 40 violin? He just arrived yesterday.

PIANO: No. I don't know him.

THE OTHER VOICES: Nor do I. I don't know him. I never saw him.

GUITAR: He's still sleeping. Maybe he made a long trip to get here
             and is still very tired.
PIANO: He must be someone who is very precious and famous. Did
             you see how careful Mister Diapason was when he was
             handling him? How carefully he unpacked him?   5
SAXOPHONE: (*laughing*) Of course, I saw it. There wasn't a place in the
             whole shop that was good enough for him. (*He imitates
             the voice of Mr. Diapason*) Near the window? Too cold.
             Near the radiator? Too hot. The big table? Too high. The
             small table? Too low. In the corner? Too dark. In the mid-   10
             dle of the shop? Too bright. Hahaha! He finally brought
             down that little antique table to put this extraordinary
             thing on! And under a glass cover!! (*he snorts*) It's
             ridiculous!!
GUITAR: Why is it ridiculous, Mr. Saxophone? You're always making
             fun of people who are dignified and respectable.   15
PIANO: (*Severely*) Yes, really, young man . . . you exaggerate!
SEVERAL VOICES: Yes. That's right. That's right. And especially when you are
             just a child of fifty-five years of age!

•   •   •

The first thing to draw to your attention is perhaps the least important. Note that the directions to the actors and to the musicians and
sound effects people are set off from the dialogue in italics. Since all
scripts for radio, TV, or film are originally typed and then reproduced in
the necessary number of copies (by photocopying, duplicating machine,
or photo-offset), stage directions are distinguished from speech by being
underlined or by being in capital letters. In scripts that are published in
book form, stage directions appear in italics as is usually the case with
the scripts in this volume. In any case, instructions that deal with the
manner of the performance appear differently from the actual words
that are to be spoken in the performance, simply so that the one is easily
distinguished from the other.

There is one further mechanical suggestion that you may wish to
follow. It isn't essential, but, as a director, I found it very handy. When
the scripts were typed, I always asked the typist to number the lines on
the right-hand margin of the page. It isn't necessary to number every
line—just every fifth line is sufficient.* This numbering makes it so
much easier for a director to identify a line or a speech when he or she
is making corrections or suggestions before or after rehearsals. It saves
a great deal of time that might otherwise be wasted hunting for the line or
speech. The numbers don't need to be cumulative; you can start numbering all over again on each page because the pages themselves are num-

---

*Stage directions do not count as lines to be numbered, only the lines of speech. If a line
carries over only one word, then that carry-over can be ignored. Because the pages are
numbered, the numbering of the lines can begin again on each page.

bered. Thus, it is easy to identify a line by saying, "just above line 20 on page 8, please." The actors will find the place immediately.

As I said at the outset, while it may be possible to consider any piece of writing as literature, a script, whether for theatre, radio, film or television, is really a blueprint for a production. Thus, anything that makes that blueprint more comprehensible is desirable. Even the idea of numbering lines is not new. You'll find it in many editions of long narrative poems, making it possible to find certain lines or quotations more quickly.

Much more important in the piece just reprinted are elements that are specifically *radio*.

The first thing to remember is that, because radio works only with sound, bits of action cannot be seen and therefore must be described. There are two methods of description—words themselves and sound effects.

Sound effects by themselves, however, often don't tell much. The sounds of a scuffle or a fight can only indicate that there is a scuffle or a fight. Listeners have no way of knowing who is winning and who is getting the worst of things. Even grunts and groans don't help much because the grunters and groaners are usually indistinguishable. Grunts and groans sound much the same, when they come from throats of the same sex, no matter who utters them. Such things, therefore, must be presented with care, recognizing that in radio we can only see in our mind's eye.

Although the narrator says in the opening announcement that the time is nearly midnight, the *feeling* of darkness and its effect on the characters is organic to the action. Thus, when the clock strikes twelve, it is no surprise but rather a continuation, a reinforcement, of the darkness and the midnight feeling.

Stumbling is identified by the one who stumbles; a striking of the head is identified by the character who does so. As each character performs an act, her or his feelings are expressed: the act isn't extraneous to the character. In the same way, an act has something to do with the story, too.

The above excerpt from a longer play is the first of a series, so its job is that of exposition, in addition to being interesting on its own. Thus the midnight-ness of the action is very important because that's the time the instruments come awake and talk together. It is for this reason that so much is made of the time of the action. Listeners can accept the fact the succeeding episodes will also take place at midnight. In the same way, the feelings of the children, feelings of anxiety and anticipation, are strongly emphasized.

Clearly part of the exposition is establishing the characters of the instruments. This is done not only by what they say to each other, but also by the way they speak and the sounds that accompany the speeches. By the end of this episode, listeners will have a friendly acquaintance with all those who have spoken. They will know the voices by their quality and manner, and they will expect that often, at least, the characters will be introduced by the sounds of the instruments who are speaking. This characterization is aided by the character description that is provided in the gossip of the participants themselves.

The piece that has been reproduced is not presented as a great piece of dramatic writing, but it does deserve study for its presentation of many aspects of writing for radio. It is commended to your attention for this reason.

Verse and Verse Drama

It is a very ancient practice among the peoples of Western European culture to tell stories in verse. The habit goes back to the stories of Homer and the sagas of the North. The stories were told aloud by storytellers, who found that they could remember the stories more easily if they were in verse. They also found they could greatly increase the effectiveness of their storytelling by the addition of music, which they played on some stringed instrument they carried with them as they wandered from court to court, from market to market, or from fair to fair. The use of musical accompaniment is an extension, perhaps, of the basic attraction of rhythmic motion and rhythmic sound. All these clearly were elements that directed the attention of the storytellers to the use of the music of language itself. This gave rise to the whole field of prosody, which deals with the music of language. When the music of language is used for presenting stories invested with imaginative imagery, it is called poetry. Thus the early narrative poems and story ballads were composed in poetry.

Telling stories in poetic form quite understandably extended beyond the feasting table and the market place, and poetry was used for telling stories on the stage. All great European literatures boast poetic dramas. The brightest star in the firmament of the English language is, of course, Shakespeare, but before him and for many years after, theatrical pieces were written in verse. One of the more recent examples is Maxwell Anderson's *Winterset.*

As we have learned, radio relies on sound and sound alone. The creative use of the sound of language is in utilizing all those elements found in poetry. Therefore, it is not at all surprising that poets and radio found each other to be most congenial colleagues. In the height of radio drama, great American poets, indeed poets who wrote in the English language no matter from which part of the culture they may have come, were attracted to the medium of radio. As I have said, Archibald MacLeish wrote radio dramas in verse; his *J.B.* was written for the British Broadcasting Corporation in the early 50s. He had been writing verse dramas long before that, however. *The Fall of the City* was produced on CBS' Columbia Workshop in 1937! Other American poets of first rank wrote directly for radio, poets such as Norman Corwin, Norman Rosten, and Marc Blitzstein. Even Stephen Vincent Benét's *Western Star* was adapted—with very slight changes—for radio as a memorial program on the first anniversary of his death; it was aired in March 1944.

Writing radio drama in verse, that is, writing radio drama and trying to use all the music and imagery of poetry, has some relationship to writing music, probably a close relationship. Perhaps this is why a considerable amount of such writing slipped over from the usual concepts of drama and came to be called oratorios—such works as Blitzstein's *The Airborne*, or the well-known *Ballad for Americans,* and the somewhat less-known *Lonesome Train*.

Radio programs that were written in verse took on new forms because they did not need to be realistic. They could have a much more formal structure, like music, and, because of this, less narrative.

As an example of this kind of program—which in the days of radio were called radio documentaries, since they dealt with ideas instead of stories—I present one short piece that I wrote a long time ago. In the third week of August 1944, the Allied Forces were approaching Paris, on their way to liberating the French capital. By Tuesday, August 22, the liberation was clearly imminent. I had returned to Hamilton, Canada, from Ottawa. I had lived in Hamilton briefly before the war had commenced and had begun my relatively brief radio career at radio station CHML in that city. Becoming quite ill I had resigned from the National Film Board of Canada and found myself working part-time at CHML once again. On Tuesday, August 22, I began writing the program.

In a sense, I wrote it backwards for I prepared the music and sound effects first. We worked in those days from discs and made up what would now be called *sound tracks* from a succession of music pieces and sound effects that we re-recorded on new discs. (Magnetic recording had not yet been invented in forms that one could utilize with ease and economy, so we had to re-record on acetate discs.) As I listened to music to choose what I should include in the show, the show itself took shape in my mind; I felt a certain kind of structure emerging. Certain bits of music, certain sound effects or possible sound effects began to line up in some kind of order. I re-recorded what might be called *sequences*, leaving places that could be elastic to make room for the as-yet-unwritten words. Such places that could be stretched were unmetered sounds like the sound of airplanes flying, marching boots, muffled drums, and so on. Not least of the elastic bits were one or two stretches of silence. In a show that had much sound and music, silence can be very dramatic.

On hearing the program again recently, it now appears to suffer from a great deal of wishful thinking. We couldn't have thought that then. At the end of August 1944, Canada had been at war just short of five years, for Canada entered the war when Germany invaded Poland on September 1, 1939. There had been nearly five years of all kinds of feelings, mutual encouragements, mutually developed hopes and aspirations, and now a certain euphoria that the war would not last forever but would end in *our* victory. If our hopes seem now to have gone somewhat astray, it was, I think, not our mistake then. It can only be because of a host of mistakes that all of us have committed since then.

Writing the program—that is, the listening to music—began on Tuesday, and the writing was totally completed, Friday evening, the day that Paris was actually liberated. On Saturday morning we recorded the show, using whomever we could find around the station—two announcers, a newsman, a couple of time salesmen and a couple of secretaries who read the female voices. We had a couple of rehearsals and then recorded the show for broadcast. It wasn't perfect because it was a kind of pick-up team that played, and they had neither the professional capabilities nor time for rehearsals that would have greatly improved the whole show. Yet it met with some success and BBC said that it preferred this show that ran about 17 minutes to its own hour-long program for the same occasion. Even if BBC was only being polite, it was very pleasant!

A Tribute to Fighting France

Commemorating the liberation of Paris, August 25, 1944

ANNOUNCER: A Tribute to Fighting France!

FANFARE*

ANNOUNCER: French freedom lives — — — — and Paris breathes again!

INSTRUMENTAL VERSION OF "*LA MARSEILLAISE.*" ESTABLISH WELL, THEN DOWN UNDER WORDS.

VOICE ONE: Arise, O sons of France,
Now dawns the day of glory!
Against us were outstretched   5
The bloody hands of tyrants;
Our homes defiled, our sons
And brothers scourged and beaten.
To arms, comrades, to arms!
Form your battle-lines,   10
That this most evil blood
Shall fill the furrows of our fields!

MUSIC UP TO FINISH

VOICE TWO: Now dawns the day of glory.
France is herself once more,
The France whose name is triple-tongued and strong.   15
Her free and equal brothers share the fight

---

*As noted earlier, stage directions are sometimes indicated by capital letters, as in this script.

	In unison with freedom's comrades. All
	To free all men from savage tyranny.
	The day of glory dawns, to cry:
	Live France! To Hell with tyranny!
VOICE ONE:	France is alive again—and Paris has been freed! 5

INSTRUMENTAL ARRANGEMENT OF *"THE LAST TIME I SAW PARIS"*

MUSIC UP, THEN UNDER.

MAN'S VOICE:	(*reminiscently*) The last time I saw Paris. . . . 10
FIRST WOMAN:	Remember the cafe in Montmartre? Where the artist with the red beard drew your picture?—and the bookstalls near the Pont Neuf?
MAN'S VOICE:	(*as before*) The last time I saw Paris. . . .
2ND WOMAN:	John, look! That's Schiaparelli's latest. And look over there! That hat box—see?—it says Lily Daché. Gee, she's cute! They're called midinettes, I think . . . the girls, silly, not the hats! I wonder if that one's for Danielle Darrieux.....
MAN'S VOICE:	(*as before*) PARIS. . . .
3RD WOMAN:	(*in classical "dumb blonde" style of speech*) Har-r-r-r-y . . . what's the French for eau-de-cologne? 15
MAN'S VOICE:	(*dreamily*) Yes . . . the last time I saw Paris. . . .

MUSIC UP TO END

VOICE ONE:	But the little man with the toothbrush moustache
	looked from his window
	In the Bavarian Alps.
	He saw the shining cities 20
	And the green and heavy vineyards—
	And he wanted them—
	as a garden for his living-room.
VOICE TWO:	(*sotto voce*) In German they say "lebensraum".
VOICE ONE:	But few took heed. . . . 25
	And those who did were scorned.
VOICE THREE:	(*conversationally*) In the Quai Dorsay, the foreign office
	Buried the head of France
	In a hole in the ground—two hundred miles long—
	And called it the Maginot Line. 30
VOICE ONE:	That was military power.

FRENCH MILITARY BAND. BRIEF REFRAIN TO END.

VOICE ONE:	But Hitler wasn't much impressed.
	He had a line himself—for show
	And pageantry
	And named it Siegfried. 35

SNEAK IN MUFFLED DRUMS BEHIND SPEECH

He went to a desk and dusted off a plan
Devised by the Junker von Schlieffen
And got his armies ready.

VOICE THREE: In the Quai Dorsay, the Foreign Office—
VOICE TWO: *(sotto voce)* Two hundred famous families pushed them on—
VOICE THREE: Made eyes at freedom's butcher.
VOICE ONE: They went to a meeting in Munich.
Neville carried an umbrella . . .   5
He thought it looked like rain.
VOICE TWO: *(sotto voce)* It did rain—Czechoslovak tears.
(pause. then slowly) The rain was salt.

SLOW, SAD, PONDEROUS BEGINNING OF ORCHES-
TRAL ARRANGEMENT OF SHOSTAKOVICH *"PRE-
LUDE IN E^b"* DOWN AFTER FULL ESTABLISHMENT
UNDER SPEECH.

VOICE THREE: The pall was carried staunchly
But the mourners were unmoved. . . .   10
The lesson still unlearned.

THE MUFFLED DRUMS HAVE REMAINED TOGETH-
ER WITH THE MUSIC.

VOICE ONE: And still the drums of death beat on
Unheard
Unheeded. (PAUSE)
Then—The Blitz!   15

ATTACCA. KOSTSCHAI'S DANCE FROM STRAVIN-
SKY'S *"THE FIREBIRD."* DOWN UNDER. WHILE UN-
DER MIX BACK TO PRELUDE.

VOICE ONE: Three weeks—Dunkirk—the lion wounded sore.
And three weeks more till Paris was defiled.
Pétain defeated France—
Her anguish shrieked aloud.

MUSIC UP AT CLIMAX THEN FALLING CADENCES
MIX WITH AIRPLANE SOUNDS.

VOICE TWO: And so France seemed to die.   20
Again the rain was salt.

MUSIC UP, MOMENTARILY SUPER *"LA MARSEIL-
LAISE"* OVER OTHER MUSIC BUT KEEP *"LA
MARSEILLAISE"* IN DISTANCE.

VOICE ONE: O, star of France—
Star crucified—by traitors sold—

(SNEAK IN MARCHING BOOTS)

Star panting o'er a land of death,
Heroic land.   25

SOUND UP . . . THEN UNDER

VOICE TWO: The bloody, muddy Aryan boots
Walked on her heart in the mud.

SOUND UP . . . THEN UNDER

VOICE ONE: And then the lackey traitor . . .
We know him as Laval . . .
Danced on the guillotine.

VOICE TWO: And the little man—
They thought him funny, once—   5
Posed by the Eiffel Tower.

SNEAK IN "RIDE OF THE VALKYRIE" UNDER

VOICE THREE: He was the modern Siegfried,
The leader of gods and men,
The lesser gods rode with him—
And his arms would cover the earth.   10

MUSIC UP . . . THEN IS DROWNED BY THE SOUND OF
AIRPLANES. THESE SOUNDS CONTINUE UNDER
THE SPEECH, WHICH BEGINS AFTER THE SOUND OF
A BOMB EXPLODING. PLANE SOUNDS AND OCCA-
SIONAL BOMB NOISES STAY IN BACKGROUND.

VOICE ONE: But Freedom was not dead,
And free men lived to fight.
They breathed
And gathered strength
And joined their strength together.   15

VOICE THREE: Now fighting side by side,
Advancing strong and sure,
A certain shield their clear determination
To throw away forever
The yoke of thralldom and the tyrant's goad.   20

VOICE ONE: Nations united, striking ringing blows—
Tunis—Bizerte—Sicily—
And Stalin's Volga City,
Whose crumbling, smoking ruins defeated half a host.

VOICE THREE: The paltry strutting Duce,   25
A puppet pantaloon,
Hauled by the puppet master to safe Trans-Alp seclusion.

VOICE ONE: Rome free again—the Eternal Tiber city—
Her seven serried hills
At peace once more.   30

VOICE THREE: And as the noise of battle
Rings louder—ever nearer—
Its clamor sounds reverberate through Europe
Underground.
Now Normandy and Brittany—   35
The High Savoy—Bordeaux—Marseilles—
And Paris lives again.

VOICE ONE: The day of Glory dawns—to cry
Live France!
To Hell with Tyranny!   40

INSTRUMENTAL VERSE AND CHORUS OF "HYMN OF
THE UNITED NATIONS" UNDER SPEECH

VOICE THREE: France lives again and marches free again

To build, with freedom's comrades, on this earth
A tower of peace and love and liberty
To shine forever and to light men's hearts.

VOICE ONE: Buttressed foursquare by names in consonance—
Quebec and Casablanca—Moscow—Teheran—   5
Nor can it ever fall.

MUSIC UP AS SINGER SINGS CONCLUSION:

SINGER   *As sure as the sun meets the morning*
ON   *And rivers go down to the sea,*
RECORDING: *A new day for mankind is dawning,*
Our children shall live proud and free.
United Nations on the march with flags unfurled
Together fight for victory, a free new world.

MUSIC UP TO END

In the foregoing there is an amalgam of speech, music, and sound effects. Music and sound effects were of sorts that were very familiar to an audience that had lived through five years of wartime radio broadcasts, newsreels, and war story fiction films. All the music, therefore, had immediate relevance. In the same way, the names were not then strange, although now they probably need to be explained.

The line of defensive fortifications built by the French under the military leadership of Marshal Pétain was called the Maginot Line. The corresponding German fortifications were called the Siegfried Line. The von Schlieffen plan had been drawn up in the nineteenth century and proposed the successful invasion of France by German forces by means of simply going around the end of whatever French fortifications might remain in the way. That this meant conquering Belgium to enter France by way of Flanders caused no consternation to the Nazis. Laval was a Premier of France who was really a puppet of Hitler. Mussolini, the dictator of Italy, had antedated Hitler as dictator by a decade, but soon after Hitler's rise to supreme power, Mussolini became second fiddle and henchman. In their respective languages, each called himself "Leader"—in German, *Der Fuehrer*, and in Italian, *Il Duce*. As the Allied armies advanced up the boot of Italy and Rome's liberation was imminent, Hitler arranged an airborne escape for Mussolini from the Allies. A Hungarian Officer, named Skorzeny, flew a plane into Italy and brought *Il Duce* and his mistress to Germany. The place names, except for the last four, identified Allied successes. The last four names—Quebec, Casablanca, Moscow, Teheran—were of the sites of four major conferences of the Big Three—the heads of state of the USA, USSR, and Great Britain, that is, Roosevelt (later Truman), Stalin, and Churchill. Danielle Darrieux was a beautiful French actress who, it had been learned, was a collaborator of the Nazi Gauleiter of Paris. Such inclinations would not have been apparent to a pre-war tourist.

As discussed earlier, music is used to reinforce the feeling and fullness of an experience. Two pieces, the Shostakovich and the Stravinsky, would have been known to musicians but would have been unfamiliar to most listeners, and therefore their musical *mood* quality could be relied on without the intrusion of other associations. All other music had a clear cultural associative function. The sound effects were also familiar to the audience, and this familiarity was relied upon.

Insofar as a pick-up team of performers permitted, the voices were chosen for the quality that would serve most usefully in the delivery of the several speeches. Once again, voice quality demonstrates the need to write for the ear and to recognize it in performance.

Radio drama is not dead, even in the United States, and certainly not in third world countries. It must be remembered that this country is a nation of automobile riders, and it isn't possible to watch television comfortably when one is an automobile passenger; even without comfort, it isn't possible to watch TV when you're driving! It is surely quite likely that more and more radio drama will be broadcast in the months and years to come.

Finally, a note about punctuation in writing for radio. . . .

Of course it's a truism that all punctuation is for the purpose of indicating pauses in reading, and English has a formal system of punctuation in which the comma, semi-colon, colon, and period form a series of longer and longer pauses. Additionally, there are other signs that indicate other instructions, such as "read this as a question" or "read this with surprise." Further, there are additional formalized meanings for signs, for example, a period signals the end of a sentence and a colon indicates that what follows is a list. And so on.

In radio punctuation is used for much the same purposes, but there is a basic difference. The signals are for the eye of the person who is to *read aloud*, not for each reader to govern when he reads privately and silently. Thus, we do not need to adhere religiously to the literary values of punctuation marks. In fact, it works better if we don't! Written English has a much more formal structure than does speech. We often speak in unfinished sentences because new thoughts come to us while we are speaking and we begin again, or leave unfinished what doesn't need to be finished. We can learn this from the expressions of the person with whom we are talking. In radio this kind of body information isn't available. Thus, new kinds of indicators for the person who reads aloud are needed. Radio punctuation is very open. While we don't contravene the more formalized rules of punctuation, we use fewer of the usual punctuation marks and tend to replace them with dashes or repeated periods. Dashes are more identifiable to the eye, for instance, than are parentheses. Incomplete sentences and other kinds of hanging speech are indicated by the repeated periods— . . . .

It must always be kept in mind that the reading will be aloud, and the function of the visual presentation of the material is to make reading-aloud as simple as possible. We are not writing literature for printing and private reading.

2

Films

As we have seen, radio is a medium that utilizes only sound; it is, therefore, an audio medium. The other media with which we shall be dealing—film, television, slidefilms, and filmstrips—are said to be audio-visual media. They use visual images as well as sound of all kinds, thus providing writers with an additional spectrum with which to generate audience responses.

Before discussing how one must approach the audio-visual media in writing for them, I must draw attention to one of the overriding considerations for the professional writer. Visual media are expensive to produce. The audio medium is a simple one requiring technical crews of small numbers and limited areas of responsibility. They must know about recording original sounds either in a studio or on location, and they must know how to mix different kinds of sounds to make composite sounds, for example, voice with music behind it. That's about all. The actors work only with their voices while standing in front of microphones. They don't have to look like the characters they portray; they only have to sound like them. They don't need to have costumes nor makeup, nor do they have to study body movement nor learn blocking to move about the stage. They have relatively simple jobs, albeit very important ones, and many of them learn to become skilled craftsmen.

The audio-visual media use all of the elements of radio, plus a host of others. It is because of them that costs of production skyrocket. Where the production cost of a radio commercial announcement may run to a few hundreds of dollars, the average cost nowadays of producing a one-minute announcement on film for television broadcast is much, much higher. The vast majority of TV commercials that are currently produced are 30 seconds long. It seems that their impact is about the same as that of longer announcements, and the cost of broadcast time is more accessible to advertisers. The production costs of such a commercial announcement—generally called *spot announcements* or simply *spots*—appears to average at this time between $20,000 and $35,000. Sometimes spots that are made for local advertisers and shot on 16mm film can cost as little as $7,000, and some that are made expensively for national clients cost as much as $400,000. If $25,000 is considered the usual cost of a half-minute spot, the costs of production are proportionately equivalent for a spot and a feature film of about 90 minutes.

I have drawn attention to the matter of costs to provide a stern and vigorous warning at the outset that one of the major problems in all of the audio-visual media is the cost of production. Because a script is, as has been pointed out, a kind of rough drawing from which a producer, director, and all the crew and cast develop a finished work, the basic cost structure is established in the script, and therefore it is the writer's responsibility to be aware of costs from the outset.

Fiction Films

The producer is the person who raises the money for a film or for a TV program. It is he, also, who engages the writer (or buys his material), the director, probably the stars, and perhaps the director of photography and the scene designer. He may engage these people after discussion with the director, or he may hire them before he finally hires the director.

The scene designer needs to have sets built, and this means a crew of teamsters to bring the material to the shops and to the sound stages or locations, carpenters, scenic painters, and the property people who find the furniture, the pictures for the walls, the table props (everything that is found on any table), and the hand props (everything that may be handled in the performance as part of the business of any performer). A property master is in charge of this crew and of the storage of the props once they have been found. There is a costumer, who may have to have a whole dressmaking department to make the costumes and a department to maintain them and to clean and press them; a make-up crew will also include hairdressers.

The director of photography has a crew of camera operators who actually operate the cameras during the filming. The director of photography is responsible for the lighting. (He will also be the camera operator for most industrial films and on all other low-budget films.) The camera operators have assistant cameramen to load and unload magazines of film and to do a host of other chores. Stage carpenters also man the set, move scenery, and help in many other aspects of the filming. Allied to them are the people who are responsible for any plants or shrubbery; they are called *green men*. There is a whole crew of electricians who are responsible for moving and placing all lights wherever the director of photography requires them, keeping the lamps fully operative at all times, and so on. Carpenters and stage hands are called *grips*, and electricians are called *gaffers*. There are assistant directors who help to control the logistics of a production. If the film is a western, there will be a whole staff of hostlers. The list goes on almost interminably, and this covers only the actual shooting of the film.

After the film has been exposed on the various sets, it must be developed and then a working copy, called a *workprint*, is made. The original is never again handled until final copies of the finished film are ready to be made, for if it should come to any harm, even the slightest scratch, every copy made from it would exhibit this same defect. It is the workprint that is called *rushes* or *dailies,* and which is viewed by the director and producer to make sure that nothing needs to be remade. It is the workprint that is edited by the cinema editor and her or his staff.

Meanwhile, a sound crew has been recording the original sound track of dialogue, sound effects, and music; additional members will take part in mixing whatever sounds have been selected by the editors for the final film. *Mixing* means that all the sounds are blended together into one sound track.

And there are still many more people such as the secretarial staff, the legal staff, and so on. It is because of the cost of hiring all these people and their attendant expenses (including transportation, food, and lodging if the locations are distant) that the costs of film-making and television-making have become so very high.

Regardless of all this, however, stories must be written so that they can be presented on the screen or on the TV tube. Usually they aren't presented to the potential buyer in any kind of finished form.

The simplest form of a story is a *synopsis*. This is the briefest kind of outline, the barest sort of summary of the characters and the action. When you see the acknowledgement on a film that it has been developed from "an idea by . . . . ," this probably means that the synopsis was prepared by so-and-so. Such a presentation may be only three or four pages long, perhaps less. It is always written in a completely nontechnical kind of language, using everyday colloquial speech. If you happen to be well-known to a film producer, or to the producer of the television show for which you are proposing a story, the synopsis, or story idea, may well be the initial piece of writing that you will submit. It is the basis for further discussion, further development, and nothing more. Its brevity and simplicity make it easy to "kick around." A group of people can easily have a meeting about it, each with a copy, which can easily be committed to memory for the purpose of the discussion.

The next stage of the development of a story is called a *treatment*. As its name implies, it is a detailed statement of how the film, or the show, will treat the story. In contrast to the synopsis, in which only the main characters may have been introduced, all the characters who will appear in the film are introduced in the treatment. The relationships among them are clearly indicated. The relative significance of the characters and the incidents are revealed. Equally important, some fairly clear suggestion is made concerning the *cinematic treatment* of the story, that is, there will be some indication of the visual treatment of the story and the use of sounds that have important significance.

Here are several scenes of an original screen story by Lillian Wilentz. The emphasis is on action, and there is very little dialogue.

Note also that the present tense is used throughout; this emphasizes the feeling of action and of motion for we must never forget that we are dealing with *motion* pictures. The entire story was 25 typewritten pages. This is longer than some synopses because this is a kind of combination of synopsis and treatment. A treatment for a feature-length film could run, perhaps, as long as 100 pages and may appear very much like a script.

The Man Who Died Twice

A melodrama, © copyrighted 1934 by Lillian Wilentz

Characters

Saardi ....President Bank of Paris
Rene ....A "vagrant"
Collette..A "star"
Madame Saardi...Saardi's wife
Bonat ....Prefect of Paris
Henri ....Madame Saardi's Lover
A prisoner   Bank Directors
Butler   Maid
Student
Policemen . . . Political students . . . Night-club habitues . . . Theatre inmates . . . Street crowds . . . Sightseers . . . Tenement families . . . Fair-crowds . . . Airplane pilot . . . etc.

Scene: Paris, from morn till midnight.

In the central police station of Paris, officers sit about in the squad room smoking, playing cards, etc. It is night and the men have had a lazy day. Suddenly the air is shattered by a screaming siren. The call to duty finds them ready. Cards are swept aside in the dash for action.

Paris streets shriek with the echo of police cars driving frantically to the scene of crime. . . .

In the semi-darkness of a man's den, figures are seen in quiet consultation. A bearded official looks up from a figure buried in blood—"dead!"

"Suicide!" hurriedly interpolates the officer in command. "His name is . . ." they crowd around the officer in questioning anticipation . . . then draw back, fearful and wide-eyed . . . at the name whispered to them.

In the sub-cellar of a Montparnasse cafe, a secret group of political students, known as the "Martyrs" are in session. They walk about in nervous tension . . . awaiting news of some sort. Their leader sits impassive . . . alone!

Suddenly the siren of police-cars passing overhead. The students stop short. "It is done!" cries their leader savagely.

From the darkness, a voice . . . intensely triumphant: "France is relieved of her greatest enemy."

Every face turns toward that voice. A figure appears from nowhere: "Tomorrow France will be free!" The figure leaps to a table: "Our day has come!

We must set the populace shrieking for retribution!" savagely: "And we will!"

Arms arise in stiff salutation . . . tense with suppression . . .

Already the streets of Paris are alive with newsboys' shouts: "Extra! Extra! Read all about the Saardi Suicide! Extra!" . . .

Night-club festivities stop! Bankers . . . executives . . . politicians . . . playboys . . . forget their sweethearts . . . in agitation and panic!

The radio flashes the suicide to housewives . . . husbands . . . children . . . who survey each other in trepidation . . . electrified!

Industrialists . . . Diplomats . . . arise in hushed fear . . . scandalized! . . .

Furtively . . . cautiously . . . a figure climbs the roofs of Paris . . .

In the bedroom of a palatial home, a woman in her early thirties throws herself across her bed . . . weeping. Her maid quietly retrieves a newspaper crumpled on the floor. We notice the "Saardi Suicide" headline, as the maid leaves with it . . . first stopping at the door, to gaze back at her mistress with compassion. . . .

Silently, the figure of the roofs slips into this room . . . stealing across to another door furtively . . . as the woman tosses in grief.

In an adjoining room, we see the figure before a safe. Certain of himself, he removes documents . . . jewels . . . bills. Suddenly the light from an open door spreads itself across the floor. The figure crouches quickly out of sight. The maid we saw a moment before peers in quizzically . . . then, as if reassured, closes the door again. The figure hurriedly escapes through a French-door.

On the balustrade, the figure tiptoes resolutely on. As he creeps past the window of the room where the woman lies weeping, he hesitates . . . then peers in. The light vividly reveals his grief-shaken face . . . a man in his late thirties . . . distinguished! A moment of penitent gazing and he disappears into the blackness of the night. . . .

On the outskirts of Paris, in the gloom of a farm-house, a beautiful girl rushes to embrace a man just arrived . . . the figure of the roofs! . . . Hardly has the warmth of their embrace cooled, when the hum of an approaching airplane is heard. "It is for us!" the man announces happily, yet with a touch of remorse.

Down swoops the plane to a halt before the waiting figure. The pilot climbs out, offers goggles and uniforms to the two and with a turn of the propeller, starts them off. . . .

High . . . high . . . above the dark earth, the man removes his goggles, turning with a curious apprehension toward his companion. The girl smiles at him expectantly . . . lovingly. He is about to say something, but the sound of his motor recalls him. He fingers the dials eagerly . . . violently! The girl watches . . . frightened. The motor begins to stutter . . . miss . . .

"Darling!" he turns to her terror-stricken, "There's something you must know. . . ."

His words are lost in the sudden mad gyrations of the plane. It drops swiftly . . . silently . . . somsersaulting . . . through space. . . .

In a bedroom, of a home similar to the one where we saw the woman weeping, a man is being awakened by his butler, "Mr. Saardi!" The butler shakes him, repeating his name, "Mr. Saardi!" . . . the slightest bit of exasperation in his voice.

The figure in bed rolls over . . . his eyes heavy with sleep . . . and dissipation. He is the man of the roofs!

"Yes?" he asks tiredly.

Apologetic: "The bank has been calling all morning, sir. It's desperately urgent, they say!"

Saardi takes the phone unwillingly. . . .

At the bank, directors frantically gesticulate and shout into the phone. Others cluster around the board-table scanning books hysterically. A rotund, pock-marked official gestures helplessly: "Fifteen Million Francs!" . . . and falls back into his seat in tremors.

Another looks up in dismay, "Our little game is up!"

Imperceptibly, they form a huddle. Whispering passes among them . . . ominous . . . passionate. . . . Gradually we hear: "Saardi . . . Saardi . . . he . . . must pay. . . ." The syllables die out in a hushed, inscrutable accusation! . . .

Suddenly Saardi is here. Directors fall away as leaves in a storm. His magnetic presence fills the room. He says nothing.

For a moment they stare at him . . . awed! Then one of the more courageous officials begins: "Unless we have fifteen millions by . . ." Another cuts in with an expressive gesture . . . completing the awful portent which awaits them.

Suddenly the pock-marked official rises . . . his nerves shattered: "You! It is all your fault!" . . . his trembling finger in Saardi's face.

With a single blow, Saardi sends him crashing to the floor: "That goes for all of you! . . . unless you stop your whining cowardice!" The effect is magical. They return to the boardtable like beaten children. "Now let's see what we can do about it!" . . . opening the books obdurately. . . .

In the Latin-quarter. A limousine draws up to an apartment house. A beautiful woman . . . the one we saw weeping . . . alights and passes quickly and apprehensively into an apartment. A man greets her. They embrace like secret lovers. The woman draws back suddenly: "Henri darling. I have a feeling of calamity. The bank phoned him!"

The man reassures her, "But nothing can happen to us, dear."

"But think, if there should be any disgrace . . ." reluctantly.

"Then you could have a real excuse for leaving him." He says it without the slightest awkwardness.

She turns helplessly away. After a moment, "You know, he and I haven't spoken to each other for weeks.

He takes her in his arms, "My poor child!"

"If only he would give me a divorce!" . . . she moves away . . . inarticulate with emotion . . . impenetrable . . .

And now we are at the bank again. Saardi sits enigmatic . . . hunched. Facing him across the table stands a director delivering an ultimatum: "There can be no other way! It is either you . . ." Saardi meets his glance without the slightest change of expression . . . ". . . or the bank! And you know why it can't be the bank!"

Saardi turns leisurely toward the others. They stare back at him . . . their faces masks of obtuseness. Saardi smiles . . . as though at some unseen joke . . . then rises, and in an indifferent voice asks: "It's either fifteen millions by to-night . . . or . . . me?"

The gazes which meet his question are uncompromising in their silence. . . .

At the Théâtre Racine a dress rehearsal is in process. Smiling faces and full bosoms float across the screen. Suddenly a masculine voice: "Enough! . . . take that first number over again."

Chorines step into line tiredly . . . accompanying the vivacious music. Beauty prances by in extravagant complacency. . . .

In her dressing-room, Collette, the star, prepares her make-up. "Don't you think I'm beautiful?" she asks her maid, across the room.

The maid looks up from her sewing, "What would you say if I said no? . . . sometime!"

Collette smiles through her mirror, "Don't you dare!"

The maid returns to her task submissive.

Collette hums to herself applying mascara the while. Slowly . . . as though out of a mist . . . there appears in her mirror . . . the figure of . . . Saardi! She turns, coyly expecting him.

Saardi tries to embrace her. She repulses him petulantly . . . murmuring excuses about her make-up. Saardi seems wan. He overlooks the formality and watches her for a moment in the mirror preparing her features. Then, very soberly: "I'm afraid there'll be no more rehearsals."

She turns toward him as though she had not heard aright: "Surely you're joking?"

He lights a cigarette; "On the contrary!"

She watches him inhale the cigarette smoke before replying: "The stock market again?"

"Much worse! The bank!"

She tries to hide the disappointment in her voice; "But you've made up the money before."

He stands there resigned . . . almost indifferent. She motions to her maid to leave the room . . . then attempts to cajole him: "Darling! You know how much I counted on this play! Isn't there some other way. . . ."

He smiles cryptically . . . then rebuffs her: "You haven't heard the worst!"

She pauses . . . stung by the force of his words. They stare at one another in indecision. Almost apologetically: "I'm afraid . . . your apartment . . . too!"

Her hand goes to her breast in fear: "You can't! You can't!"

He turns away to avoid her eyes: "It's not me . . . I'm helpless!"

She cries out fitfully: "They shan't! I won't give it up!"

"It will be taken from you . . ." he says it slowly without looking at her. . . . "like many other things!"

She recoils in fright: "No! No!"

He looks at her . . . recalling for a moment their past together . . . in all its nostalgic fragrance . . . then . . . as if to get it all out of his mind cleanly . . . turns abruptly and leaves. . . .

The music from the stage . . . wails a weird cacaphony to Collette's weeping figure on the floor. . . .

And now we are at the office of the Prefect of Police. The Prefect is intent upon illustrated travel booklets. He looks down at his secretary and observes pleasantly: "This year, nothing shall stand in the way of my vacation."

The secretary looks up at him from the corner of his eyes as though to say: "I've been hearing that for the last five years."

The Prefect ruminates aloud: "The Alps! . . . Venice! . . . Africa! . . . Aah!" . . . he daydreams. Suddenly the clang of the telephone. The Prefect is recalled to his duty.

His secretary answers. "It is Monsieur Saardi!" he calls to the Prefect.

The Prefect takes the phone . . . after a moment his face undergoes a swift metamorphosis. Animated, he shouts into it:

"At the Restaurant Tulleries? Yes! I shall be there! Yes! I shall ask" . . . he looks up slyly to see if the secretary is listening, then reassured, he continues in a lower voice: "I will ask the life-prisoners. Yes! It is possible . . ."

The secretary looks up in surprise as the Prefect stamps out toward the cell . . . his official face agitated . . . his travel booklets already forgotten. . . .

In such a treatment the dialogue is minimized, but its lines are indicated clearly. The filmic editing of the finished work should be sufficiently implied so that its significance is also felt. In this regard technical terms, which are certainly not essential, are helpful because by the time you have arrived at the point of preparing a treatment, you can be sure of having technically competent people reading it. Obviously, the sequences are clearly indicated and proportioned; the scenes and perhaps the shots as well are also implied.

Technical Terms

Again some terms need definition. A *sequence* is "a section of a film which is more or less complete in itself, and which sometimes begins and ends with a *fade*. However, sequences frequently end with *dissolves* or even *cuts*, which give a better flow of action than fades. In a comparison with writing, a *shot* may be taken as equal to a sentence; a *scene*, a paragraph; a *sequence*, a chapter."*

A *shot* can be considered the basic element of a motion picture. It is accomplished by continuous running of the camera to record continuous action, that is, it is an element of film in which the continuity of space and time is preserved. In general commercial language, the word *shot* is often replaced by the word *scene* (just to confuse the issue!) especially when reference is to portions of the script.

The apparent distance of the camera from the subject, and the position of the camera relative to the subject, constitute the *camera angle*, and shots are characterized by reference to the camera angle. Note that I have said "apparent distance from the subject." All descriptions of camera angles are relative. To achieve a close shot of a locomotive, the real distance of the camera from the subject will be vastly greater than the distance needed to achieve a close shot of an ant.

Keeping in mind the total inexactness of the nomenclature, here are more common variants. When writing a script, the different kinds of shots are identified, usually, by initials.

Close shot or *Close up;* CS or CU: A shot that appears to have been taken from a short distance from the subject. It is, more often than not, a shot in which a face fills the screen or in which a hand performs some task.

---

*Raymond Spottiswoode, *Film and its Techniques* (Berkeley and Los Angeles: University of California Press, 1964), p. 462.

Extreme close shot or *Extreme close up;* ECS or ECU: This appears to have been taken from a shorter distance than a CU. It is the way in which a detail is exhibited. Perhaps it may be a shot only of the eyes, or of a finger, or an ear, or of the proboscis of a bee, or the indicator of a dial.

Medium close shot or *Medium close up;* MCS or MCU: Not so close as a CS nor so distant as a medium shot. (How's that for being inexact?) It is perhaps a shot in which the head and shoulders are seen or perhaps a full bust shot (that's a shot that includes the upper portion of the body from head to waist).

Medium shot; MS: This can also be called a *mid shot.* It is a shot showing a person at full height, just a little less tall than the height of the frame. It represents the nearest thing to a sort of normal viewing distance between the viewer and the subject.

Then there are a succession of shots that are more distant than MS. The relative distances between camera and subject-apparent distances is clear from their names. There is a *medium long shot* (MLS), a *long shot* (LS), and an *extreme long shot* (ELS).

A *high angle* is one in which the camera is higher than the subject that is being photographed. This can be increased to an *extreme high angle.* Shots from these positions are called *high angle shots* (or *high shots*) and *extreme high angle shots* (or *extreme high shots*). In the same way, there is a *low angle* and an *extreme low angle* from which shots can be made.

A *reverse angle* places the camera on the opposite side of the subject from the previous shot, and a *half reverse angle* is approximately 90 degrees from the original shot, that is, a kind of profile in relation to the original shot.

When the camera moves towards, or away from, the subject it is said to *dolly,* because the movable platform on which it is mounted is called a dolly. A shot made with such movement is called a *dolly shot,* and one can *dolly in* (towards), or *dolly out* (away from). The same kind of movement can be achieved with a zoom lens (although there is an optical difference that is only apparent after considerable training in perceiving the projected image). Such shots are *zoom shots,* and one can *zoom in* or *zoom out.*

When the camera moves transversely in relation to the subject, it is said to *truck,* and such a shot is called a *trucking shot.* Such a shot would be used, for example, if we were seeing a line of soldiers from the point of view of an inspecting officer as he walked down the ranks of men on inspection. Such a shot, being *his* view, and not the view of a kind of third person observer, can also be called *subjective camera;* it is his subjective view of what is transpiring.

During a dialogue sequence, a view of someone listening, as opposed to the person speaking, is called a *reaction shot.* Reaction shots can also be shots which show the reactions of anything to some occurrence, for example, a brief view of a dog as he cocks his ears in response to some sound that may have originated *off camera,* that is to say, out of sight off stage, or a face exhibiting horrified disbelief as it looks at an erupting volcano. Brief shots of this nature, or of a kind that add some kind of explanatory or commentary material, are called *cutaways*. Some cutaways are also called *insert shots* because they are inserted into the action. These are usually some kind of explanatory detail, like a piece of printed material (a newspaper headline, a calendar date) or a dial of a thermometer or a speedometer.

A *two shot* is a shot showing two characters, and in most cases the term indicates that the characters are pretty close to the camera. A *three shot* has corresponding meaning.

An *establishing shot* gets its name from its function of establishing an environment. It is a long shot, generally at the beginning of a sequence and generally an exterior, although it can be a long shot of a large room, or a factory, for example. The terms *interior* and *exterior* simply refer to the relative location of the action and imply specifically the presence or absence of some kind of roof, strangely enough, for one can have an interior in a cave, although the cave is not inside a building. Generally, however, an exterior is outdoors and an interior is indoors. The two terms are commonly abbreviated to INT. and EXT.

It is the variability of the camera distance and the variability of the camera angle that distinguish cinema from any kind of stage presentation. In the legitimate theatre, whether we watch dance or dramatic presentation, or even if we watch a performance of mime (the theatrical equivalent of silent cinema), we are always the same distance away from what is going on. We bought our tickets, and these identify the seats in which we must sit. We cannot move about during the performance. Our distance is always relatively far away from the performers, and we recede as our ability to pay diminishes. We are at approximate eye level if we sit in orchestra seats, and our angle becomes somewhat higher as we sit in the various balconies. But, wherever we sit at the beginning of the performance, there we must remain until it is over. Dramatists select for us what scenes and what sequences we are to watch, but they have no control over where we find ourselves for the watching. The screenwriter and the film director, on the other hand, select for us every view of every element in the drama, and they can change this view from moment to moment.

Because of this potential of changing from one shot to another from moment to moment we can have a totally different kind of drama in the cinema from the kind of drama that happens on stage. I have already identified the reaction shot, which is almost invariably a close shot. The reaction can be shown by a raised eyebrow (the singular number is emphasized) or by tensed hand or raised finger. None of these would be possible on stage because they would not be seen by most of the audience. Everything on a stage has to be large, and even the voices have to project so the people who sit in the top gallery can hear what is said. Dudley Nichols, a great American screenwriter, said it this way:

"Unthinking people speak of the motion picture as the medium of 'action;' the truth is that the stage is the medium of action while the screen is the medium of reaction. It is through identification with the person *acted upon* on the screen, and not with the person acting, that the film builds up its oscillating power with an audience. . . . At any emotional crisis of a film, when a character is saying something which profoundly affects another, it is to this second character that the camera instinctively roves, perhaps in close-up, and it is then that the hearts of the audience quiver and open in release, or rock with laughter or shrink with pain, leap to the screen and back again in swift growing vibrations. The great actors of the stage are actors; of the screen, reactors."*

The possibility of the close-up implies discontinuity of the spatial relationship between the audience and the thing observed. As we have seen, the position from which the action is observed can be changed from moment to moment. This possibility also provides a new source from which new rhythms can be generated. There is not only the actual rhythm of the action or the speech, there is the variation on the rhythm of action that emerges from the variability of our distance from it. The dynamic of the rhythm of a railroad engine is different when we observe it passing within a yard of us from the rhythm observed when it passes half a mile away. Additionally, there is a rhythm that can be generated simply by controlling the tempo of the changes from shot to shot. In film there are two possibilities of creative control—the discontinuity of space and the discontinuity of time.

Other relationships can also emerge from these potentials. There is *the way* one changes from one shot to the next. We can just *cut* from one shot to the next; this is simply joining the two shots, one after the other, so that the viewpoint is changed suddenly. (Such physical joining is called *splicing*). Or we can allow one shot to fade out to a black screen and the subsequent shot to fade in from black. (These are called *fades*—a fade-out or a fade-in.) The fade-out-fade-in seems to separate what has gone before from what follows, much as does an unfilled page at the end of a chapter of a book from the subsequent chapter heading. But the fades can also overlap, so that the fade-out occurs *while* the fade-in is taking place. This is called a *lap dissolve* or just a *dissolve*. It is as though one shot were melting into the next. It does not have the sense of temporary termination that one gets from the fade-out-fade-in.

Another way of changing from one shot to the next is by means of a *wipe*. Imagine that the windshield wiper of a car is disclosing the new shot as it wipes the old one off; imagine, too, that the old shot does not move from its place but is simply replaced by the new one. This is a wipe. If, instead of disclosing the new shot to replace the old, the new shot enters from side of the screen and pushes the old shot off the screen, this is called a *push-off.*

All these ways of moving from one shot to the next—and a multitude

---

*John Gassner and Dudley Nichols, eds., *Twenty Best Film Plays* (New York: Crown, 1943), pp. xxxiii-xxxiv.

of others as well—are, with the exception of the simple cut, called *opti-cals* or *optical effects*. Each has its own capability of generating certain feelings in the audience, feelings of tempo, smoothness or abruptness, or close or distant relationships of one kind or another.

There are a few more camera movements you should be aware of. When the camera remains in a fixed position and pivots horizontally, it is said to *pan* (from panorama), and if, from the same position, it pivots vertically, it is said to *tilt*. If the mount of the camera should rise, this is called a *crane shot;* a crane shot can lower the camera, too.

The more you can think visually when you write—and, of course, the more familiarity you have with the cinematic medium—the more detailed you can be in your directions to the director and the film editor. (But you must be warned that they may never follow your instructions.)

These are some of the elements that are particularly cinematic and that should be part of your armament as a cinema (or TV) writer.

However, there are a few more words you ought to know. At the beginning and end of each film or television program are printed announcements that inform the audience of the name of the film or program and the names of all the people and companies that have been associated in its production. These are called *credit titles* or *credits*. The name of the film itself is called the *main title*. Whoever it is that presents the film is named on the *presentation* title. The remainder of the credits are the *production credits,* except for the title that says "The End" or its equivalent; that is called the *end title*. The placement of the credits and the number of names on each *card,* as well as the relative size of the lettering, is generally established by the terms of the contract governing the engagement of a person. For example, the name of the director must be all by itself, and the director's credit must be either the last credit before the beginning of the film or program or the first credit after the completion of it. This is set out in the contract of the Directors Guild of America. A star is more important in the performance hierarchy than is a featured player, and therefore her or his contract will call for a larger display, or more favored position, or both, than the featured player, who, in turn, is higher up the ladder than those whose names appear on a fairly long list of supporting players. As a writer becomes better and better known, or more and more highly paid, his agent also negotiates more favorable credits. It is clear that the credits for a film or a TV show are just about the same as the by-line of the newspaper writer or author of a book. Position, size of type, and prominence of display demonstrate both how important the writer now is and help to promote him or her to further heights.

Cinematic Story Presentation

Returning to the actual craft of writing, we come to the next stage of the story itself. This is the *scenario* or *shooting script*. In the shooting script everything that has been said or indicated in the treatment is developed and set out in specific detail. Complete descriptions of the visual images and the full dialogue are set out in order, and the scenes and speeches are numbered. Because of the logistics of film-making, scenes are not shot in sequence, and the numbers before each shot identify the scenes for everyone on the shooting area and to all the post-production staff (editors, sound people, and so on) and indicate their position in the entire film.

A shooting script is really pretty technical in its manner of writing because the people who will use it are technically competent. They are the producer, the director, the technicians, the actors, the editors, the sound people, and so on.

Placing visual image and dialogue in two or more columns facilitates reading by such technical people because things which are concurrent appear side by side. Most scripts prepared for reading by non-technical readers, such as the film scripts that are published in book form for sale in book stores, are usually set up as though they were a rather special kind of theatre playscript. It may make for easier reading, but it also makes for harder film-making!

Lewis Jacobs, the film historian, was a screenwriter in Hollywood for a good many years. Here is a brief part of the first sequence of his motion picture adaptation of Hendrik Ibsen's play *An Enemy of the People*. I'll discuss it as an example of cinematic writing after you've had a chance to read it.

An Enemy of the People

After last credit title fades out—

FADE IN:

1. INTERIOR. MEETING ROOM.
   Camera PANS around long directors' table, at which are seated a group of very austere Directors of the Baths, all facing toward the speaker at one end of the table. We hear the sonorous voice of the speaker during the pan. The camera reaches him—it is Peter Stockmann, Chairman of the Board and Burgomaster of the town. We hold on him for a few moments as he reads his report on the excellent condition of the Baths and the great benefits it has brought to the people of the town.

   BURGOMASTER:
   I regret, gentlemen, that the medical officer of the Baths is not here to give us his regular report.

Suddenly the camera dollies fast away from the Burgomaster. His voice fades.

CUT TO:

2. INT. HOSPITAL ROOM. Camera dollies back from a bed, on which a patient is lying. We hear two voices whispering, and the camera rides between two men, including them in the scene. One is a doctor, the other Dr. Thomas Stockmann, medical officer of the Baths.

> DOCTOR: (Softly)
> Yes, Dr. Stockmann, I'm certain that it's typhoid.
> DR. STOCKMANN: (Worried)
> That's the fifth case within the past three weeks.
> DOCTOR:
> And all those gastric attacks have us mystified, too. You know, one of our typhoid patients died this morning, Doctor.

CUT TO:

3. MEDIUM SHOT along directors' table toward the Burgomaster. Camera slowly takes in beaming faces of directors.

> BURGOMASTER:
> —And we are proud of the health which the Baths have brought to countless visitors.

CUT TO:

4. INT. HOSPITAL. MEDIUM CLOSE-UP of Dr. Stockmann and Doctor.

> DR. STOCKMANN:
> This is serious, Brandes. I must take some definite action to stop it.
> DOCTOR:
> But, do you have any idea as to the cause, Dr. Stockmann?
> DR. STOCKMANN:
> Yes—one idea. (Making sure no one is near.) Have you failed to notice that every one of these cases has resulted after the patient used the health baths?

Doctor Brandes puts his hand to his mouth to stifle the exclamation.

DOCTOR: (Whispering)
The Baths—!

Dr. Stockmann nods.

DR. STOCKMANN:
Not a word. I'm not sure, you know.

Dr. Stockmann leaves.

CUT TO:

5. EXTERIOR OF THE HOSPITAL. Evening. MEDIUM SHOT of two young boys playing near the door. They are Stockmann sons; Morten, 10, and Eilif, 8. Dr. Stockmann exits from the hospital, and the boys rush up to him.

MORTEN: (Breathlessly)
Where do we go now, father?
DR. STOCKMANN:
We'll walk up to the Bath house.
MORTEN: (Jokingly)
Fine! Eilif's neck is dirty. We'll give him a bath.
EILIF:
Hey, you!

Eilif runs around after Morten, who dodges behind his father.

DR. STOCKMANN:
Here, here, Gentlemen! We have business to attend to.

Both boys straighten up, serious. They start up the street, one on each side of Dr. S., apparently "gentlemen". Slyly reaching around behind his unsuspecting father, Eilif slaps Morten on the back of his head. The latter whirls around, wondering where the blow came from.

WIPE OUT:

6. INT. OF WHAT LOOKS LIKE A SWIMMING POOL. There is a sign marked "HEALTH BATH." Camera PANS down from sign, along water to edge, where a hand is holding a small bottle in the water. The hand pulls the filled bottle out, and the camera PANS to take in Dr. Stockmann wiping the bottle with his handkerchief. He puts the bottle into his pocket, and leaves.

CUT TO:

7. THE MEETING ROOM.
The Burgomaster at the head of the
table. MEDIUM CLOSEUP.

> BURGOMASTER: (Smiling)
> —And, in conclusion, gentlemen, one may
> say, on the whole, that a fine spirit of
> mutual tolerance prevails in our town—

CUT TO:

Series of fast montage flashes of smiling faces of individual directors, as the
voice continues—

> . . . an excellent public spirit. And that is
> because we have a great common interest
> to hold us together . . . an interest in
> which all right-minded citizens are equally
> concerned.

CUT TO:

8. FULL SHOT OF ALL DIRECTORS
from the Burgomaster's position. They
rise, facing the camera, and exclaim
as one . . .

> DIRECTORS (In unison)
> The Baths!

DISSOLVE TO:

9. INTERIOR. DR. STOCKMANN'S
HOME DINING ROOM.
Camera PANS around the room, indicating that it is obviously a scholar's
home. At the dinner table, Billing is
finishing one course of a meal. The
table is littered with dishes, as after
a meal. When the camera reaches a
door leading to the kitchen, Mrs.
Stockmann comes thru it, carrying a
large joint of roast beef. She goes to
the table and sets it down.

> MRS. STOCKMANN:
> If you come an hour late, Mr. Billing, you
> must put up with a cold supper.
> BILLING:
> Oh, I don't mind at all. I was detained at
> the newspaper office.

We hear a knock at the outside door.
Mrs. Stockmann calls into the
kitchen.

MRS. STOCKMANN:
Hedvig! Someone at the door!
BILLING: (Eating)
Perhaps that's George. He knows Petra
gets home about this time.

As he is saying this, a smudge-faced
maid comes out of the kitchen and
passes thru to the front room to answer the door.

CUT TO:

10. INTERIOR. MEDIUM SHOT AT
OUTSIDE DOOR.
Maid comes up and opens it. The Burgomaster is standing there. At that
moment a cat runs into the house,
tween the Burgomaster's feet, frightening him. The maid turns away
slightly and snickers. The Burgomaster looks at her sternly. She swallows,
and curtsies.

HEDVIG: (Meekly)
Good evening, Burgomaster.

The Burgomaster enters, the camera
DOLLYING back before him. Hedvig
closes the door, and walks hurriedly
past him. He is moving slowly, looking
over everything in the room disdainfully.

CUT TO:

11. FULL SHOT OF DINING ROOM
TOWARD FRONT ROOM.
Hedvig hurries in and goes directly
toward the kitchen, not even stopping
as she announces . . .

HEDVIG:
The Burgomaster.

Mrs. Stockmann brushes herself off a
bit and goes toward the front room, as
the Burgomaster appears in the doorway.

BURGOMASTER:
Good evening, sister-in-law.
MRS. STOCKMANN:
Oh, good evening. It is good of you to
look in.
BURGOMASTER:
As a matter of fact . . .

He looks toward Billing, who is still
eating at the table in the foreground.

> I see you have company.

Billing turns around.
He goes right back to his food.

CUT TO:

12. MEDIUM SHOT OF BURGOMASTER
AND MRS. STOCKMANN AT DOOR
BETWEEN THE ROOMS.
The Burgomaster disdains Billing's
lack of respect. He turns back to Mrs.
Stockmann.

> BURGOMASTER:
> As I was saying, I dropped in to learn why
> Thomas did not attend the meeting of the
> Directors tonight.
> MRS. STOCKMANN: (Apologetically)
> Something serious must have detained
> him, I'm sure.
> (Hurriedly) Won't you sit down and have a
> little bite?
> BURGOMASTER:
> I? No thank you. Hot meat in the evening!
> That wouldn't suit my digestion.
> MRS. STOCKMANN: (Smiling)
> Ah, for once . . .
> BURGOMASTER:
> No, thanks. I'll stick to my tea and bread
> and butter.

CUT TO:

13. CLOSEUP OF BILLING AT THE
TABLE.
He hears the Burgomaster say—

> It's healthier in the long run . . .

and pushes a big slice of meat into his
mouth, in defiance.

CUT TO:

14. SAME AS SCENE 12.

> . . . And it's rather more economical, too.
> MRS. STOCKMANN:
> You musn't think Thomas and I are
> spendthrifts, either.
> BURGOMASTER: (Feigning unconcern)
> Far be it from me to pry into your private
> affairs.
> MRS. STOCKMANN: (To change the subject)

Come in until Thomas gets home. He'll probably be in any minute.

CUT TO:

15. EXTERIOR. BUSINESS STREET OF THE TOWN.
Dr. Stockmann and the two boys are walking along, camera DOLLYING before them. Occasionally they pass a storekeeper in his doorway, who greets Stockmann very cordially. The boys are carrying on behind his back, hitting each other, then dodging back to their father's side. One storekeeper steps out.

STOREKEEPER:
Good evening, Dr. Stockmann. How are you feeling?
DR. STOCKMANN:
Fine. Fine. And how is your business, Mr. Werling?
STOREKEEPER: (Cheerily)
Never better, sir. Business has been fine. The Baths have done that. We've paid up a lot of old debts. More customers . . . better prices. Yep, we're grateful for what the Baths have meant for us, Doctor.

During this conversation, Morten and Eilif have been carrying on behind their father. The storekeeper now turns to them.

And how have the two young doctors been?

They both immediately straighten up to military attention.

MORTEN AND EILIF:
Fine, thank you, sir.
MORTEN: (Glancing down the street)
Look, father, here comes Captain Horster.

Dr. Stockmann excuses himself hurriedly to the shopkeeper and walks fast down the street.

CUT TO:

16. MEDIUM SHOT OF CAPTAIN HORSTER APPROACHING.
Dr. Stockmann and the boys walk up. The two men shake hands heartily.

DR. STOCKMANN:
Well, well, Captain. Glad to see you. When did you return?
HORSTER:
Just this afternoon, Doctor.
DR. STOCKMANN:
Another voyage chalked up, eh? Come over to the house with me and have a bite to eat.
HORSTER: (Hesitating)
Eh . . . eh . . .
DR. STOCKMANN:
Come now, we won't take no!

He takes the Captain by the arm and they turn down the street. The two boys follow behind. The camera DOLLIES along.

HORSTER:
Everyone's been telling me how prosperous the Baths have made them. Certainly an achievement for you, Doctor.

As he speaks, the camera DOLLIES past them and continues down the street; we hear the voice of the Burgomaster.

BURGOMASTER:
That's true. Its gratifying that the taxes . . .

CUT TO:
17. CLOSEUP OF THE BURGOMASTER
seated near the doorway of the dining room in the S. home, speaking.

BURGOMASTER:
. . . have been lifted from the well-to-do.

CUT TO:
18. MEDIUM SHOT OF MRS. STOCKMANN AND BURGOMASTER.

MRS. STOCKMANN:
Everyone is expecting a gala season. I hope so for Thomas' sake. He works so hard.
BURGOMASTER:
As one of the staff, he's done more than his duty.
BILLINGS:
The creator! you mean.

CUT TO:

19. CLOSEUP OF BURGOMASTER as he
draws himself up in protest.

> BURGOMASTER:
> Was he? Indeed! I should have thought
> that I too had a modest share in the under-
> taking.

CUT TO:

20. CLOSEUP OF MRS. STOCKMANN
who has been made uncomfortable by
Billings' remark.

> MRS. STOCKMANN:
> Yes, Thomas is always saying that.

CUT TO:

21. MEDIUM SHOT OF THE THREE.
Mrs. Stockmann exits. The camera
PANS with Burgomaster who goes to
the table. There it follows him back
and forth as he paces.

> BURGOMASTER:
> You've come on business, I presume, Mr.
> Billings?
> BILLINGS' VOICE
> Partly. Also about an article for the paper.
> BURGOMASTER:
> I imagined as much. I understand my
> brother contributes frequently to the
> *People's Messenger.*
> BILLINGS' VOICE
> Yes. When he wants to unburden his mind
> of one thing or another, he usually gives
> our paper the benefit.

The Burgomaster is about to reply
when noise from an outer room stops
him.

CUT TO:

22. MEDIUM SHOT AT OUTSIDE
DOOR. Doctor Stockmann, Captain
Horster, and the boys are just entering. A hubbub of conversation and
laughter. The smudged-face maid appears and takes their hats. Dr.
Stockmann wants to call her but can't
remember her name.

> DR. STOCKMANN:
> Er, Oh, what is your name again?

MORTEN: (Interpolating)
Hedvig! father.
DR. STOCKMANN:
That's it. All right, Hedvig. Tell Mrs. Stockmann I've brought a distinguished guest.

The maid exits toward the dining room. The others start to follow.

CUT TO:

23. FULL SHOT OF DINING ROOM TOWARD LIVING ROOM. We hear the voices nearing, then Dr. Stockmann and Horster appear in doorway.

DR. STOCKMANN:
Hello, Mr. Billings.

Yelling toward the kitchen.

Katrina, here's another visitor for you.

Mrs. Stockmann enters as he calls.

MRS. STOCKMANN:
Captain Horster!

The captain bows. Dr. Stockmann takes him by the arm and leads him to the dining room table, passing the Burgomaster standing off just inside the doorway.

DR. STOCKMANN:
I caught him on the street, Katrina, and could hardly get him . . .
MRS. STOCKMANN: (Interrupting)
But Thomas, don't you see . . .

Dr. Stockmann turns suddenly around and sees the Burgomaster. He lets go of Horster's arm and walks up to the Burgomaster holding out his hand.

DR. STOCKMANN:
Oh, is that you, Peter? Capital!

CUT TO:

24. MEDIUM SHOT OF THE BURGO-MASTER AND DR. STOCKMANN.

BURGOMASTER:
Unfortunately I have only a moment to spare.
DR. STOCKMANN:
Nonsense! You must have a drink with us.

Turning towards the table.

> You're not forgetting the drinks, Katrina?
> KATRINA'S VOICE:
> Of course not. In a moment.
> BURGOMASTER:
> Drinks, too . . . !

Haughtily, the Burgomaster starts to leave, going through the doorway into the living room.

CUT TO:

25. SHOOTING FROM LIVING ROOM THRU DOORWAY INTO THE DINING ROOM. The Burgomaster is just entering and Dr. Stockmann calls after him.

> DR. STOCKMANN:
> Peter!

•   •   •

Now that you have read this cinematic adaptation of Ibsen's play, please read the first act of the play itself. You'll be able to find a copy in the public library, I'm sure. Read the whole play if you wish, but certainly read the first act to be able to compare it with the shooting script.

The most obvious observation in this comparison is probably that in the stage play there is only one location, one set—the living room of Dr. Thomas Stockmann's home. This set serves also for Act II. Act III moves to the editorial offices of the journal, *The People's Messenger,* Act IV is in a large room in Captain Horster's house, and Act V is in Dr. Thomas Stockmann's study. On the other hand, in the space of a few minutes in the movie script there are several exterior places, and a number of rooms inside different buildings. Onstage we are limited to the physical requirements of the stage itself and to the cost of production, which limit the stage possibilities. In film there is really no limit to the geography in which the action can take place, and the economics are entirely different. A stage play must play to a few hundred people every night for a long series of nights. A film can play to many thousands of people simultaneously, and, if it is broadcast on television, to many millions.

Thus, while the costs of production are always of primary consideration in making a film, they are of an order that is vastly different from the costs of a stage play. Writers can, therefore, be liberated from geographic limitations in their sequence of scenes and use the marvelous potential for ubiquity that is peculiarly cinematic.

Not only can they be liberated from a confined geography, but they can move about from moment to moment. See how many different locations there are in this brief film sequence. More than that, see what this kind of liberation from spatial confinement, and from temporal confinement, permits the writer to do with his story presentation. He presents three different threads of the story contrapuntally, almost simultaneously. He gives the feeling of simultaneity. Through this potential for counterpoint, writers can establish conflicting interests and conflicting occurrences immediately and establish the suspense on which the development of the plot relies. The audience does not have to wait for it to be explained to them through conversation.

By this same means, they can *see how the characters react* to the conflicting interest. They can see them exhibit themselves through these reactions and begin to know them immediately. They do not have to be told about them as they do on stage. For example, on stage Dr. Thomas Stockmann *needs to tell us* of the typhoid and other ailments that occurred last summer. In the film we *see him reacting* to their ominous presence.

Lewis Jacobs has taken advantage of all of the potentials of his medium in preparing this tiny portion of a film sequence. Moving pictures move, and motion and action are continuously going on. But they are not going on just for the sake of motion. One cannot confuse motion with activity, even in the motion picture medium. Within the fullest meaning of the dramatic sense, each character must face a succession of tasks, and his activity must always arise out of the attempt to perform those tasks. It is out of this continuing attempt to perform a succession of tasks that the motion arises, for it is the evidence of the activity. The mobility of the camera makes it possible for the audience to become active participants with the characters in the performance of their tasks. This is the movie medium.

Even though this brief script of *An Enemy of the People* is called a shooting script, the film may not be shot as indicated in it. There may be more or less shots than are called for by the writer for a great number of reasons. The actual scenery on the sound stage, or the actual conformation of the location, may require that there be more or fewer *camera set-ups,* that is, camera positions. The variations may be caused simply by the creative need of the film director. In the script just read, the 25 scenes that have been enumerated in it would most likely be increased to 40 to give even more plasticity and rhythm.

(By the way, the word *montage* that appeared in the script means *creative editing,* and in this particular context it means a relatively rapid sequence of short, individual shots.)

Clearly, screenwriters must know their medium so that they can use it to the full in presenting their ideas. But, no matter how well they may know the medium and be able to work in it, they still must have ideas if they are going to write anything more than trite formula material. Unfortunately, in a brief book such as this, all I can do is to indicate the needs of the medium and its potentials. I cannot help the would-be writer develop something to say.

The particular comparison presented—the adaptation by a skilled screenwriter of a play by an acknowledged master—will well repay careful study. Each knows his medium and is able to utilize it fully. There are other comparisons that might also serve. There are many published screenplays. Those that have not been prepared for publication to a general audience will be most rewarding to study, if they can be found; but all will draw attention to the nature of cinema if they are read with a sense of inquiry.

But you don't have to compose a complete shooting script, or scenario, when you are writing a dramatic fiction film. You can write it very much like the published scripts of films that you will find in bookstores. The reason is simple. Until you are yourself a director, or until you are working directly with a director, you have to assume that it is the director, and not you the writer, who will select the shots that are to be made, the manner of editing that is to be planned for, and the rhythms of action, sound, and editing that will eventually make the story a film.*

Here is the opening of a dramatic fiction film script by Bernard Edmonds.

Fifty-Seventh Street

1. EXT. 57th ST., N.Y., N.Y.—LATE AFTERNOON—PRESENT

It's rush hour. The street is crowded with cars, cabs, and busses. It's September and the temperature is dropping as the sun lowers itself into the Hudson River. The sky is a dark grey, everything else is a deep orange; it's as if Edward Hopper painted the stark background and Walt Disney provided the frenzied activity.

All of this is revealed from the air in a helicopter shot that begins on the piers of the Hudson and continues across town to the East Side. Without actually hovering, the camera picks out some key buildings and landmarks. We pass over the CBS broadcast center, the Hearst magazine operations center, Carnegie Hall, the Art Students' League, the Fifth Avenue stores—Bergdorf's, Bendel's, Tiffany's—the old IBM headquarters, the art galleries, the Galleria, the Universal Pictures Building, and then crossing Second Avenue, the massively elegant co-op and condominium apartment fortresses.

We hear the traffic below as it would sound from several hundred feet in the air: muted and comforting. We also hear a sonata for flute and violin by Telemann (No. 2 in D Major) and we are not sure of its origin. But we sense that it is real and not background trickery. (As we crossed Fifth Avenue the music began to drown out the distant traffic sounds.)

---

*Writers Guild of America, East, Inc., has published a pamphlet entitled *Professional Writer's Teleplay/Screenplay Format,* in which is displayed and explained the layout on the typed page that should be followed for teleplays and for screenplays. The pamphlet can be purchased for a nominal amount from the Guild, 22 West 48th Street, New York, NY 10036.

The camera finally comes to rest above 322 E. 57th St. and begins a slow descent along its Italian Renaissance facade as the music continues to swell. One massive window is open and embroidered draperies are gusting through it. The camera comes to rest in front of this window. Over this continuous shot are supered the main title and the key credits of the film.

2. INT. 322 E. 57th ST.—HENRI STORCK'S STUDIO—LATE AFTERNOON—SAME DAY

In a reverse angle we see the draperies blowing out the window. The camera begins a slow continuous dolly, defining both the character of the room and the three characters in the room. It's a gigantic space: double height ceilings, a curving staircase leading to a wrought iron balcony overlooking the room, full height French doors at one end, floor-to-ceiling bookcases at the other end.

Near the center of the room sits a full size Steinway concert grand piano glimmering with a high gloss French polish. Sitting on the piano bench is Henri Storck. He is a large, physical man feeling the constraints of his formal concert attire. He's 75 years old, handsome, with a wise countenance. He has been intently listening to the Telemann Sonata.

As the camera circles the piano, we see reflected in it, standing on one side, a young man playing the violin. Robert Brothers is approaching 30, with sensitive good looks. He's dressed in lean jeans and a lumberman's plaid shirt with the sleeves rolled up. The camera follows his intent gaze across the piano to find Claudia Perkins, the flute-playing other half of the duo. Claudia is in her mid-20's and is primly dressed in a white blouse and mid-calf length black wool skirt. Whereas Robert was intently gazing at Claudia, Claudia is just as intently studying her music.

The camera dollies into an extreme close-up of her tongue rapidly gliding over the flute's mouthpiece. Gleaming licks of spittle are discerned as she opens and closes her lips. She is obviously transported by the music which she and Robert are making. Her total absorption in what she is doing renders her cool and distant—her self-confidence is apparent.

As she continues to play, her subtly erect nipples push against the crisp cotton of her blouse. She is oblivious to the change in her appearance. (The audience is unsure collectively of what they are seeing, but they know individually they are seeing something happen.) Claudia's tongue continues its swift glides while her lips tensely hold a fixed "O" position. The camera surveys the reactions of Henri and Robert. Henri admires her—her talent is obvious—and he nods knowingly on the condition of her breasts. As the camera nears Robert, the frame is quickly shattered by the sharp angle of the elbow of his bowing arm. The camera dollies farther and his violin and chin are seen. The taut forearm muscle of his bowing arm is bristling with fine downy hair. The camera tilts up to find his expression. Robert is watching everything: the tongue, the breasts, the flapping draperies, Henri's hungry eyes, his own wooden posture. The camera completes the circle and returns to its perch in front of the window as the Telemann Sonata comes to a coda.

Henri picks up the score he has been following and brings it to his face, completely covering it while he breathes in deeply, dramatically drops the score and exhales loudly. Henri reaches out with his hand to touch Claudia.

> HENRI
>
> (in a thick and charming accent)
>> Claudia! Claudia! *Liebchen! Ma chérie!* Darling Claudia! You can make an old man hear new music. You've got a clarity that can only compare with pure light. If there is such a thing—and I'm no scientist—your music is like a laser in outer space: it seems to penetrate to the heart of the universe.

Gets up and embraces her.

> HENRI
>> I'm so proud of you . . . and of myself for eliciting such pure sound.

He glances over to Robert as they share an unspoken thought.

> HENRI
>> But . . .

Claudia tenses. She's heard it before.

> CLAUDIA
>
> (anticipating)
>> Yes?

> HENRI
>
> (rushes on with determination)
>> There's more to life than music, even your music. I know you're from Minneapolis, but that's no excuse.

> ROBERT
>
> (interrupting)
>> Henri, Claudia is from St. Paul, not Minneapolis. You never want to make the distinction.

> HENRI
>
> (ignoring Robert)
>> I wish I could be delicate, *Liebchen* . . . and please excuse the analogy, but remember the TV news producer from your hometown—Mary . . .

> ROBERT
>
> (helpfully)
>> Richards, Henri. I think it was Richards. Or was it Grant.

> HENRI
>> It's Richards. Well, she had a career and a life, too.

> CLAUDIA
>
> (defiantly)
>> My life is my career!

> HENRI
>> *Exactement.* You know you sound like Katharine Hepburn in one of the favorite films of my youth, *Christopher Strong*. She played an

aviatrix—a woman pilot—killed herself, you know, rather than give up her career for a man.

CLAUDIA

Perhaps. But she went on to garner three Academy Awards.

ROBERT

That's not what Henri meant. And you know it.

HENRI

(with mild sarcasm)
Thank you, Robert. I think I can handle this myself.

ROBERT

The only thing you want to handle is Claudia. And I don't mean her career.

CLAUDIA

(amused)
Now boys, let's restrict this conversation to me.

HENRI

Thank you, Claudia. But let me prove my point. What do the initials "S.F." mean to you?

CLAUDIA

San Francisco? Sante Fe?
(thinking harder)
Solo flute? Silent film?

HENRI

Exactement! Places and things. Not people and ideas. To educated Europeans of my generation, "S.F." . . .

Henri gestures to a signed and framed photograph of Freud.

HENRI

(continues)
. . . can only be Sigmund Freud. Maybe to the less educated, *savoir-faire.*

Henri walks over to a post-impressionist painting by Vuillard of a sitting room.

HENRI

(continues)
Or to the uninhibited, sexual freedom.

Henri indicates himself.

HENRI

(continues)
Claudia, *liebchen,* as a musician you must know these facts of life. Look at Rubinstein, Stravinsky, Stokowski, Fiedler, Toscanini, Casals. They are or were still at their creative peaks well past 70. And I have faithfully followed their example.

CLAUDIA

Henri, your modesty is only exceeded by your sex drive.

                              HENRI
  Yes. But you. It's practice, play, practice.

Henri indicates Robert.

                              HENRI
  (continues)
    Why not give your friend a chance?

                             CLAUDIA
  (indignantly, in the voice of Katharine Hepburn)
    But surely, you all must know I'm going to be the greatest flautist of
    my generation. James Galway, step aside. Jean-Pierre Rampal, I do
    love you but . . . it's my turn.

                             ROBERT
  (teasing like an older brother)
    Your modesty is only exceeded by your cockiness.
      (surprised)
    That didn't come out quite right. Sorry.

                              HENRI
    Don't apologize, Robert. It's true. She can't make love to a flute.
    Unless, of course, she's an entrenched admirer of the *Sensuous
    Woman.*

                             CLAUDIA
  (blushing)
    My love comes out of the flute in pure music, and you both know it.
    Henri, you're just an aristocratic sexist. Quick, who are the three B's
    of music?

                              HENRI
    Beethoven, Bach, and Brahms. Or Berlioz, Bruckner, and Bizet.

                             CLAUDIA
    Right. Perfect for you.
      (mockingly)
    Exactement. All men. All composers. All dead. I prefer musicians
    who bring music to life. Bernstein, Boulez, and Brico.

                              HENRI
  (warming to the challenge)
    And I suppose you prefer the bold, brash, brilliance of Lincoln Center,
    excuse me, Avery Fisher Hall, to 57th Street's own romantic Car-
    negie Hall? To me, a concert hall named after a steel magnate has the
    firmer ring of substance than one honoring a radio maker like Fisher.
      (in exasperation)
    You modern youth. In ten years they'll change the name from
    Fisher—that is, when radios are obsolete and replaced by tran-
    sistorized integrated diodes—and honor the inventor of the tran-
    sistor, Schockly. And you know what that will mean don't you? Don't
    you?

                             ROBERT
  (playing along, with a smile)
    No, what?

CLAUDIA

(interrupting Henri)
  Schlock. Schlocky music, right?

HENRI

  You said it, not me. Come here.

Henri gets up and crosses to the other end of the room, beckoning Claudia and Robert to follow. With a great flourish he unrolls a poster.

HENRI

  See. Here it is. Finally.

The camera dollies into a close view of the poster and we recognize Claudia and Robert. It's an announcement of their upcoming concert:

CLAUDIA PERKINS AND ROBERT BROTHERS
THEIR FIRST NEW YORK CONCERT
DECEMBER 6/CARNEGIE HALL
WORKS OF BEETHOVEN/BACH/BRAHMS

As the audience begins to read the three B's, off-camera is heard . . .

HENRI

  It's only three months away . . . you won't let anything obstruct your
  career—convictions, conscience, or concert halls.

Fade out.

3. INT. HENRI'S STUDIO HALL—MINUTES LATER

Robert and Claudia are waiting for the elevator to go down.

CLAUDIA

  Bob, you will have to learn to control your erotic imagination. My
  family will be here any day now, they're bringing Claire to Barnard,
  and while she might find you arousing, my parents won't. Besides,
  you're so wrong it's pitiful. Henri Storck is one of the world's finest
  musicians, a noble and inspiring teacher, and besides, I love him.

•   •   •

The first thing to notice is the amount of space that is given to setting out the quality of the environment, the quality of the actions, and the quality of the personalities and their interrelationships. This is done by indicating in considerable detail what the camera sees and how it sees what it sees, but it does not insist on how many shots are to be made nor from where each shot will be taken. However, all the colors of the scene are made evident, clearly and dramatically, by the indications the writer has given. It is true that he has used a kind of third person narrative description to provide a visual image of the room and its furnishings and to some extent also the people of the scene. But this is for readers of the script. In the film itself the people will disclose themselves by the way the camera sees what they do and by the way the microphone hears what they say.

Because the script has not been broken down into a shooting script with the individual shots described, the numbers in the left margins refer to what are called *sequences,* or scenes in a play. Meanwhile, each location, each place in which the action is to take place, is identified in capital letters to make its appearance unmistakable. Then the description of the action and all the writer's color descriptions, although provided in smaller, lower case letters, are indented in relation to the scene identification. The dialogue is set off by being still further indented. Its presence is thus clearly indicated. In this presentation, the name of the character, in capital letters, is in the middle of the line directly above that character's speech.

A few sequences later in the script, we meet Arthur, who is Claudia's father. He is visiting New York with his wife—Claudia's mother—and their second daughter, Claire, Claudia's younger sister. Arthur is a successful meat salesman who works for a large conglomerate called DATAFAX, and the purpose of his New York visit is to attend a large company meeting.

19. INT. REGENCY ROOM—HILTON HOTEL—THE NEXT AFTERNOON

Arthur is in the Regency Room: gilded French Provincial moldings, crystal chandelier, flaming red carpet. He is among a hundred other men all sitting on folding chairs, facing the dais. Above the dais is a wide banner proclaiming that "The Difference Is You". Flanking the banner are two huge signs, like marquees, with alternating lights. The one on the left says "Datafax:" and the one on the right reads "A Company with a Difference". In the middle of the stage is a movie screen. Projected on it is Datafax's annual President's message film.

This scene begins with a tight shot of the Datafax screen filling our screen. As the scene develops, the camera dollies down the center aisle, revealing Arthur Perkins and the rest of the audience.

DATAFAX FILM
VOICE-OVER NARRATOR
Datafax, yes . . . a company with a difference. That's not an idle thought, a glib remark, a public relations posture. No. Datafax does make a difference. In our lives, in the lives of our children. And, yes, in the life of our country.

Today, it's so easy to launch a sarcastic attack, a rude barrage of unkind verbiage, to utter an indifferent sneer at the basic root of American society—the corporation. Easy for some. But here at Datafax we take pride in knowing that truly, our company, is a company with a difference. And, that difference is you.

The Datafax film begins with a graphic montage of Datafax's far-reaching empire: world headquarters in Minneapolis, stockyards in Chicago and Omaha, supermarkets around the country, trucking fleets on the move, cattle ranches, and, of course. Datafax people.

As the sequence closes, the screen breaks up into a dozen smaller screens, each filled with a Datafax employee: men and women, blacks and whites, blue collar and white collar. As the narrator says ". . . that difference is you . . ." the dozen screens fade to black and the title, "The Difference Is You" fades in.

The theme music builds as the narrator continues by introducing—still on film—the Chairman of the Board of Datafax. He is seated in the Datafax boardroom.

DATAFAX FILM
CHAIRMAN OF THE BOARD
Here, at world headquarters, we've got our feet firmly on the ground. We don't allow ourselves to daydream, to relax, although dreaming and relaxing do have their place. We're committed to building a strong country, a viable economy, and securing the individual needs of our employees.

The Chairman continues speaking in glowing, inspirational tones as Arthur gets up and hurriedly leaves.

20. EXT. HILTON HOTEL—LATER THAT AFTERNOON

The camera is perched high above the street, and we see Arthur Perkins briefly consult with the doorman and get a cab. The camera follows the cab as it enters the heavy traffic on Sixth Avenue.

CHAIRMAN OF THE BOARD
(continues over)
That's why I take special pride today in welcoming our top 100 sales people to New York. Congratulations to each and every one of you. For without you—and I mean this—there would be no Datafax. Each of you has earned the right to be at the top through the diligent application of the Datafax credo: "Success is the reward for disciplined ambition."

The cab pulls up in front of a building on West 51st Street and Arthur gets out and goes in the building.

21. INT. SMALL BUILDING—FOYER AND CORRIDOR—SAME AFTERNOON

Arthur rings the bell and a door is opened by a young black woman.

BLACK MASSEUSE
Hello stranger. Come in. Take a load off. Who recommended you?

ARTHUR
The Hilton.

The masseuse, mildly impressed, raises her eyebrows. Arthur enters the corridor and notices a gallery of black-and-white glossy 8x10 photos of a half dozen young women. Beneath each photo is her name in capital letters: SHERI, AMY-SUE, VIVA, MARIE, DONNA, BOBBIE. He studies the portraits before asking for one of the girls.

• • •

Early in the script, the writer had demonstrated that Arthur is stuffy, closed to new ideas, a male chauvinist in relation with his daughters, and filled with establishmentarian clichés. In the above brief piece of the script, we enter the large auditorium in the hotel where the company's meeting is taking place, the reason for Arthur's New York visit. The total establishment ambiance is clearly established.

While the company president's voice drones on, Arthur leaves the great hall of the hotel and takes a taxi to another location. We are surprised to discover that he has gone to a very elitist massage parlor. The continuing voice of the company president, which is heard "over" the trip in the taxi, emphasizes the environment in which Arthur has found his success and serves as a comment upon this new adventure on which he has embarked. It is an adventure that contravenes all the righteous attitudes that he addresses to his daughters, yet it is, at the same time, an adventure that is, perhaps, expected of a certain kind of successful salesman in American society. All this seems to have been compressed in the brief portion of the script just read, bound together as it is with the contrapuntal voice. This is because the voice is not just a mechanical linking of the scenes. On the contrary. Because the voice is the voice of the company president speaking at the annual company meeting, it is organic to the flow of the film, and, at the same time, directly commentative.

The next excerpt from the script of the film entitled *Fifty-Seventh Street* takes place later. Claudia has been having dinner with her family (on her father's expense account) and with Robert when she suddenly remembers that she has left her music score at home and rushes out to get it and to meet her family at the concert hall where she and Robert are to play with the symphony. Failing to find a taxi, she accepts a lift from a good looking young man in an oversized Lincoln Continental. Claudia does not know, although the audience has been able to infer, that her driver, Steve, is also the owner of the massage parlor. Steve had just previously taken heroin and now, instead of driving Claudia where she wants to go, takes her into the dark, quiet recesses of an underground garage where he makes vigorous efforts to seduce the equally vigorously unwilling Claudia.

37. INT. AVERY FISHER HALL—SAME NIGHT

The concert has begun.

ROBERT

(whispering to Claire)
Maybe she couldn't find a cab. But don't worry, she'll be here soon. She'll play with them after the intermission.

38. INT. LINCOLN CONTINENTAL—SAME NIGHT

Steve pulls up at the light in front of Lincoln Center. Claudia tries to open the door, but can't because it is locked. Steve flashes his Swiss Army knife at her. He turns the corner and drives the car into the Lincoln Center Garage, exiting down a ramp.

39. INT. AVERY FISHER HALL—SAME NIGHT

The concert music continues. The camera pans the faces of the audience. It passes over Arthur, Audrey, Claire, and Robert. It pans the orchestra players. It stops in the flute section on Claudia's vacancy.

40. INT. LINCOLN CENTER GARAGE—SAME NIGHT

Concert music continues full up.
Steve drives the car into an empty space and closes the windows electronically.

The camera remains outside of the sealed car. Steve and Claudia are seen, but all that is heard is the concert music.

Steve lunges at Claudia. She struggles against him. Her face can be seen through the window and she is screaming, but it cannot be heard. The concert music continues. She turns away from him. He grabs her from behind. His hands pull her head lower and lower. She disappears from view and he can be seen loosening his pants. Quick flashes are seen of parts of Claudia— her foot kicking, her hand clawing the air. She is not yielding to his demands, and her resistance is making him angrier.

The cocaine has transformed Steve into a simplex circuit, his mind sending one message through his body, over and over. Sounds echo in counterpoint to the concert music.

ECHOING OF STEVE'S VOICE
This one's for you, Ms. Iowa.
This one's for me.
This one's for you, Ms. Iowa.
This one's for me.

These lines are echoes of what Steve said to himself while he sniffed cocaine.

The circuit finally overloads and breaks. Claudia can't be seen sprawled on the seat, but she obviously says something because Steve turns quickly and screams at her. His face distorts with rage again.

He leans down out of view for a second and reappears with the flute case. Opening it, he pulls out the flute and drops the case. It looks like he's going to break it in two, but instead he holds it like a shovel and straddles Claudia, still unseen. Light glints off the gleaming flute as it abruptly disappears and reappears from view.

Suddenly Steve stops, leans over Claudia and flings open her door. The edge of the door barely misses the camera. He shoves Claudia out of the car onto the floor of the garage, where she lands in a pool of grease.

The camera is lowered below ground until it is eye level with Claudia's face, lying where it landed on the greasy concrete. Tears roll down her cheek, and when they land on the floor they mix with the oil to form abstract swirls of color. One of the musical selections from the concert has just ended, and thunderous applause is heard.

Steve meticulously cleans the seat of his car, straightens his clothes, combs his hair, and wipes off the flute. He is breathing heavily.

He holds out the flute, offering it to the prostrate Claudia. She reaches up to take it, but he slowly pulls it back. She stretches up and reaches further for it. When her hand is in the car's interior area, he slams the door on it. Then he opens the door, tosses out the flute and the case, and shuts it quickly. The buckle of the seat belt is caught outside the car door.

41. EXT. LINCOLN CENTER GARAGE ENTRANCE—SAME NIGHT

As Steve pulls out from the bowels of the garage, we hear the dangling seat belt scraping on the asphalt pavement. He notices the sound too, and changes the tape on his eight track tape player. This time the music is Bach's Mass in B Minor. He enjoys the music.

42. EXT. STREET—SAME NIGHT

Steve/Paul drives up Broadway. When he reaches 118th Street, he pulls over to the curb in front of Barnard College. Several women students on dates walk past the parked car. He waits patiently. A girl walks up to the car and gets in. The Bach music continues.

GIRL
I've been thinking about what you said last week . . .

PAUL
Good.

GIRL
. . . about personal freedom being an illusion. You may be right. It's all an illusion. That's right, isn't it? You said that I was burdened, that I carried my middle class bourgeois values around like a 65 pound back pack.

This passage of the script has been selected so that I might be able to demonstrate to you the importance of sight and sound in *thinking* motion pictures. While it is true that the scenes you have just read are almost all in third person narrative, they do not deal with what Steve was thinking or feeling, nor with what Claudia was thinking or feeling, except insofar as those immediate feelings make clear *to the reader* the actions that are occurring. In the film it will be the sights and sounds, the actions and the reactions, that will make clear the thoughts and the feelings of the participants in the drama. The writer has given the reader, who may be the producer, director, actor, or cameraman all that he or she needs to visualize what will be seen on the screen. Yet the writer has not intruded himself into the crafts of those specialists who will eventually translate the script into a film.

I have already pointed out the difference between a shooting script and a treatment. You will readily see, therefore, that the three excerpts from *Fifty-Seventh Street* are from what is in reality a very detailed, complete treatment, indeed, it is what is called a *scenario*. When a producer will eventually arrange to film the script, a detailed shooting script will then be prepared. Moreover, this will probably wait until the director has agreed to the models of the scenery that the designer will have designed, or until he has arranged the locations in which the filming will actually take place. It is not possible to break any filming down into a sequence of individual shots if one doesn't know where that filming will take place.

To sum up our ideas of fiction film writing, we can say that a fiction film must be so conceived that all that we need to know about the characters must be apparent in what they do and in what they say as well as that rich comment on their doings and sayings that can be made through the creative use of sounds and music.

A word about commentative use of music—perhaps the most discussed use of music as commentary has been Richard Wagner's invention of the *leitmotiv*. It is not appropriate here to go into the uses to which he put the *leitmotiv*, beyond saying that he used themes that identified, for example, Siegfried, the Rhine maidens, or the Holy Grail, and played them at times in the operas when the action was not directly related to the themes. In this way, Wagner provided a commentative mnemonic ("While this is going on, remember Siegfried") or a contrasting characteristic or quality as a kind of emotional counterpoint to the action. There are two examples of this in the excerpts from *Fifty-Seventh Street*: the voice of the company president and the echoes of Steve's voice as he begins to rape Claudia.

Creative activity is not limited in form or style. Allow yourself to think freely, but learn about your medium so that you can be even freer because of your knowledge of its unique potentials.

Non-Fiction Films

You may be surprised to learn that there is a film industry that is as large or larger than the fiction film industry. It is engaged in making what are called non-theatrical films, a category that includes television commercials, documentaries, all kinds of business films, public information films, and, not least, hosts of instructional films. This part of the industry is so large that there are perhaps a thousand non-theatrical producers listed in the various telephone books in the United States—perhaps more.

Instructional Films

Instructional films, which are also referred to as classroom films or educational films (and in Europe as pedagogic films), are films that are made to relate to a school curriculum and are expected to be used as teaching tools. This also means that such films are directed to certain age levels or grade levels.

I have chosen an example that was made by a young man who had been my student, Henry Cheharbakhski, for a distributor of classroom films, International Film Bureau, Inc., in Chicago. The film was entitled *A Film About Film Editing,* and I include portions of this script for two main reasons. First, its subject matter will be of some instructional value to potential screenwriters who are not fully familiar with the film medium. Additionally, it is a script whose form is, perhaps, classic. It begins by making a clear statement of what will be demonstrated. The body of the film follows, and in this the basic processes of film editing are set out. Finally, there is a summary in which a piece of edited motion picture is to be seen. The subject matter is such that there really isn't any other way of showing it clearly and convincingly except in a film.

A Film About Film Editing
by Henry Cheharbakhshi

ABBREVIATIONS

V means *Villain*   H means *Hero*   HE means *Heroine*

VISUALS	SOUND
1. MLS pan L to R to MS establishing V, who spots H and HE	APPROPRIATE MUSIC
2. MS establishing H-HE-V in background	
3. MS V from behind approaching H-HE	
4. CU HE—talking to H	
5. CU H—talking	
6. CU V—watching the two	
7. LS H-HE talking	
8. CU V—moves towards H-HE	

9. MS V—approaching

10. MS V—approaching

11. CU H

12. CU HE—smiling

13. MS V—approaching H-HE

14. MS H—beginning of chase —H jumps over railing of porch

15. CU HE—expression of alarm

16. Full Shot—splices being operated

MUSIC DOWN FOR BEGINNING OF NARRATION

17. MCU H—looking around for HE

THEN MUSIC OUT

18. CU film running through moviola

19. MLS V dragging HE running from H

Editing is the process of arranging the shots of a film.

20. CU synchronizer-pan from footage counter to mag track and film running through*

It is generally considered

21. CU H chasing V

the most important and

22. MS girl editing

powerful element

23. MS synchronizer

of filmmaking.

24. CU synchronizer spinning

Editing gives

25. MC from a front angle—V running away

a film its sense and continuity so that it can tell its

26. Cut away to trees—dolly shot

story clearly. Good editing keeps a film

27. MC take up reels

interesting.

28. CU editor's face

29. CU side view of editor

In this film you will be shown how the editor

30. MS editor

arranges shots into a finished film.

31. CS viewer

The basic equipment of the film editor includes a viewer and a

32. CS rewinds

pair of rewinds.

33. MC side view of editor

The viewer is good for seeing the

34. CU screen of viewer demonstrating the difficulty of pull-

composition and action of a shot, but

---

*"Mag track" means magnetically recorded sound film and, in this case, perforated 16mm film to be carried on the synchronizer.

ing film through viewer at a consistent speed	because it is hard to move the film constantly at the correct speed, it is difficult to evaluate the rhythm and pace of the film.
35. MS projector	For this purpose the film should be run on a projector unless
36. MS man working moviola	you have access to a professional motor-driven editing machine which will run at constant speed.
37. Full Shot—splicer being used	Splicing is the basic mechanical task of film editing.
38. CU editor's face	Since splices
39. MS front view of editor	must be strong and accurate, a good
40. Full Shot—splicer (no action)	splicer and skill
41. MS front view of editor	in its use are very important to the film editor.
42. MS synchronizer	The film synchronizer has two basic purposes.
43. MS footage counter of synchronizer	It has a footage counter for measuring,
44. MS front of synchronizer showing 40 frames per foot	and the front sprocket wheel is marked to show the 40 frames in each foot of 16mm film. One revolution of the synchronizer spindle equals one foot of film of 40 16mm frames.
45. MS film and mag. tape running through synchronizer	The synchronizer is also used to move two or more pieces of film and/or sound track together frame by frame.
46. MS side view of editor	Editing is usually done with a "work print", an inexpensive print made from the original film which was shot in the camera.
47. CU editor's face	A workprint is used to prevent
48. MS side view of editor	damage to the original film by scratches, finger marks or other accidents. The editor can also experiment with
49. CU footage counter	cutting and recutting the film
50. MS side view of editor	without losing frames or having unnecessary splices in the original.
51. CU editor's face	Only after the
52. MS side view of editor	final editing of the workprint does the editor work with the original camera footage, conforming or matching it to the edited workprint.

53. CU film pulling through synchronizer showing A-B rolls

Most often in working with 16mm film, the original picture is edited into two rolls called A and B. Individual shots in a sequence are alternated between the two rolls and are separated from each other by black leader. When prints or negatives are then made from these A&B rolls, the splices will be invisible.

54. LS V and HE running away and out of frame supered over CU of gun

Using A&B rolls also allows editing special effects such as superimpositions and

55. Diss. to LS-V-H-HE running to the top of a hill

dissolves.

56. Diss. to title frame—naming the four major categories of editing effects

Editing effects can be grouped into four major categories: spatial, temporal, point of view, and transitions.

57. Diss. to title frame: SPATIAL

The first of these groups, spatial effects,

58. MS H-HE facing camera in a posed stance

has to do with the composition and

59. MCU Camera behind HE on H face, as V comes up behind and hits H

movement of the objects in a shot.

•   •   •

After the exposition has been completed, the summary ends the film. In this case the summary is the finished film as finally edited. We'll only look at a short part of this.

MOVIE BEGINS

The edited sequence, with appropriate music, runs for a couple of minutes to the end of the film.

156. LS establishing shot of house where story takes place

157. Diss. to MS-H-HE walking on porch to where HE sits down

158. Match-cut to MS.—HE sitting down

159. CU HE's face smiling

160. CU H's face talking

161. MS H-HE talking while V appears in background—spots H-HE

162. MCU V pulling mustache while studying situation

163. MS H-HE talking—V moves in background to begin sneaking towards H-HE

164. MS back view of V moving towards porch where H-HE are talking in background

165. CU V looking at couple

166. MS camera angle below and through porch railing as though from the V's point of view—H-HE talking

167. CU V watching-moves towards porch

168. MS V moving towards porch (camera angle from porch through railings) — peers through railing

169. MCU H sitting talking (camera angle from V's point of view)

170. CU V peering through railing

171. MS V creeps around porch towards couple

172. MS V creeps up the steps of the porch

173. MS V creeps around corner of the porch

174. LS H-HE talking (camera angle from V's point of view)

175. MS V creeping along railing towards H-HE (camera angle from V's point of view)

176. MCU H's face—V sneaks up behind and hits H (camera angle slightly below and to right side of HE)

177. CU HE's face—expressing surprise and alarm

178. CU V holding gun

179. CU V grabs HE up from the chair

180. MS V chases HE out of chair

181. MLS V pulling HE down steps of porch and they run away

182. LS H lying on porch

183. MS V pulling HE along

184. LS H getting up after being knocked out on porch

185. MCU H gets up—looking around

186. MS empty chair where HE was sitting

187. MCU H looking around putting on hat

188. MCU V pulling HE (camera angle from the front)

189. MS H running to railing looking around (camera angle from below in yard)

190. CU H looking around

191. MS H jumping over railing off the porch (camera angle from below looking upwards)

192. LS V pulling HE running

193. MLS H begins to chase V—stumbles and falls

194. CU H running (side view)

•   •   •

The film continues until scene 219 and the credit titles.

One of the most difficult problems for an about-to-be screen writer to overcome is the problem of words! All of us are used to writing and speaking, and we have learned to follow a flow in the direction towards which the words we use lead us. There is a logic that is inherent in words and the flow of verbal ideas. Unfortunately, this may NOT be a logic that is congenial to motion pictures or any medium other than words. Ideally, writers must learn to SEE what they write when they write movies and make sure that the *visual flow* is such that it leads viewers' eyes in the directions they want the audience to go.

Let me give an example of what I mean. Suppose that your idea needs to state something about geese and the kind of environment they like to be in and then needs to say something about a different kind of countryside in which there are field birds and thistles. There is no problem with such a juxtaposition if we are writing; we simply write whatever it is we want to say. In films, however, our eyes must be led in certain ways, somewhat analagous to the movement of our eyes induced by the skill of a painter. In films we can also go from geese and grass to rough countryside and thistles—but we do it cinematically: perhaps, by calling for a shot of the feet of a goose walking on grass past some dandelions that have turned to seed and which are setting their silky floss free, and then following this shot by the down of a thistle in the air and retracing the course of the thistledown to the plant itself. Maybe this illustration is forced and mechanical, but it is given to draw attention to the idea that it is possible to provide some kind of visual flow in writing a film, and it is this flow that respects the nature of cinema, instead of being overborn by the written words.

This is really why you must learn to think visually when you write film scripts and why you must think visually when you read film scripts. It is why a competent writer of instructional films or other non-theatrical motion pictures learns to write the left side of the page before the right. This is not to say that one writes the left side of the entire film before writing the right side of the page, but it is desirable to write several scenes on the left BEFORE writing the dialogue or narration that is to go with them. Remember, film is a visual medium.

It is true that the director of your film will take it as his or her responsibility—as indeed it is—to visualize whatever you have written. It will be the director who will make sure that the shooting is planned so that the editor will have the shots that will make possible the most creative kind of film. To do this the director will, among other things, see to it that the action follows an appropriate direction across the screen from shot to shot, that the tempo of action is appropriate, that the forms and compositions of each shot are creative and appropriate. Nevertheless, the more visual aid you can give the director, the more of your own creativity you will have imparted to the film and the easier you will have made everybody else's job.

It will surprise most people who are not familiar with the motion picture medium to see how many scenes there are in this film-editing script. This script is really a special kind of thing, however. It is what is called *as-shot*. This means that the script reflects the film after it has been finished: the script was, in fact, written *from* the final film. For this reason, every piece of film was identified in its proper place, *after* the film editor had added to the filmed footage all his creativity. The original script, *before* shooting, would have had perhaps 25 percent less scenes in it—maybe even less than that. The film would have developed as it progressed during production and as new ideas and details were added by the director and the editor: after all, *their* creativity, too, can enhance a film. In the final analysis, there are about 11 cuts per minute in the finished film. If the actors had spoken their dialogue and the speeches had been recorded, each scene would have lasted a far longer time on the screen, because of the nature of direct speech.

Note also that the right-hand side of the page appears to have no respect for the way a sentence ought to *look* when it is set in type. As a matter of fact, it doesn't! The right hand side of the page is set out so that the reader can see what words occur during what shot. The cinema logic is dominant, not the literary. When writing narration, or dialogue, remember this and set it down so that the line of spoken words appears opposite the description of the scene to which it has relevance.

The visual detail that is set out in this script should make your job of visualizing that much easier. Try to *think* the pictures as you read. In any case, you can find a kind of crib, because, as I said earlier, you can borrow the film from the producer, International Film Bureau, Inc., (332 South Michigan Avenue, Chicago), and compare the film and the script.

Every instructional film, every classroom film, must bear the endorsement of an educational advisor who will have been, in some degree, the on-going authority on whom the producer and director will have relied for technical advice and consultation during the production of the film. When a film is issued under the imprimatur of such an educational advisor, the anxieties of the teachers and instructors who may want to use the film in their teaching are laid to rest, for it has been declared, by a worthy and competent authority, to be correct and useful! In the case of *A Film About Film Editing,* I was the consultant.

When an educational film is planned, a list of concepts to be included in it is prepared in consultation with the educational advisor. In the film under discussion all the concepts that we agreed had to be included are set out in a clear and fluid procession.

Finally, note that the narration is said to be "voice over"; that is, the voice is heard over the pictures and there is no direct nor immediate relationship between the *person* of the narrator and the persons within the film. When, as in this film, the narration *is* voice over, it is possible to manage the visuals (photographically and in editing) as if the film were, in fact, a kind of silent film. The length of each shot doesn't depend upon the words that must be said as it would if we were shooting and editing synchronous dialogue. The pacing of the editing and the actual choice of the shots to be made need instead relate only to the inherent *action* of the sequence.

A Film About Film Editing is really a kind of illustrated lecture, however, and its didacticism is forthright. Such films are intended to be didactic—the audience is captive, and the points of reference of the film are accepted by the consensus of the group. Further, and most important, classroom films, pedagogic films, didactic films, are always presented in an environment that permits what is called "immediate utilization." A teacher or a discussion leader presents the film, usually with a brief introduction that puts a framework around the presentation so that the attitudes and attention of the audience are focused. Then, immediately after the film ends, the teacher or discussion leader conducts a discussion in which the salient points are exposed and explored, with all the associations that will have special meaning for the immediate audience. By this means, points that may have escaped the notice of some members of the audience are brought to their attention and the comprehension of everyone is assured.*

Industrial Films

Equally attitudinal, equally educational, although not involved with classroom instruction or other direct didactical purpose, are a host of films that are considered in the general catgory of public education. In a real sense, these films are often true documentaries. Frequently, such films are made to satisfy a special need, to fulfill a special purpose, to perform a special task.

The script that follows is called *Fighting Ships;* it was written for a very special need during the time of World War II. Then, as now, the production of many things in our lives is a very complicated process that is achieved only by a great deal of specialized labor. Often the maker of one part, or the performer of one operation, doesn't have the slightest idea of how his or her work really fits into the whole, nor on what other jobs it may depend. When the unit that is produced is as complicated as a ship that goes to sea with a crew of hundreds inside it, the estrangement of one tiny group of workers from another, the apparent alienation of their jobs from all the others, is severe. In those days I was working for the National Film Board of Canada and I was asked to write a script for a film that would focus on this problem by explaining to a steelworker in Hamilton, Canada, who made the plates for the hull of a ship, what all the other jobs and parts and processes might be. By extension, the film would provide the same information to all those other workers.

For this film, as for most industrial films that deal with the processes of production, the first step is what is called a *scripting trip.* The writer, probably accompanied by a technical advisor from the company—or, as in my case, from a government department—goes to visit all the plants in which salient production processes take place. The writer is given a very detailed guided tour so that he or she can SEE what is taking place and UNDERSTAND the processes. The writer will do well to take a camera along for a collection of many polaroid still photographs, taken from every corner of every room and of every portion of every process, will be an invaluable *aide-mémoire.* It will also be of invaluable help to the director and cameraman who will need some kind of forewarning of the problems they will encounter so that they can properly prepare for them. (Wherever it is possible, and wherever the writer has even the tiniest semblance of competence, she or he should attempt to discover where the nearest main source of electric power may lie for each of the rooms, and, if possible, find out how much power is available so that enough cable can be brought to serve whatever lights may be needed. With this information, and with the photographs, the writer should consult with the producer, the cameraman and the director—all of them, if possible; if not, with

---

*The functions of instructional films are discussed under Non-Theatrical Films in chapter 8.

whomever is available—so that he or she does not write into the script any sequences that either can't be shot, or that might be too expensive to shoot.)

After a number of discussions with the producer at the National Film Board who had already had a number of discussions with the appropriate people in the government department concerned, I visited a large number of factories in a large number of towns in Ontario and Quebec, the two most industrial provinces of Canada and the ones in which all the elements we needed were to be found. I visited the steel plants of Hamilton, Ontario, and, in the same province, I saw the making of electric cables of all sizes and kinds in a plant in Peterborough, the making of all sizes of propellers in a plant in Owen Sound, and many others. I obtained some idea of the sequence of operations in each factory and of the kinds of labor performed by the workers. I also got a sense of how all of these different products—propellers, gauges, pumps, cables, and so on—were themselves part of something larger and more complex; and I absorbed a feeling of their interrelationships. These were the things I would have to deal with in the script.

On the other hand, I had already learned another lesson that all film writers must learn. Factories don't wait for you to make your film; they must continue to operate. It may be weeks or months between the time of the scripting trip and the actual shooting. This lapse of time is real, honest, and legitimate. It takes a while to write a script, and it takes another while to get the complete approval of the sponsor or client. Then production has to be scheduled by the film production house. This scheduling may depend upon the availability of its own personnel, it may depend also on the activities of the factory whose production may have changed only somewhat in the interim, or may have changed a great deal indeed. In any case, for this reason the sequences in each of the locations that deal with operations or processes, are not written into the script at this time. Half a dozen scene numbers are allocated to each such sequence to indicate a kind of elasticity and to provide some kind of nomenclature for the scenes. If not enough numbers have been provided, the director will add letters to some of the numbers, for example, 77, 77A, 77B, 77C, and so on.

Before presenting parts of the script for *Fighting Ships,* let me point to several abbreviations that have not yet been defined: *BG* stands for background, *FG* stands for foreground, *F.O.* means fade out, *F.I.* means fade in, and *freeze frame* means that the action of the scene is "frozen" so that it appears to be a still photo.

FIGHTING SHIPS

VISUAL	NARRATIVE
1. A convoy is shown going out to sea . . . suddenly it is at-	Out into the grey Atlantic, laden with tools for the new offensive warfare, sail

tacked by air and submarine, there is a fierce battle during which a tanker is struck and sunk. Survivors are seen bobbing about in the winter sea . . . some are on a life raft, shivering in the unmerciful cold . . .

1A. The scene loses animation, freeze

the convoys . . . week in, week out, squat freighters and tankers head into the winter sea with cargoes of food and munitions for the expanding front lines of the United Nations. Shepherded by fast destroyers and corvettes, these ships of freedom sail on over the dark horizon into the dangers of tempest and attack.

FADE IN DICK'S VOICE READING: . . . and that was all I could see . . . just a bit of flaming wreckage that sank very quickly and a handful of men, their faces black with oil, shivering on a raft . . . and way off in the distance was a lifeboat looking for others . . . and bouncing about like a walnut shell . . .

Dissolve to

1B. Man's hand as it crumples paper.

cut to

2. MCS Dick
cut to
3. MCS Harriet
cut to
4. CS Dick
cut to
5. MS both at table

cut to
6. CS Dick

cut to
7. Full-face Dick, from over H's shoulder
Dick begins to smile and says:

cut to
8. MS Harriet gets up and goes to Dick at the door; they kiss each other goodbye.
cut to
9. MLS from outside . . . door is open; both D & H are visible . . . D comes down steps and H slowly closes door.
cut to
10. Series of shots showing Dick on his pedestrian progress to work . . . during which
11. his voice delivers the accom-

DICK: They're doing real things out there.

HARRIET: You're doing things, too, Dick—

DICK: Yeah?
How?

HARRIET: You're helping to build the ships aren't you?

DICK: Ships! It might as well be frying pans as ship plate.

HARRIET: But, Dick, the steel plates you make, they're just as important as the guns . . . why, if it wasn't . . .

DICK: Yes, I know . . . but, when you do the same job every day, you sort of lose sight of what it means . . .

HARRIET: You mustn't feel that way Dick . . .

DICK: I know, dear, . . . but if we could only see what they did with our stuff.

DICK: (Voice off camera begins to be heard as D approaches the camera): That's the trouble with the whole thing . . .

Our plates go into ships—but we're so far away from the ships, we lose sight of 'em. Seems funny, though . . . you'd think doing the same thing all the time panying rumination . . . his arrival at the plant

12. coincides with the last two sentences of the rumination . . .

would bring you closer to it . . . but I guess it just becomes a habit, like biting your nails . . . That's the way it is now . . . if we could only find out just how they use the plates we make . . . if we could really see those ships they're building . . .

• • •

24. MLS inspection group . . . lieutenant, superintendent and another . . . the group approaches Dick . . .
    cut to MCS

25. Super. introduces Dick and lieutenant

SUPER: Mr. McFletrick, Mr. Bing-ham . . .
LT: How are you?
DICK: Fine.

26. CS Lieutenant—nods towards it
    cut to

LIEUTENANT: What's this plate for?

27. CS Dick—indicates number

DICK: We don't know much about it . . . it's just an order number to us . . .

    cut to

28. CS order number on plate
    cut to

LT: Just a number, eh?

29. MCS Dick and Lieut.

DICK: Yes . . . you can't get very close to a number.
LT: How do you mean . . .

    cut to

30. CS Dick

DICK: You take in the paper this morning that story about the convoy . . . we feel out of it here . . .

    cut to

31. CS Lieutenant
    cut to MS

LT: Out of it?

32. group . . . Lt., Dick, Tom . . . Tom tries wordlessly to silence Dick. Dick indicates plate
    cut to

DICK: Sure . . . if we only knew what what this was for . . . or where it goes on the ship . . .

33. MCS Lt., smiling . . .
    cut to

LT: It'd be a bit tough to tell you that.

34. MS Dick . . . he turns back to work . . .

DICK: Yes, . . . I guess so . . .

35. CS Lt.
    cut to

LT: (Softly) But I think we could arrange . . . yes . . . we might at that.

36. MS Lt. and Dick
    Dick straightens up . . .
    cut to

How would you like to see a ship launched? . . . a ship that's got some of your plates in her?

37. CS Dick

DICK: Would I? Sure I would . . . but there's a fat chance of that . . .

38. CS Lt.
    F.O.
    F.I.

LT: Well, we'll see . . .

39. MS front view of Dick and officer looking up at corvette. Officer points
    cut to

OFF: There she is. Better take a good look . . .

40. MLS hull of corvette on ways with back view Dick and officer in FG

DICK: So that's the baby. Well, when do I start.

41. Officer points to trigger blocks
    cut to

OFF: Hold on now. You see those triggers there. . . ?
When the time comes, there'll be men standing by to cut the ropes.

42. MS trigger blocks and pan along holding dogs
    cut to

43. CS trigger block

DICK: Isn't she ready yet?

44. Three shots of general activity on the hull of

OFF: Don't sound so glum. There's quite a bit still to do . . . but you'll be in at the finals.

45. vessel—welding; drilling; rivetting.

46.   cut to

SOUND EFFECTS UP.

47. MS front view Dick and officer. Officer pulls Dick's sleeve. Dick still stares absorbed at corvette; Officer starts to move off. Dick snaps out of it and follows him. Camera pans with them till they round some convenient object.
    cut to

OFF: Come on. There are other things to see.
DICK: Other things?
OFF: Sure. Ships have to be built before we can launch them.
DICK: You think I don't know that?

48. Either pan shot with men as they walk through yard OR trucking shot of what they see OR pan and truck shot in sequence.
    cut to

SPRIGHTLY MUSIC THROUGHOUT THIS SEQUENCE

49. CS Dick and officer
    cut to

OFF: You take propellers now.

50. Pan down from stern to men adjusting propeller in drylock.
    mix to

That one weighs about a ton and a half, but they come as high as 13 tons.

51. Inclusive to cover Owen
to Sound material

They cast them all in one piece.

58. (Propeller factory located at Owen Sound, Ontario)

DICK: They pour it, eh, just like we do at the mill.
OFF: Not exactly. You see, you make ingots, but they have to cast a whole propeller, with delicate curves, sharp edges and so forth. So they pour from the bottom up, as it were.
DICK: That cuts out splash and helps the mold keep its shape?

mix to

59. MLS Officer and Dick threading way across piles of steel. Off. helps Dick up

mix to

60. Inclusive to cover Engine
to factory footage
66. at Montreal

mix to

67. MS Dick and Officer pausing before BG of ship skeleton or other dockyard scenery to sit down. Officer gesticulates to Dick.

mix to

68. Inclusive for steam gauges
to and valves
72.

OFF: That's it. Then they break the mold, chip the rough casting with a cold chisel, and it's ready for machining.

DICK: That's casting in a big way. But how about the engines to turn these big propellers.

OFF: The engines . . . watch out or you'll be tripping over your own steel plate. . . . the engines of course, have to be big stuff too, even for a 300 ton minesweeper . . . An average marine engine weighs nearly 150 tons.

DICK: Why that's tremendous.

OFF: Yes, but it's really three engines: one for driving, one for turning and one for reversing, and all three have to be delicately held together with eccentrics and connecting rods.

DICK: How long does it take to build one?

OFF: It varies. About three months is good. They have to machine the base and level it; they have to get the main bearings bedded, the crankshaft put in, and believe me, that's some crankshaft. Then the business of dropping the cylinders into the columns is pretty tricky. That single operation may take ten men 8 hours.

DICK: Bit different from a land engine.

OFF: Well, it has to turn a shaft maybe 90 feet long and 18 inches wide with a propeller on the end of it, and drive a 1000 ton vessel through the sea at nearly 30 mph.

OFF: Let's sit down for a bit.

DICK: Must've covered all of five miles.

OFF: Yeah. But what gets me about these engines is the delicate work that goes into the pressure gauges and valves.

DICK: It's no more delicate than boring cylinders is it?

OFF: No, but here you've got two units both starting from the same thing. Poured metal—and yet utterly different in every way . . . One weighs up to 150 tons; the other may weigh only a few pounds and be a real precision job—like a pressure gauge or a temperature indicator. They pour these gauges from small carbon arc furnaces.

DICK: A bit of the steel mill in that.

OFF: Maybe, but the tooling is a lot more

precise, if you'll pardon me. And drilling the correct movement for the gauge is work that can only be done by people with a watchmaker's skill. The same applies to the assembly. When you see a gauge broken down you realize how accurate they have to be.

DICK: You mean men's lives depend on

mix to

the right head of steam?

73. CS pump in marine stores

OFF: Yes, the same as they might depend on that pump there.

DICK: Pumps, I thought they only used them when the ship was full of water?

mix to

74. Inclusive to cover pumps and
to   filters
79.

•   •   •

The film continues through sequences at the pump factory, the manufacture of generators and the insulating of cables, the launching of the corvette and its test run, and, finally, an appropriate ending to the film.

As you can see, this kind of script is somewhere between a treatment and a final shooting script. It is as final as one can make it in the face of uncontrollable environments and events. At the same time, it provides a firm framework within which the director and the crew can work productively to achieve the purpose of the film.

The direct dialogue sequences occurring between people who have the appearance of reality give the audience the means of identifying with those people. The purpose of the film, as I said at the outset, was to develop some kind of understanding of a worker's work and of a worker's place in the scheme of things. This was to increase morale during wartime, clearly a job of attitude building. Thus, we took advantage of the means afforded by the motion picture medium to provide characters with whom the audience had some kind of identification and thus, through them, developed some modification of attitude.

Yet, having used the sync sequences as the means by which to accompany Dick and the officer on their travels and sight-seeing tours, the officer, who is the guide, becomes the voice-over narrator for the sequences in the various factories and plants. In this case, the distance that usually occurs between an off-screen narrator and the audience is overcome because the audience has come to know the narrator as a person, and viewers put themselves into Dick's place during each of these sequences.

The screen instruction *mix to* is just another way of saying *dissolve to,* and it would be the director's job to find forms and shapes in the various shots so that dissolves could flow with some similarity of composition in each of the two shots concerned.

Throughout the script there is an attempt to provide some kind of motivation for the movement from one sequence to another and from one plant to another, and the script attempts to indicate as vigorously as possible a *visual* as well as narrative means of progression.

If the dialogue between the characters in *Fighting Ships* seems to be stiff or written with somewhat less care than might have been expected, you may have made a keen observation. The film was to be performed by non-professional actors, people who were indeed the workers at the respective jobs. Dick was to be, in fact, a steelworker; the naval lieutenant was to be a real naval lieutenant. The dialogue that was written into the script was an *indication* of what we wanted the characters to say. However, most non-professional actors have a great deal of difficulty remembering lines of dialogue and delivering them in a manner that sounds natural. It was our expectation that when we did the actual filming, we would discuss the brief sequences of dialogue with the participants and let them develop the speeches that would carry the same content but would also be comfortable in their mouths and therefore believable to the audience.

A Note About Narration

In the foregoing scripts, two different ways of handling narration have been presented. In the first example, *A Film About Film Editing*, the narration is all voice-over: in the second, *Fighting Ships*, it is voice-over, but in the voice and person of someone with whom the audience has become familiar because he has spoken sync sound on camera before speaking voice-over narration. Each kind of narration serves its own purpose and develops its own kind of relationship between the narrator and the audience. Hopefully, these special qualities will have become apparent to you from studying the scripts.

Do not be dismayed by the fact that the narration for *Fighting Ships* hadn't yet been written. It is a common way to make a documentary or an industrial film. The writer first writes a treatment with great or little detail—in the film being discussed, it was written with great detail. Then, since the shooting has been indicated as clearly as possible to the director and cameraman, the shooting takes place. After this, the editor puts it together. Then, and only then after the film has been edited, does the writer write the final narration. While this may seem strange and filled with obstacles, in actual fact it makes possible a very creative process. When writers can see the footage for which they must prepare the narration, they can draw a special benefit. Working directly with the images that will be projected on the screen, writers can be moved by those images and find inspiration in them. They can let the images help them write.

How do the images help? Remember a basic rule: motion pictures are dependent upon motion and derive their dynamic from it. *All movement is expressed in verbs and the quality of movement is expressed in adverbs*. Images can thus suggest dramatic, sensitive, evocative verbs and adverbs to a writer, and these will enrich the narration beyond belief.

This kind of enrichment can be further enhanced if the writer refrains from duplicating in the narrative what appears on the screen. It is not necessary to say, "Here is so-and-so" or "Now we see so-and-so." If it can be seen, the writer doesn't have to say it. If it has to be said, it has been visually presented badly. Remember, again, in motion pictures it is the motion that provides the dynamic. When we watch a film, it is the pictures that fascinate us because of their movement and because of what we can see moving. The words have less dynamic, and their function in narrative is *complementary*. Repeat: narrative is complementary! Thus, it should not duplicate the pictures. If we see a South Sea Islander climbing a very high coconut palm, there is no need to say "Moana is now climbing a coconut palm." That would be redundant and boring. On the other hand, it might be interesting to be told whether there is more than one crop a year, how many nuts a single tree might yield, how many trees might be picked by Moana in a day, a week, or a season, and to learn how many kinds of artifacts and foods are derived from the coconut tree and its fruit.

Just as counterpoint tends to enrich musical statement, so a complementary relationship between images and words enrichs the impact of a film.

If this idea is extended to another level, we can suggest that the verbs, and the complementary narrative, can also serve as metaphoric statements to provide even further enrichment. An illustration of this idea was taught me by John Grierson, the founder and leader of the documentary film movement in Britain, Canada, Australia, and a lot of other places. In a film I was making there was a scene in which we were in a very large shipbuilding yard in Vancouver, British Columbia. Our camera was placed high on the top of a ship that was almost finished, and we were watching a large plate of steel being lifted by a huge crane, high above another nearly finished hull, over that hull, and on to a third. There was no need to describe what was happening in this tremendously exciting and beautiful scene. Everything was evident—the unbelievable size of the shipyard, the number of hulls under construction, the awesome lift and carry of the crane as it took the sheet from place to place. I wrote the narration with little direct reference to the action. It talked about the need for the ships and the purpose of their building. They were to take their place in the North Atlantic convoys in which so many ships had already been sunk by the Nazi submarines. It talked of the need for these many merchant ships "filled with the goods of war, bearing across the winter sea their cargoes of hope and victory." We were careful to synchronize the words "bearing across" with the visual image of the transverse movement of the sheet of steel plate as it was carried by the gigantic crane high over the ship's hulls. The phrase "bearing across" was thus a metaphoric adaptation of the action we were watching. The audience response to the action can be greatly intensified by the use of this technique.

Although that film was made during World War II, the mode in which it was made is not out of date. Unfortunately, not even the subject is firmly behind us.

There are several other aspects of the structure of the script you have just read that are important to note again. One is the use of believable people speaking in sync, on camera, so that the audience can be induced to empathize more deeply. Second, is the recognition that, in some instances, there is only an indication or outline of the actual speech that will be recorded. Third, is the knowledge that some of the writing will have to be done after the filming is completed because the writer didn't know precisely what would be photographed since he couldn't control it completely.

The film script from which the following excerpts come was written more than 30 years after *Fighting Ships*. Yet two of these same three structural aspects appear in it: direct sync dialogue and sequences that cannot be written about until they have been shot. The script was written for a shipping company that had developed a new kind of carrier system for freight to and from the Mediterranean and Black Seas; it was prepared in 1975 by Bernard Edmonds. The title is *LASH: The Ship for Any Cargo.*

Because the film production company had to assume that a good number of the people in the shipping company would have to read the script in order to approve it, and because they also had to assume that these people might have little or no experience with film scripts, the actual script is preceded by an Introduction/Glossary. Even though some of the terms in the brief glossary were provided earlier in this book, it is appropriate to reprint the introduction to the film just as it originally appeared.

Three notes before you read: The word *montage,* which has appeared before, is French and is pronounced mon-TAZH. The word *segue* is Italian and is pronounced SEH-gway, it means "follows." Traditionally musical instructions are written in Italian. Finally, in this script the first scene is numbered 101 in the left margin, instead of 1. It is of no great importance, but to start numbering with three digits eases the job of the typist who can keep the numbers and the beginnings of the instructions equally spaced without effort.

LASH: The Ship for Any Cargo

INTRODUCTION/GLOSSARY

This shooting script is divided into two columns: VISUAL and AUDIO.

VISUAL   Each scene (or shot) is numbered consecutively except where one shot serves as a master scene and short vignettes or type are intercut or supered over. In that case, the shot number remains the same and a letter designates the change.

Animation indicates artwork/photos rephotographed under an animation camera.

Live action signifies normal activity.

Optical stands for the rephotography of live action material in a different mode, i.e., freeze frame, split screen, slow motion.

ECU	Extreme close-up
CU	Close-up
MCU	Medium close-up
MS	Medium shot
MLS	Medium long shot
LS	Long shot
ELS	Extreme long shot
Wide Angle	Very broad field of view
Tight Shot	Close field of view
Pan	Camera revolves horizontally
Tilt	Camera revolves vertically
Zoom	Lens changes its field of view optically
Dolly shot	Camera travels on movable vehicle: crane, dolly, car, wheel chair
Travelling shot	Camera travels: walking or as in dolly shot
Dissolve	One shot merges and becomes the next shot (overlap)
Montage	Several shots tightly edited together to form a pictorial sequence

AUDIO   All narration, i.e., spoken by the NARRATOR, will appear in the film as it is written.

Other voice-over narration and dialogue (RADIOMAN, COMPANY PRESIDENT, CAPTAIN, MILITARY SEALIFT COMMAND OFFICER, TERMINAL MANAGER, CUSTOMER, et al.) will also be based upon this script, but will reflect the style of speech natural to each individual. This script can only outline the subject areas and indicate their visual treatment—the final wording (and phrasing) of specific dialogue must come from the individual. Thereby, the use of *real* Company personnel will lend credibility to the whole film.

SFX	Sound effects. Either recorded sync or wild or pre-recorded
Sync	Synchronous. Sound recorded at same time as picture
Wild	Sound recorded without picture
Segue	A sound dissolve
Voice over	Voice without the speaker being seen

VISUAL	AUDIO
101. Animation. Title fades in . . . *LASH: The Ship for Any Cargo*.	SFX: fade in sea ambiance—wind and gulls.
102. Live action. LS fade in from title. Bird's eye view of mildly rough Atlantic a few miles from New York harbor.	MUSIC: Fully orchestrated "international" theme gently fades in over SFX and grows in intensity.
103. LS similar to 102 but ship	MUSIC CONTINUES.

enters frame on left and passes through on right.

104. MS of interior of engine room.
105. LS of access tunnel. Walking shot down corridor.

SFX: The continual whir and drone of a deep-sea cargo ship under way.
MUSIC CONTINUES.
SFX: Engine room—rhythmic rumbling.

SEAMAN (voice over): Ay, Ay, Sir! Ahead two-thirds!
MUSIC CONTINUES.

106. MS of radio room with Radioman at console.
107. CU of Radioman from behind.

SFX: Radio room ambiance.
RADIOMAN (voice over): Whiskey, Juliette, Able, Juliette. Whiskey, Juliette, Able, Juliette. We are approaching Ambrose Light and should be docking at the 29th Street pier at 1400.
(Pause, in an informal voice) Bob, tell Richie I'll call him tonight.

108. MS. Slow pan of radio room pausing on relevant equipment and weather facsimile report machine.
109. ECU of radio speaker.
110. CU of Radioman responding to call from the officer on the bridge.

SFX: Beep . . . Beep . . . Beep . . . Beep.
RADIOMAN: (in his official voice again) Ay, Ay, Sir! I'll call the pilot and get the information right now. . . . (continues conversation with officer on bridge).

111. CU of Navigating Officer on phone. In background we see other officers and Captain on the bridge.

MUSIC FADES DOWN AND OUT.
SFX: Bridge ambiance. Buoy bells and gongs. (Off-camera, very distant)

NAVIGATING OFFICER: (on phone to RADIOMAN) . . . Right, and please let me know when you've contacted headquarters. Thanks.

112. ECU of weather map of storm.

CAPTAIN: Well, except for that storm on Wednesday, this has been a really smooth crossing. Considering what the Atlantic can be like—this time of year. These LASH ships do make a difference out here when the wind decides to test its strength.

113. CU of Captain listening.
114. LS of passing ship.
115. LS of Ambrose Light as seen from the ship.

MATE: I know what you mean Captain.
SFX: Passing ship in Hudson Canyon.
SFX continues

116. CU of "LASH BARCELONA" sign on exterior of bridge.

SFX: Bridge exterior.

117. LS of bridge as seen from forward deck through bridge windows. Pilot enters.

MUSIC FADES IN AND BUILDS.
SFX: Ambrose Light ambiance. Pilot boards LASH ship and enters bridge.

118. LS of the aft end of the LASH Barcelona with lighters and containers in view as seen from the conning tower and then slow 180° pan towards the bow as ship passes under Verrazano Narrows Bridge.

VOICES: Ship's crew on bridge exchange hellos and news with Pilot—a brief reunion.
MUSIC CONTINUES.

VOICES CONTINUE.

SFX: LASH Barcelona passing under the Verrazano Narrows Bridge.

119. Extreme zoom out from tight shot of the LASH Barcelona after she passes under the bridge—revealing complete New York Harbor and continuing to zoom through the window of President's office in the World Trade Center. Pan over to desk as the President looks up and recognizes the camera. Slow zoom in to MCU as he begins talking. Title super: CHAIRMAN AND CHIEF EXECUTIVE OFFICER.

MUSIC: Concludes with logical coda.

SFX: Busy New York Harbor.

SFX: Harbor sounds segue to office ambiance.

COMPANY PRESIDENT: The LASH Barcelona is completing its 72nd Atlantic crossing and will be docking within the hour. Our Company has built and is running a fleet of five LASH ships providing weekly service to and from the Mediterranean. We are a United States flag carrier with a century-old tradition of service. We have always been proud members of the American Merchant Marine. And, we have always made that extra effort to be a leading force in the shipping industry.

• • •

The voice-over narrator only begins to speak a couple of pages later and this voice, while providing explanatory information, is structurally only a kind of linking between "indigenous" speakers.

As the film progresses we learn that LASH means *L*ighter *A*board *Sh*ip, that is, the large, ocean-going ship carries barges (lighters) as unit loads. We also are given a feeling of the kinds of cargoes in the various Mediterranean ports and information concerning the whole business of freight shipping in this tremendous and varied area.

At one point we come across this portion of the script:

201. LASH ship discharging lighters at Iskenderun.

MUSIC: Persian theme fades in.

202. Animation. CU of overland Turkey-Iran truck route.

203. Live Action. Project cargo being unloaded on a pier in Iskenderun.

209. LS of company tug MOHAWK pulling up to LASH ship at 29th Street pier.

Zoom into
CU of Tugboat Captain as he begins talking.

NARRATOR: An increased demand for project cargo in Iran sparked our interest. We checked out the overland truck route through Turkey: found it rugged but possible. Now, we call at Iskenderun, Turkey, and interface with an inland truck route directly to Iran.

NOTE: A brief case history section could go here. More detailed explanations would appear in the specific cargo modules.

SFX: New York Harbor. Dockside ambiance. Tugboat tying up to a LASH lighter: crew voices, engine boom, lines being thrown. In background is the purr of the LASH gantry crane off-loading barges.

TUGBOAT CAPTAIN: (Tugboat Captain discusses his role in the LASH system and emphasizes the availability of customer waterside facilities).

. . . there are so many unused docks and piers in and around the New York Harbor area . . . lots of spots for these barges . . .

• • •

After one or two more sequences, there is a summary and then the film ends. On careful study it will be seen that each sequence presents a certain concept that had been felt by the client (the sponsor) to be important for his audience. The film has speaking actors to develop the action within these sequences. The sequences are linked and summarized by the narrator—voice-over off-camera. As in *A Film About Film Editing* and *Fighting Ships,* the film begins with what is called an *action opening.* This is just what its name implies: it is a beginning of a film in which the viewer jumps mid-stream into the action.

When I spoke, much earlier, about writing for radio, I drew attention to the use of familiar theme music to introduce certain programs. The return of familiar music reassured the audience that they were in fact tuned to the right program. The use of such music at the beginning and end of each program served as a kind of curtain that, at the theatre, is raised at the beginning of each performance and lowered after it. This practice works well when there is an audience that is devoted, expectant, and habitual. The question now arises: how does one seduce people who may be turned away by a particular curtain? In movie theatres, before World War II, it was common to begin a film with all the credit titles. This was thought to serve several purposes. First, it gave people a chance to settle down in their seats before the story began. Second, and by no means of little importance, it became possible for the studios to emphasize the importance of their "properties"—the actors and actresses, and perhaps, the director. In those days, all these people were under long-term contracts to the studios and were considered very real properties. The studios spent a great deal of money building their names and reputations and, in fact, even subsidized the fan magazines.

This "opening curtain" of credit titles in the theatres did not prevent the audience from enjoying the film. They were prepared. They had dressed up to go to the theatre as was the fashion, and they had a psychological pre-set for the acceptance of the presentation.

Since World War II, there has been just about 30 years of television programming. The opening curtain, whether it be music or titles (with one exception that will be discussed later), is a hazard that the broadcaster does not want to provide. Clearly, if the audience is not "hooked" immediately, its members are likely to turn the dials of their TV sets to find another program. This loses the audience of program A to program B; more important, it loses the audience of the advertisers on program A to the advertisers on program B. The audience must be held at all costs!

The solution to the problem was soon found. All one had to do was to start the story *in medias res* and "catch the fancy of the king" in the momentum and excitement of action already in progress. The credits were then usually relegated to the end of the film (at which time people file out of the theatre or the TV room, failing, most of the time, to take any notice of those who have actually created the presentation!).

The habit of action openings is now firmly established, even with classroom and industrial films. It is still not necessary in the theatre to have an action opening because people are not going to leave before the film gets under way after they have paid a considerable amount of money for the ticket. Anyway, the theatrical feature film will eventually be seen on TV.

But the classroom audience and the industrial audience is what is called a *captive* audience: they are there willy-nilly and really can't go away. This means that a proportion of the audience is negatively predisposed to the presentation, and, for those members whose fancy may be just as hard to catch as the king's, an action opening may very well entrap them.

In *LASH—The Ship For Any Cargo,* the script just read, as in *Fighting Ships,* it is clearly stated that the dialogue is only indicated. Real people speaking real words that they find comfortable to speak provide greater credibility than other modes of presentation. Thus, the dialogue is indicated in great detail, but only as a frame within which a real, non-acting performer will recast the content to his own comfort.

Finally, both scripts provide for major portions of the film to be shot before the dialogue or narration is written, for all the reasons already discussed. In this last script, note scene 119 and the indication of the company president's speech and the sequence of scenes following 107.

The Mediterranean and Black Seas are certainly colorful and exotic, and to heighten this quality the script suggests that some of the narration be delivered in the languages of the different ports at which the vessels call. The images are specific and are themselves the translation of the narration. The visuals provide the information, and the narration provides the additional color. From time to time additional color is also provided by identifiable ethnic music or ethnic musical sounds.

I return to a suggestion made earlier: the more detail you, as the writer, put into your script, the clearer will be the perception of your intent. This is obviously important when you must discuss what you have written with your producer, your client, your director of photography, or others.

Institutional Films

In spite of what has been said, not all industrial films are shown to captive audiences. There is a category of film called *institutional* that you should know about. An institutional film is made by a large company or a public service organization, and its purpose is to provide some kind of public education. This service, too, has its purpose. By providing some kind of public education, a large corporation gains for itself a great deal of goodwill; thus, institutional films are excellent means of developing good public relations.

It Happened on Long Island was produced in 1976 for the Long Island Lighting Company, New York which had decided that a film could be an excellent contribution to the United States Bicentennial. The script was written by Bernard Edmonds. The Long Island Lighting Company has been making the completed film available to schools and community groups throughout the largest part of Long Island that is not in New York City; Saxton Communications Group, Ltd., the producing company, is distributing the film everywhere else. Therefore, it is available for you to see.

The producers describe the film this way:

The film is a chronological overview of Long Island's history and the history of the Nation. The film utilizes paintings, drawings, photographs, stock footage, documents, and maps. Live action photography of landscape and architecture add to the visual impact. The visual material is woven together with the sounds of history: letters and diaries, poetry and prose, and instrumentals and songs.

IT HAPPENED ON LONG ISLAND is structured around these highlights:

- Pristine wetlands and beaches
- Verrazano's and Hudson's discoveries
- Colonial growth of towns and families
- Battle of Long Island / Revolutionary War
- William Sidney Mount's genre paintings
- Sag Harbor's whaling boom

- Walt Whitman's beatific vision
- Lincoln and the Civil War
- The Centennial of 1876
- Theodore Roosevelt and conservation
- World War I and the Jazz Age
- World War II and Post-War expansion
- The 50's and 60's
- The Moon Shot

The film ends with a series of vignettes of contemporary Long Islanders talking about their Island.

The first scene of this film, too, is numbered 100.

It Happened on Long Island

VISUAL	AUDIO
100. Animation. Title fades in . . . LONG ISLAND: ALIVE WITH HISTORY.	MUSIC: Seventeenth century European chamber music fades in softly.
101. Live Action. Exteriors. LS fade in from title. Misty scenes of pristine Long Island: shoreline from the Atlantic Ocean.	MUSIC: continues.
102. Live Action. Exterior. Dissolve to LS of shoreline from Long Island Sound. (North Fork)	MUSIC: continues.
103. (As in 101) Dissolve to MLS of waves breaking with white caps. (Jones Beach)	MUSIC: continues.
104. (As in 101) Dissolve to MLS of Sunken Forest. (Fire Island)	MUSIC: continues.
105. (As in 101) Dissolve to MS and pan of virgin timber stand. (Gardiner's Island)	MUSIC: continues.
106. (As in 101) Dissolve to MS and pan of rolling terrain without signs of human habitation. (Shinnecock Hills)	MUSIC: continues.
107. Animation. Dissolve to European painting (Dutch or Flemish) of rolling countryside with fields and farms. (Painting should be evocative of the live action in 106)	MUSIC: continues.
108. Animation. Dissolve to Euro-	MUSIC: builds and increases in pres-

pean painting of chamber musicians performing. Slow zoom into CU of lead musician.

109. Animation. Dissolve from CU of musician's head in 108 to ECU of different person in another European painting. Zoom out to reveal full painting of individual within urban environment.

ence as we see musicians—the source of the composition.

SFX: muffled sounds of urban situation: talking and laughing, wagon wheels, footsteps, horses neighing (whatever is appropriate for the painting).

MUSIC: continues slightly under.

110. Live Action. Exterior. Dissolve to LS of another Long Island landscape. Ospreys flying over water. (Gardiner's Island)

SFX: Exterior wilderness: ospreys and wind rustling tree leaves.

111. Animation. Dissolve back to European painting of English wildlife.

MUSIC: continues slightly under.

112. Live Action. Exterior. On the sound of a shot cut to a species of wildlife found on Long Island: deer, fox, etc. (Gardiner's Island)

MUSIC: continues slightly under.

113. Live Action. Exterior CU of clam shells on the beach.

MUSIC: European chamber ensemble segues slowly.

114. (As in 113) Cut to CU of oyster shells on beach.

MUSIC: as in 113.

115. (As in 113) Cut to CU of scallop shells.

MUSIC: as in 113.

116. (As in 113) Cut to CU of mussels, snails, crabs on beach at low tide, a small wave washes over them. Zoom into remaining Quahog shell.

MUSIC: segues as sync sound of wave rolls in, then fades out.

MUSIC: under.

117. Live Action. Slow pan of Indian Wampum.

MUSIC: continues.

118. Live Action. Dissolve to ECU of European sovereign (coin) showing bas-relief of ruler (English or Dutch).

MUSIC: continues.

119. Animation. Dissolve from European ruler on coin to European painting of their conception of Indians as the noble savage.

MUSIC: continues.

120-130. Animation. Montage of Indian artifacts (arrowheads, tools, costumes, masks) intercut with European artifacts as seen in paintings of nobles (sceptres, crosses, ermines, jewels and crowns, books, castles and cathedrals).

MUSIC: continues.

131-134. Animation. Montage of portraits of European monarchs who ruled in the late 1500's and the early 1600's: James I, Charles I, etc.

135. Animation. Dissolve from last portrait in 134 to European painting of an American Indian. He is proud and tough. Slow zoom into ECU of his face.

NARRATOR: Many years ago people seeking new frontiers migrated to an Island they called Paumonok. They built their homes, hunted, fished, and farmed there for 5,000 years, passing on through stories the history of their island. The written history of this island begins with the arrival of the Europeans 400 years ago. It tells how they became the new Americans and how they developed their own civilization. It's history now, and it happened on Long Island.

136-138. Animation. Dissolve from ECU in 135 to ECU of face of another Indian from a European engraving. Montage of European engravings. On last one zoom into CU of face of one of the Indians. Dissolve back to CU of face in 135. Slow fade out.

•   •   •

For everyone whose background isn't either Indian or Eskimo, the history of Long Island began nearly 400 years ago, almost 200 years before the beginning of the American Bicentennium. To recall Long Island during the first 300 years there is no choice but to use artwork and to represent the last century and a quarter with photographs. Therefore the first sequences of the film intermix live action scenes of physical exteriors that might approximate the appearance of Long Island a long time ago with animation. Throughout all this there is very little narration. Color is provided by appropriate music and sound effects.

I have omitted the next portions of the film and present now a part of the script in which the narration is composed of quotations from historical documents. Each separate quotation is spoken by a different voice. Scenes 220 through 224 follow.

VISUAL

220. Animation.
Rum running.

AUDIO

". . . Be it enacted, . . . That there shall be raised, levied, collected and paid, unto and for the use of his Majesty, . . . upon all rum or spirits of the produce or manufacture of any of the colonies or plantations in America, . . . which shall be im-

221. Animation.
Tradesmen.

ported or brought into any of the colonies or plantations in America, . . . the sum of nine pence, money of Great Britain, . . . for every gallon thereof . . ."

"Be it enacted that there shall be raised, levied, collected, and paid, unto his Majesty, . . . the several Rates and Duties following: For every hundredweight avoirdupois of crown, plate, flint, and white glass, four shillings and eight pence.

For every pound weight avoirdupois of tea, three pence."

222. Animation. British soldiers forcibly entering a Long Island warehouse looking for hidden goods.

"By an act of parliament, it is lawful for any officer of his Majesty's customs, to take a constable, and go into any house, shop, cellar, warehouse, or room or other place and, in case of resistance, to break open doors, chests, trunks, and other package there, to seize, and from thence to bring, any kind of goods or merchandise whatsoever . . ."

223. Animation. Documents, papers with official stamp.

MUSIC: continues.

VOICE: (Stamp Act) "For every skin or piece of vellum or parchment, or sheet or piece of paper, on which shall be ingrossed, written or printed, any declaration, plea, replication, rejoinder, demurrer, or other pleading, or any copy thereof, in any court of law within the British colonies and plantations in America a stamp duty of three pence."

NARRATOR: The English parliament, through the Navigation and Stamp Acts, tried to control and curtail economic expansion . . . but life and work went on as usual.

224. Live Action. Exterior. CU of thoroughbred racing horse in action. Camera pans horse—horse is continual blur.

SFX: indistinct cheering of racing fans.

MUSIC: Handel continues under.

NARRATOR: The New Market Race Course, Hempstead Plains, 1665.

• • •

Still farther on in the script animation and live action continue to alternate, but when the film comes to a recent enough time in history, it can use still photographs of the period as well as artworks. At scene 551 the audience begins to hear real voices of real people recalling that history. Until then a mixture of music and sound effects has been indicated with only very brief pieces of narration. At the end of this sound sequence is the recorded voice of Alice Roosevelt Longworth.

Once again, remember that a sound film is just that, and writers must use every possible element if they are to be fully creative.

VISUAL	AUDIO
500-506. Live Action. Exterior. Fresh vegetables and fruit grown on Long Island and trucked into the city. ECUs of strawberries (Mattituck), cauliflower, asparagus, Brussels sprouts, cucumbers, and potatoes (from Suffolk County).	SFX: exterior ambiance—farmer's field: crickets, birds, the wind rustling the grass. MUSIC: Symphony of John Knoles Paine of the "New England School."
507-512. Animation. Continuous dissolves of line drawings with watercolor washes of shellfish (scallops, clams, oysters, crabs, lobsters) and fish (striped bass, bluefish, trout, salmon).	SFX: shallow waves lapping. MUSIC: continues.
513-517. Live Action. Continuous dissolves (as in 507-512) of Long Island farm animals raised in the post-Civil War period (turkeys, sheep and a few ducks).	SFX: barnyard sounds. MUSIC: continues.
518-522. Animation. Continuous dissolves (as in 507-512) of Long Island wildlife of the post-Civil War era.	SFX: exterior ambiance of forests and meadowlands. MUSIC: continues.
523. Live Action. Exterior. Traveling shot (from car or train) of natural vegetation of Long Island (no visible signs of human endeavor).	MUSIC: continues. NARRATOR: In 1866 Long Island was a paradise for farmers, fishermen, and hunters. At the end of the 19th century, Long Island was still an idyllic retreat from the rush and roar of industrial America. The whaling boom was over, busted by California gold and Pennsylvania petroleum. Light and energy would now come from the newly emerging gas and electric companies. The next boom industry to hit Long Island was tourism. Everybody summered there: wealthy New Yorkers, well-known writers and artists, aspiring social climbers, avid sportsmen. Even Europeans.

524-534. Animation. Paintings, photos, tintypes and souvenirs of the 1876 Centennial as celebrated on Long Island.

MUSIC: Star Spangled Banner (an 1876 arrangement).

535-540. Animation. Photos of Coney Island and Long Island resort hotels (Oriental, West Brighton, Manhattan Beach) intercut with dance bands and the J. P. Sousa Marine Band. South Shore resorts.

MUSIC: Star Spangled Banner segues into rousing Sousa march.

541-548. Animation. Paintings of views of Long Island at turn of the century. (William Merritt Chase, Winslow Homer, Childe Hassam, Thomas Moran, William Davis).

MUSIC: continues.

549. Live Action. Exterior. ECU of thoroughbred racing horse, background blurred.

NARRATOR: Sheepshead Bay Track, 1890.

550. Optical. Freeze frame of 549 and slow zoom in on head of horse.

551. Animation. Dissolve from 550 to another horse's head. Pull back to see Theodore Roosevelt astride his horse, grinning at camera.

MUSIC: continues.

VOICE: (Alice Roosevelt Longworth reminisces).

Before the first excerpt from this script, the producer provided some description of the film. You will see that 15 ideas are illustrated by the various sequences. They begin with shots of Long Island as it may very well have looked before the first Europeans arrived, and the history ends with the Moon Shot. The fifteenth sequence is composed of "vignettes of contemporary Long Islanders talking about their Island."

You may recall that, when I was talking about pedagogical films, films for the classroom, I spoke of the need to prepare a list of the concepts that had to be included in a film. This list of highlights around which It Happened on Long Island is structured is just such a list of concepts.

The Client and the Client's Approval

At this point it is necessary to issue a warning so that you will not be dismayed by your clients. I have already mentioned that your script will have to be approved by them. This will take place as soon as you have a presentable draft. The draft must be duplicated, and a copy provided to each member of the client's group who will have to pass judgment and make suggestions. If you have the extraordinary good fortune to find that your client is only one person, thank your lucky stars. He or she will cause you far fewer problems than will a committee and will require far fewer changes and take far less of your time.

If there is only one person, she or he will read your script and perhaps have a few suggestions to give you when you meet together. You will make the changes and give them to the client who will read them and probably let you know that he or she has approved the script. It would not be unreal to receive a copy of the final form of the script with the approval initialed on it within a couple of weeks.

When you have to deal with a committee, the problem is magnified many times. While it may take you only a couple of weeks to secure the approval of a client who is a single individual, for a committee it would be wise to add not less than one week per person—and it may likely require twice that amount of time. In business as in government, members of a committee all play roles. They all must make relatively "large" suggestions to prove that they are thinking about the problem before them. So, you will find each member of the committee making suggestions with some degree of emphasis. If the committee is relatively large, perhaps five or six or more, then the problem becomes even more involved. Not every member can attend each meeting for usually quite legitimate reasons. But, in someone's absence, suggestions will be made that you will follow in doing a re-write or a series of modifications. The absent member will be unaware of these suggestions, and at the next meeting, you and the committee members will have to explain what was intended. Now be prepared for his or her total disagreement and for another re-writing or remodeling job. I once wrote a script that had to be approved by a committee of about a dozen people; it took 13 months and 4 complete re-writes! I can only remind you of the definition of a camel: it is a horse put together by a committee!

Research and Intended Audiences

It may be going backward to discuss how to go about doing research for an instructional or industrial script after this long examination of later aspects of the craft, but research really is the beginning of your association with your client. In pedagogic films, your client may be your distributor (if you are working on a film that already has a distribution agreement of some kind), or your client may be, by a kind of analogy, your advisor or consultant. On the other hand, your client may be a commercial or industrial organization that has commissioned you to prepare a film for its use. (Perhaps it has commissioned the production company for whom you are writing.) In any case, your first approach to the job of writing any such film is to gather all kinds of information. I have found that it works best for me to ask my clients for all the printed material they can provide that has anything to do with the film. Until I have gone through this material, I don't even have enough information to ask productive questions.

It has also proved to be of value to me, especially when I am working on classroom films, to ask the advisor or client to give me two lists of concepts. The first list should contain those concepts or ideas that are essential to the film, concepts or ideas that simply must be included. The second list contains those ideas and concepts that would enhance the film if they were to be included, but which could be left out of it if the structure, cost, or length of the film would make their inclusion impossible.

This leads to one further warning that must be given to clients who have had little experience with films. A window of Tiffany's displays only one article. A window at Woolworth's shows a collection of nearly everything. Which items do you remember? Films work much the same way and should not be overstocked with ideas or concepts.

Once I have arrived at the point of asking questions about the subject matter of the film, there are other questions that I must remember to ask as well. To what kind of audience is the film to be addressed, and how will the film be presented to that audience? What is the film supposed to do to, or for, that audience? What are the ideas that appear to be most important or relevant to the client and to the proposed audience?

Knowing what kind of audience will be expected to view the film is just as important as knowing anything about the subject matter because it is the key to the question, "How shall I present the material?" Clearly, a classroom film for third grade will have to be presented in a different manner, and even with a different vocabulary, from a film for tenth grade. It will suppose an audience possessing a much less developed background of knowledge, and thus it will require relating to very different reference points. A film to be presented to a general audience, such as the audience for *It Happened on Long Island,* will treat its material differently from a film for a specialized, highly trained audience, such as the people interested in learning about more efficient and more economical ways of transporting freight by sea.

Once I have asked questions about the film's audience and purpose, once I know where and how the film will be viewed, I can begin to collect more information, and this additional information will in its turn generate still more questions. It is important to realize that one must have at one's fingertips a great deal more information than one will ever be able to use in a script before being able to write anything really usable. This may sound odd, but it must be remembered that every kind of communication, every kind of artwork (if the script and the film become that good), is the result of careful and artful *selection.* Selection cannot be made unless there has been an energetic collection of vastly more material than will eventually be used. It is from this storehouse of information that it becomes possible to draw the concepts with which the film will deal.

There are a host of special non-theatrical audiences and a large number of special purposes for which non-fiction films are made. Industrial films, for example, are made, as indicated, for a variety of purposes. There are films for training sales personnel; there are films for training dealers. Such films may be used to present new sales techniques to the audiences or to make them aware of new sales aids or advertising campaigns. Or such films may introduce new products or new models of old products. The presentation may take place at large annual sales meetings, in which case the films will probably be very expensive and very pretentious, even using well-known Hollywood stars in their casts. On the other hand, the films may be shown at much smaller regional meetings. There are also films called *point-of-sales* presentations. These are films shown in a store, or dealer's showroom, or some other place where a customer can see them. Such films make a detailed presentation of a new line or a new model of a product and may be shown on a small kind of portable projector behind a screen about the size of a home TV set instead of on a large screen with an audience between the screen and the projector.

There are films that may simply be "a trip through the plant" whose purpose is to generate interest in a more indirect way by presenting something that is, for its audience, somewhat exotic. Or there may be a film which, by means of the trip through the plant, can present how carefully the manufacturer is engaged in "quality control." (You'll find that this is the most universally valued "value" cited by clients as a reason to buy their products.) Such films, which may be called *public information*, are often shown at the meetings of luncheon clubs (fraternal organizations like Rotary International, Kiwanis, and so on). These organizations, which hold meetings over luncheon once a week, are always seeking interesting programs for their meetings. Remember, their meetings take place in every city or town in which a chapter exists, and there are 52 meetings a year in each such place! What a way to get indirect advertising benefits by presenting an interesting film!

Films for luncheon clubs are usually about the same length as sales training and dealer training films. They usually run just less than half an hour. (At a luncheon meeting this would allow someone—the representative of the sponsor, the local dealer, the film-maker, the fund raiser —to lead a brief discussion and answer questions about the subject of the film. This, of course, further ensures the "educational" value of the presentation.)

Point-of-sales films are presented to small audiences, usually of the same size as the audience for a radio or TV show. One, two, or three people either in a showroom or waiting room of a sales office, or even in their own home, watch a film whose objective is to modify their attitudes sufficiently to induce them to buy whatever it is the salesperson is trying to sell. Such films are much shorter than the other films and might run from three or four minutes to perhaps ten minutes or so.

One of the most famous of all institutional films was *Nanook of the North* by Robert Flaherty. This was filmed in 1920 and 1921 near a trading post at Hudson's Bay for Révillon Frères Fur Company. Another

Flaherty film, *Louisiana Story,* was an institutional made for the Standard Oil Company.

Institutional films can be of special interest—films about fishing, hunting, bird watching, the care of wildlife, sports, motoring, motor boating, and so on—or they can be designed to be of general interest and for public instruction—such as films that deal with ecology, conservation, pollution, race relations, and other such topics.

Institutional films can be meat for the programs of luncheon clubs, but they can also be made so that they are appropriate for church groups, meetings of Parent Teacher Associations, and other special interest groups.

It is not too much to expect that a good screenwriter (or director) of all such non-fiction films—classroom and industrial—will become a master of his or her own trade and a jack of everybody else's.

3
Television

Although television is much more recent than movies or radio, there have been television broadcasts for a far longer time than most people realize. In the mid-1930s there was a two-hour daily experimental broadcast of television from Alexandra Palace in London, England, by the British Broadcasting Corporation. The BBC had already become sophisticated by this time for in this very period it broadcast a live performance by Paul Robeson in *Emperor Jones!*

In the United States experimental telecasts began just after the end of World War II, in the late 1940s, and in Canada even later. Regular television broadcasting began in the States about 1950.

The early years of American experimental broadcasting before 1950 consisted mainly of telecasts of films, because the experimentation was primarily technical, having to do with the actual processes of broadcasting and receiving. Experimental programs were produced in the early and middle part of the 1950s. Live programs really were live in those days, and it was not uncommon to see a microphone momentarily appear in a scene through the error of the microphone boom operator. Many dramatic forms had not become fixed, and television "Chicago style" contributed a great deal of innovation through its very flexible approaches to programming in the new medium. The *Garroway Show* and *Studs' Place,* both originating in Chicago, were a kind of *commedia dell'arte,* because very often the performers would improvise their dialogue and even their "business" within a plot structure that had been agreed and worked on by the group.

Apart from live broadcasts, which, today, are generally limited to news, sports, actual events, and talk shows (with only a very few live specials, which will be dealt with later) programs originate in a variety of recorded modes. Motion pictures account for many hours of TV air time. Another way of recording motion and sound is on videotape. (*VTR* stands for videotape recording.) Visuals can also be on slides—transparencies—or cards that display information in type or artwork. Photographs are generally made into slides so that viewers are not disturbed by the glare of reflected light that so often intrudes on photos. It is not at all infrequent for a program, or a commercial, to be made up of a variety of different modes: tape, film, and slides, for example. When that happens, however, it may be deemed wiser and cheaper to re-record everything in its proper sequence and for its appropriate length onto a new piece of tape. This would be done before the broadcast. Thus, no errors will occur accidentally on the air, and no special operators need be available to control all the different elements.

Drama

Drama is rarely presented live on present-day television. It is broadcast from film or from VTR recordings. Obviously, the writer doesn't make the choice, and the difference is not very apparent, even during broadcast, unless you are trained to see it. After you do learn how to "see" better what is happening on the TV tube, you will notice that some programs, especially the series or serials, are lit quite flat. This will probably mean that what you are watching has been recorded on tape. The reason is that taped programs are shot with three cameras, as a rule, although sometimes there may be more. The performance can be presented straight through, as in a stage play, and the director will edit the film in the booth by telling an operator, who is called *the switcher*, to cut from Camera One to Camera Three, and so on. This makes for far less expensive recording than film, in which almost invariably every shot requires a separate set-up. In a film shooting takes place with many interruptions; in fact, it may not even be shot in sequence! For each shot everyone stops, and the camera is moved and the lighting changed.

When you have the opportunity of lighting for only one camera at a time, you can light for rich modelling of the subject and its environment. When lighting for three cameras at a time, you must be careful not to light the subject and its environment in a way that creates a deep shadow in the field of one of the other cameras; thus, the lighting tends to be much flatter.

There may be other considerations too. When lighting for three or more cameras, it is well nigh impossible to have a setting in which all four walls can appear. Think about it for a moment, and you will see that if you were to come around 360 degrees, the logistics of moving cameras out of the field of view of the reverse-angle camera would be tremendous. In movies, because there are new set-ups all the time, actual walls can be moved in and out of the setting. While at any one time only three walls can be used, one that has been seen can be removed and another that would have appeared to be behind us can be moved in, so that reverse angles can be easily shot.

If a series or serial can be devised so that there are very few settings, or so that settings can be used over and over again, then tape might very well be the mode of choice for many of the reasons already cited. Generally, too, it is much more difficult to transport all the necessary VTR electronic equipment to far-off locations than it is to transport motion picture gear, so this may be another valid criterion for making the choice between VTR and film.

Since television is simply a projection system for either film or tape, and since the choice will probably never be made by you in your capacity of a writer, you do not have to worry about the filming method when you sit down to write.

Longer television dramas are subject to the same observations made previously for feature fiction films and can be written keeping the same kinds of advice in mind. They are expensive, whether they are prepared on film or on tape. With rare exceptions, they are no longer produced as live shows for reasons of cost and because live shows are not as controllable as those that have been filmed or taped. If an actor "boots" a line, or if the camera movement isn't smooth, or if the editing isn't just right, there is nothing the director can do about it in a live production. If the production is on film or tape and such mistakes occur, it is very simple to do the portion over again, to "make another take."

In 1967, the Columbia Broadcasting System telecast a play entitled *Do Not Go Gentle into That Good Night*. The broadcast ran for an hour and a half. Shortly thereafter the script was prepared for publication. Here is the page of credits as it appeared in the book published by CBS.

DO NOT GO GENTLE INTO THAT GOOD NIGHT, broadcast in color on the CBS Television Network from 9:30 to 11 PM. EST Tuesday, October 17, 1967. Written by Loring Mandel, produced and directed by George Schaefer, taped at Television City in Hollywood, and sponsored by General Telephone and Electronics.

The Cast:

PETER SCHERMANN	Melvyn Douglas
HELOISE MICHAUD	Shirley Booth
GEORGE	Warren Stevens
DR. GETTLINGER	Lawrence Dobkin
JOSEPHA	Claudia McNeil
EVELYN	Lois Smith
PHIL	Gene Blakeley
MARGARET	Martine Bartlett
YOUNG ROSE	Mildred Trares
ARTHUR SELIG	Art Smith
MARIAN	Amanda Randolph
DR. KELLER	Karl Swenson
MRS. STONE	Mary Jackson
MRS. ERMISH	Nydia Westman
MCDERMOTT	Val Avery
SLOCUM	Jacques Aubuchon
RAGLE	Don Beddoe
MRS. FLAGLER	Madge Kennedy
MARY	Almira Sessions
LAURA	Sara Taft

You can see from the magnitude and importance of the cast that this would have been an expensive production. The director, George Schaeffer, wrote in the preface to the book:

I was delighted when CBS asked me to write a preface to this volume because it gives me a chance to thank Loring Mandel publicly for having written such a profound and touching play, and to include a few production statistics and some private thoughts on television originals in general.

"Gentle," as it was familiarly called, was taped last May [1967] in Los Angeles at CBS Television City. A cast of eighty-five spent five days on camera following three weeks of rehearsal, and was supported by twenty-two engineers, two thousand nine hundred eighteen hours of stage set-up and lighting, and seven hundred fifty-seven and a half hours of wardrobe handling. The play was divided into forty-five separate scenes and recorded on high band video tape. Ten reels of tape were then flown on separate planes to Reeves Sound Studios in New York City, where another three weeks were spent in electronic editing, scoring and mixing the final sound track.

"Gentle" is an excellent example of some of the differences between a play written for the stage and one written for television.

The relationship between a director-producer and a writer varies greatly from one medium to another, but is at its best in electronic television. In the theatre the writer commands; he selects his producer, approves the director and the cast, and no word of his play can be changed except by him. This is a system of mixed merit. In films, with rare exceptions, the writer has a lesser role while the director, star or producer dominates the final results. In the pressure-cooker tension of electronic TV, both writer and director know that without cooperative collaboration some vital juices will escape, which makes this the most constructive atmosphere in which to create.

"Gentle" is highly episodic, lingering on most segments only long enough for a point to be made and then moving rapidly forward, much like film. However, when episodes came along with the length and content of a stage scene (such as those between Peter and Heloise, or the argument in Gettlinger's office), they were played and photographed non-stop as in the old "live" days. It is now possible to capture "living performances" and still achieve fast and fluid montage, due to the revolutionary technical advances that have been made in editing tape within the last two years.

"Gentle" also demonstrates another difference between television and other forms of theatrical writing, a difference of which the director must always be very conscious. The performance is aimed at a non-paying audience of individuals, either alone or in very small groups, and not to a mass of people who have gathered at considerable expense to participate in a contagious experience. Most of us who have worked in theatre la-ment the loss of collective audience reaction to our television efforts, but we should balance that by admitting that there is one great advantage, particularly in the realm of problem drama. Every aspect of a situation can be shown with extreme honesty and the individual viewer invited to react in direct relation to his own experience.

In theatre, the director has failed who does not elicit a unified response; even an extreme black-and-white statement is preferable to a confused and fragmented audience. This is not necessarily true in television. In Loring's drama, many different attitudes toward geriatrics are dramatized, yet no character in the play is either absolutely right or completely wrong. The viewer is expected to participate; to reject or approve what he is watching in the light of his own knowledge. "Gentle" is a play that can only be a complete success if it evokes different reactions in different members of the audience.

The script itself demonstrates the same kinds of attributes that have been discussed before. The qualities of the characters and of the environments cannot be made apparent by *talking about* them. All characters who are in any way important must be made to appear as three-dimensional personalities by what they do and by how they react to what is done to them or near them. While the physical environment must, of course, affect what a character does, that environment is also itself interpreted by the ways the characters act and react within it. This reiterates what was quoted from the observations of Dudley Nichols earlier in the discussion of fiction films.

On the other hand, neither the description of the scenery in the script, nor even its appearance during the performance, needs to contain any more details than are necessary for the kinds of interactions that will take place between it and the characters. I must repeat, and repeat often, that making any kind of artwork is a process of *selection*, not collection. Never use ten words, if three will do! Note carefully, also, the conditions the small screen of the television set impose on the visibility of the image. Much of the tiny detail of a scene, detail that is valuable on the large screen of a theatre, becomes either indistinguishable, or just too busy, in the diminution of the TV image. Compare the numbers of glasses and bottles on the backbars of western saloons in films made before and after TV.

Here are the opening sequences of *Do Not Go Gentle into That Good Night.* No scene numbers, or even sequence numbers, appear because this excerpt is for *readers*, not TV workers. Otherwise the script remains unchanged. Note also that this begins with ACT I. Surprising as this may be, it is a perfectly reasonable way to divide a script into parts. We may or may not see the words ACT I or an identification of subsequent acts during the presentation, but it is a way to divide a script into relatively equal portions—in importance if not in length—so that breaks in the presentation can be afforded the sponsor (whose name appeared on the credit page) to present commercial announcements.

All the stage directions appear in italics. As I said before, it doesn't really matter how the directions are set out in the typescript of a radio, film, or television drama, so long as they can be easily read and clearly distinguished from the dialogue.

Do Not Go Gentle into That Good Night

ACT I

A station wagon comes down a snowy road in an old village residential area and pulls to the curb in front of the old looming frame house built by Peter Schermann. Inside the house, George Schermann, Peter's 45-year-old son, watches at the window. Seeing the car approach, he calls to his wife, Evelyn.

GEORGE: He's back.

Evelyn, sitting in the dining room at a table set for company, rises and goes toward the kitchen. There is bitterness in her voice.

EVELYN: The meat's all dry.

At the curb, the car doors are now open. Margaret, Peter's daughter, is standing on the snow while Phil, her husband, comes around to help the old man out of the rear seat. Philly, their son, runs ahead of them toward the steps leading to the house. The old man, Peter Schermann, says nothing.

Phil helps Peter up the high wooden steps. Margaret hurries past them. The old man climbs so slowly . . .

We see the entrance into the house, the stairs, and the heavy gothic newel and rail leading up to the long front porch, screened in summer and now open and crusted with ice. The white paint is peeling.

Margaret, Phil and Peter enter the front door.

PHIL: Hold the door. Hold the door.

MARGARET: Come on, Dad. Phil, get him out of the cold!

Then, calling to Philly, who has entered in a rush.

Philly! Boots off first! Come back!

Inside, there is a long center hall which goes straight to the back door of the house. At the far end of the hall the kitchen goes off to the left and a rear bedroom goes off to the right. Philly has raced down the hall and now is squealing with Beth and Scott. Evelyn is approaching the door from the kitchen. George, upstairs, has not yet appeared.

SCOTT: They're here! They're here!

MARGARET: Philly, get back here. Boots off!

Philly comes running back past Evelyn in a great hurry to reach his mother, perform the demanded chore, and get back to his cousins.

Margaret removes his boots.

PHILLY: The trains are up!

Beth runs up to Peter and Phil.

BETH: Hi, Pop.
Evelyn chases her away.
There is now a knot of people at the front door. Margaret helping Philly remove his boots. Phil, still holding Peter tightly by the arm, is helping him through the doorway. Beth and Scott crowd in to be close to Philly. Evelyn brushes the water which clings to the heavy dark blue overcoat Peter wears. The children are gleeful. All the others are tense.

EVELYN: What a mess, Pop.

PHIL: I'll tell you the roads are treacherous. Where's George?

EVELYN: Upstairs.

MARGARET: *Finishing with Philly's boots.*
There. Get out of here.

BETH: Come on.
The children rush down the hall.

MARGARET: And take the coat off!
As Phil puts his own coat in the closet, Margaret turns her attention to the old man who, partly by his silence, remains our focus of attention. She helps Evelyn remove Peter's coat.

MARGARET: His hands are ice.

EVELYN: Did you enjoy yourself, Pop?

PHIL: *Shouting up the stairs.*
George?
The women get Peter's coat off. He wears a coat-sweater underneath, Margaret moves him to a chair and he sits.

MARGARET: I'll get the galoshes off.
Evelyn stands watching Margaret, who has gotten to her knees on the wet floor in order to remove Peter's overshoes.

PHIL: *Calling upstairs.*
George, your city kin are here! The roads are a mess.
To Evelyn.
Sorry to be late, Ev, the roads are just treacherous. Holding dinner, I hope.

EVELYN: *Still watching Margaret and Peter.*
George is all tired out. Doing accounts. Wasn't feeling too well.

PHIL: *Calling up again.*
Georgie!
George comes down the stairs. He looks drawn and pale. He moves, however, with determined steps.

GEORGE: OK, Phil. Dad, how do you feel?
George reaches the bottom step. He goes to Peter, whispering to Evelyn as he passes her.
All right, I'm here.

GEORGE: *To Margaret.*
How is he, Meg?
To Peter.
How was it, Dad?

PHIL: *To Evelyn.*
I hope the dinner didn't dry out or anything, but we started on time.

EVELYN: Yes, The roads are treacherous.
Evelyn walks away, down the hall, toward the kitchen. Phil follows after her.

PHIL: Cars off the shoulders all over the place. Like dead horses.

MARGARET: Phil! There's a suitcase in the car.

PHIL: Ye Gods.
Phil grabs his coat and rushes out. George kisses Margaret sincerely on the cheek, takes the wet galoshes she holds up to him and puts them under the hall table.

GEORGE: *Not looking at Peter.*
Good to have you home, Dad.

PETER: *After considering it.*
Why?

GEORGE: *Starting to help Margaret with her coat.*
Let me—

MARGARET: Take Dad.
George loops an arm under Peter's, helps him rise, and they move off to the left of the hall into the living room.

GEORGE: Come on, Dad, get in the warm part of the house. I was going to light up a real fire but the wood is wet and the smoke's no good for you.

PETER: Shouldn't let it get wet.

GEORGE: Well, we missed you round here, that's for sure. How was it at Meg's? I'll bet her kids ran you ragged, huh! I talked to the man who—he's a doctor, too,—who runs that home, Dad . . . I know you'd like it . . .

PETER: I'm tired, George, Let me sit down.

GEORGE: *George assists Peter in sitting on a straight-backed upholstered chair which we might sense is Peter's habitual seat. George, freed, exhales deeply and looks down at his father.*
Are you hungry? It'll be a while. Ev was figuring you'd be here an hour ago. . . . You want to rest a while on the bed? I've got to light a fire or something . . . find some cellar wood . . .

PETER: You can leave me . . .
Peter looks around the room. The room is suddenly bare and unpainted, as it was many years ago when the house was almost ready to be inhabited. A sawhorse stands in the room, and a rough unfinished credenza. Rose, Peter's young wife, looks at him with admiration. She wears a cape on her shoulders.

YOUNG ROSE: More than I dreamed, Mister Schermann. A house like this can stand a thousand years . . . you're so kind to me . . . but you talk to me so little . . .

PETER: I can build, Rose . . .
Suddenly he sees a new image.
Rose?

Rose, now a very old woman, sits in a rocker. She looks near death.

OLD ROSE: Always tired, Peter. Why am I always tired?

We are back to the present. Peter sits looking across at the rocker. It is empty and still.

GEORGE'S VOICE: You can't just sit here . . .

Peter looks up at George, then back to the rocker.

GEORGE: You can't just sit here . . .

PETER: I made your crib. I built . . .

At the front door, Phil bustles in carrying the small worn suitcase.

PHIL: I'll put it in his room.

He hears George pleading with Peter, and moves down the hall. Phil brings the suitcase to a room off the hall on the right, the middle bedroom, Peter's room. The furniture is outsized and simple . . . a bed, a chest, a stiff-backed chair alongside the radiator by the window, and a small corner table with a cleared-off porcelain-enamel top of a kind familiar in old kitchens. Phil swings the suitcase lightly to the bed and steps back into the hall. He hangs up his coat, then walks to the back bedroom and opens the door. The three children are inside, Philly still wearing his coat and hat. They are all sitting on the floor playing with a set of electric trains.

PHIL: Hey, that's pretty good.

He squats by the children and watches the train.

PHILLY: It isn't smoking . . .

SCOTT: I ran out.

BETH: It looks smoking to me . . .

Cut to a close shot at floor level of the train as it comes straight for the camera. It turns abruptly just before hitting the lens and starts the curve around the oval. Camera pans slightly to follow the train around the turn. As the train begins to retreat from the camera on the highball back, the camera ends its pan and catches Beth's laughing face in the frame as she presses her head to the floor. She shared the funny terror of pretending the train was going to crash into her eyes.

Slow dissolve to black.

It is much later that night. In the dining room, before the massive rectangular table, an argument is in progress. George, Phil and Margaret are settled in the room. Evelyn, drying dishes which are stacked in the kitchen, commutes between the kitchen and the dining room through the connecting doorway. During the scene she is continually picking up a wet dish, carrying it into the dining room while she dries it, returning it to the kitchen and exchanging it for a wet dish, repeating the procedure. The dining room table is cleared of all dishes except coffee cups and saucers. Margaret wears an apron, as does Evelyn, but she's too involved in the argument to work. We begin the scene with a closeup on Margaret.

MARGARET: He's entitled to better than that from us, George. Why do you want to rob him? Has he been that bad a father to you?

GEORGE: Rob? How! Why am I—? Did I ever say that? Does that have anything to do with it? I want the same things you want!

EVELYN: *To Margaret.*
Are you keeping him? Why did you bring him home?

MARGARET: *You* said bring him home.

EVELYN: Unless you want him to move in with you.

GEORGE: Don't accuse me, Meg, unless you're ready to take on the responsibility.

PHIL: George, she's—

MARGARET: You know I can't.

GEORGE: You can't?

MARGARET: No, I can't.

GEORGE: Then God, will you stop? Will you stop with me?

PHIL: What is this? Feeding time at the zoo?

GEORGE: She's accusing me of not loving him! Why should I be defending? I love him as much as you do . . .

MARGARET: You want to ship him off to an institution, not me—

GEORGE: This place is a home, it's not an institution! I went to different places, I wouldn't . . .

MARGARET: *Continuing without pausing.*
I have a five-and-a-half room apartment, that's five rooms, five rooms. For two adults and three children. We just can't handle a bigger rent. You have nine rooms in this house, rent free . . .

GEORGE: You want my tax bill?

MARGARET: Oh, George! This is his house, built with his own hands, like this table! It was such a damn happy place. . . . He built it for Mom; he has—nine rooms; you have yourselves and two children and you can't find room for him!

GEORGE: Look at him, Meg! There's nothing left of the man who built it and he's agreed, he said I could look for a home . . .

EVELYN: When are we supposed to have a life of our own?
She holds out a hand to silence George, who is about to speak.
Do you think that man is happy now? By what right—listen, George has paid taxes and upkeep on this house for ten years. George does the repairs, the work, the deed is in his name! Plus running the agency! But we've never had a home here, and it may sound cold, but when do Peter's children come into their own? When is the man I married going to be the head of his household? Your father—and I love him, too, I do—sits like a cancer, sits in his workshop like a lump, a stone, a cancer, just sits, can't cope with the children. . . . Beth and Scott just get on his nerves, he frightens them, and you sit up in Boston and say he's not going to be put in a home? Well, he is going to be put in a home, yours if you want, or someplace where there are other old people and trained nurses and doctors and . . . I'm sorry, I'm done.

> *Evelyn, struggling with tears of frustration, goes into the kitchen. We watch her as we hear from the other room . . .*

MARGARET'S VOICE: Sending him to die! Sending him to die!

GEORGE'S VOICE: Will you look at this brochure, Meg? Look, will you?

> *The camera remains focused on the kitchen. And as the discussion goes on in the other room, we dissolve to the interior of the back bedroom. The sounds of the discussion are audible, but not fully intelligible. In the bedroom, the three children are sitting on the daybed. They are whispering and giggling to each other.*

PHILLY: Then you'll be able to play in his shop all the time.

SCOTT: *Happily.*
Yeah. If they let us.

PHILLY: I guess he's going to a hotel, huh?

SCOTT: You ever been in a hotel?

PHILLY: No, a motel.

SCOTT: No, no, a *motel—hotel.*

> *Scott and Philly both giggle at this. Beth smiles and says in mock amazement . . .*

BETH: A *moo*-tell *who*-tell?

> *The children giggle again. Philly slips out of the bed and crawls on the floor.*

BETH: Hey, where you going?

PHILLY: C'mon . . .

> *Scott leaps out of bed to follow Philly, who has reached the train transformer and turned it on. The train lights blink on and the engine begins to move. Beth watches.*

•   •   •

You have read the opening of the first of five acts of this television drama. The only thing that seems to be different from the way *Fifty-Seventh Street* was presented is that the script *Gentle* indicates less music and sounds. It isn't possible, however, to say whether this has been an overt choice because too little of each script has been quoted here. It may well be that since *Fifty-Seventh Street* presents two musicians as its protagonists, more use of music and sound is suggested by the story itself. In any case, as with all the other elements of your drama, be aware of the need, or the possibility, of sound to enhance the words of the dialogue.

Both these scripts demonstrate what we saw earlier in the opening scenes of *The Enemy of the People*—the great mobility of the cinematic image. It is not necessary to stay in one place for long periods of time; on the contrary, the action can move about without hindrance, as and when the writer wishes. A large part of the creative potential of the cinematic process is the way in which time and space can be distorted. This, of course, includes the flashbacks that appear in *Gentle*.

I have used the word *cinematic* when talking about both film and TV because it seems to be the only word that appropriately applies to this kind of dramatic presentation. The contraction, elision, or lengthening of time, the brisk changes of scenery and background, and the imposition of new time sequences and rhythms through editing—all are aspects of this cinematic quality. For this reason, while they provide great potential for creative use in drama, they are also present in other kinds of cinematic presentations.

Series and Serials

There is one limitation on all television presentations that does not control theatrical films. In television, as in radio, the time permitted for a broadcast is rigidly fixed. An episode of a series on television, for example, an episode that is called an hour show, runs only 47 minutes!* Not more, and not less. In most cases, it is the editor who fits the program into the narrow confines of this Procrustean bed. The length of time the writer feels the story ought to have is pruned, or stretched, to fit the mould. It will probably be the editor who will enhance this miracle through slower or faster cutting; he may also have to overcome obstacles raised by the style of the direction during the shooting. On the other hand, experienced television film directors develop a feel for the time in which a story must be played.

Series shows are shows in which each episode is self-contained, although the main characters are the same in every episode; a *serial* is a continuing story. Both series and serials have been available in films long before television invaded the livingroom. Serials have been in the movie theatres since even before *The Perils of Pauline*. They served the same function then as serials do now: they were intended to be a trap to ensnare the audience and induce them to return each week to the same theatre. Now, on television, they are shown to ensure the return of the audience each day to the same sponsor. Series on television serve much the same purpose, but they arose out of a somewhat different concept: if one *Boston Blackie* or *Doctor Kildare* or *Charlie Chan* movie was successful in the theatre, then another with the same major players would also be successful. Some, like *Doctor Kildare* or *Tarzan,* were recreated in television after first appearing in the movie theatres.

Series also appear in somewhat strange disguises: *Godfather* and *Godfather II,* for example, or *French Connection* and *French Connection II!*

For the writer there isn't much difference, however, between a TV series and a TV serial. It just isn't possible for one writer to write every episode of a series, much less a daily serial, although it is possible for one writer, or a small team, to write every episode of a mini-series such as the several episodes of *Roots,* from the novel by Alex Haley. In spite of what I

---

*This is to allow time for commercial announcements, station breaks, and opening, closing, and production credits.

have said about the disregard for the needs of a story that the rigid time limits impose, occasionally an episode within a series is strong enough and long enough to become a two-part episode. In such a case, the same writer will author both, writing them as if they were one story.

The most long-lived serials on television are, as they were in radio, the soap operas. On TV, however, they run for half an hour or an hour, instead of radio's 15 minutes. Because of the cost of such presentations, and the even greater cost of broadcast time, these programs boast several sponsors; no single sponsor would put all of its dollars into one program basket, even if it could. (This is also often true of longer series shows and of feature-length dramas.) It is pretty obvious, I'm sure, that no writer could write five half-hour dramatic episodes a week, let alone five hour-long episodes. Thus, soap operas still rely on stables of writers as did their radio forebears. The series programs also use a number of writers, although the methods of working are different. In serials the plot may be worked out, as it was in radio, by the person whose name is credited as author, and other writers may then flesh in the specific elements of each episode. In a series, the producer is confident of certain writers' abilities to write the kind of dramas that the series requires, and they will be commissioned to write the episodes, one to a writer. They may invent the story idea and the plot, or they may develop a story idea provided by someone else, or they may dramatize a story or a novel that has been bought by the producer.

All I said earlier about the kinds of stories that were told by the radio soap operas applies pretty well to soap operas on television. Yet, television drama, even in these serials, seems to have grown up just a little. The stories are still romantic melodramas. They deal very much with family problems: marital and premarital equations of all kinds, problems of having or not having children, adoption, and legal conflicts. But the changes in the social environment that have taken place during the past 40 years are clearly reflected. Extra-marital sex is talked about; women and their jobs are the foundations of many of the relationships; the professional capabilities of women are recognized. Children are rarely seen in these dramas, and this absence may very well be because of the great expense—child labor laws make many demands on film and television producers (they may need to provide schooling, medical care, and other benefits, for example). Nevertheless, the richness of the stories is diminished when children are involved in the plots but remain unseen. It is a contravention of cinematic dramaturgy as we have already discussed it.

Television soap opera stories still meander, progressing very slowly, for all the same reasons that governed the pace of radio soap operas. However, each day's episode of a TV serial is at least a half-hour long, as noted, and even more usually an hour in length. But, for the economic reasons that have been discussed, these shows are divided into quarter-hour segments, each of which is sponsored by a different advertiser—although that advertiser may sponsor the same segment every day.

For writers, soap operas are very much a specialty.

Continuity

Writers do have opportunities of writing continuity for television, just as for radio. What really is continuity? As was mentioned in discussing radio, it is the words that link parts of a program together. They provide continuity in the basic sense of the phrase.

The CBS-owned television station in Chicago, WBBM-TV, broadcast a series of programs, each a half-hour in length, for the Church Federation of Greater Chicago. The title of the series was *Different Drummers*. A master of ceremonies introduced the elements of each show; he opened each show, closed it, and provided the continuity of the broadcast.

Sometimes the elements were live in the studio with him—live guests whose presentations formed part of the program. Sometimes they took part in a discussion, or they played music or sang, or they danced or recited. On the other hand, other elements were photographs, or they were previously taped pieces. The previous taping might have been done because a guest couldn't appear at the time of broadcast, or maybe the part that was taped took place somewhere else as, for example, a portion of a play or some other kind of performance.

Before you read the script, which was written in the station's or co-producer's continuity department, for program number 24 in 1977 (that's what is meant by the numbers 24-77 on the top line), there are some abbreviations that ought to be explained.

V/O means *voice over.*
SOT means *sound on tape.*
2-shot means just that: a shot with just two people in it.
In coop means "in cooperation with" and refers to the Church Federation of Greater Chicago.
Limbo is a description of the scenery: there is none!
    A limbo set is one in which there is nothing to identify the locale.
    It may be just a blank wall or a gently patterned cyclorama.
Wraps in Sc. 14 simply means "wraps it up" or "ends the show."

It should also be said that the indications on the second and third lines: VTR 10/5/77 and AIR 10/8/77 mean that the whole show was taped on October 5, 1977, and it was broadcast on October 8, three days later.

Different Drummers No. 24-77

VTR: 10/5/77

AIR: 10/8/77

1. CU Live Card	RANDY (V/O):	The ancient Bible story says that all our troubles with Adam and Eve and the snake began with an apple. There's a new version of that familiar

2. 2-Shot Randy and Oscar in Limbo—Randy hands Oscar apple

story in town. And the person who's writing about apples these days is one of Chicago's most popular entertainers, Oscar Brown, Jr. Join us as we step to the tune of a different drummer.

SOT:

3. Super:
Different drummers with Randy Evans in Coop

4. CU Randy

RANDY: Bible stories have been re-told for centuries. Imaginative versions of the Bible strengthen and freshen the meanings of ancient stories and eternal values. As we grow older, our understandings and conceptions of people and stories in the Bible can change, as do our beliefs, and even our doubts.

In recent years, biblical stories have emerged on the stage and screen as musicals. *Jesus Christ, Superstar* and *Godspell* presented familiar stories in a new, exciting and innovative manner.

Here in Chicago, we can add to that list with a new re-telling of the story of creation. *"In De Beginnin"* is the new story of Adam and Eve told in music and rhyme, now showing at the Body Politic Theatre.

5. CU Oscar Brown Jr.

The writer, director, and star of *"In De Beginnin"* is Oscar Brown, Jr. A WBBM-TV award winning program called "Oscar Brown's Back in Town," produced by Scott Craig, introduced the remarkable talents of this man like this:

6. Roll wild tape "Oscar Brown's Back in Town"

7. Diss to CU Oscar Brown

RANDY: The lyrics to that song are based on a poem by Gwendolyn Brooks. And before we say

CU Randy

8. CU Jean Pace

9. CU Africa Pace Brown

10. CU Elliot Rawls

11. Randy and guests ad lib discussion
12. Randy: Lead to Africa singing "Chocolate Doll" (Randy asks Oscar to intro song)
13. Randy and Guests ad lib
14. Randy wraps

15. CU Randy

16. Full screen Address Slide

17. CU Randy

more about the multitalented singer and his illustrious career, I want you to meet his family.

Jean Pace has gained recognition around the country for singing, dancing and acting. She portrays "De Serpent" in *In De Beginnin*, and is the show's costume designer. Ms. Pace also happens to be married to Oscar Brown, Jr.

Talent runs in the family, as is evident in eight-year-old Africa Pace Brown, Oscar and Jean's daughter. Africa has received a Joseph Jefferson nomination as best supporting actress in Chicago legitimate theatre in 1977 for her portrayal of the mischievous "Eve."

Also with us is Elliot Rawls, one of our contributing editors for our program feature "Stepping Out." Elliot stepped out with me to see *In De Beginnin* at the Body Politic.

RANDY: Thanks to Oscar Brown Jr., Jean Pace, Africa Pace Brown, and Elliot Rawls for being with us today. Thank you, too.

And, we'd like to hear from you. You can write to us at Different Drummers, Room 300, 116 South Michigan, Chicago, 60603. That's Different Drummers, Room 300, 116 South Michigan, Chicago, 60603.

Next Week on Different Drummers . . . Learn how you can talk back to your television set and even become a TV Critic. I'm Randy Evans. Have a good week.

18. Standard Close Tape—SOT:
19. Super Credits

To attract and hold its audience, every program must have an underlying idea, some kind of basic concept. This is true of the dramatic series that relies on the return of the same characters, and it is true of the individual half-hour show. This basic underlying idea will provide the criteria for the selection of the elements of which the program will be composed. In this episode of *Different Drummers,* the selection of Oscar Brown Jr., and his family and of the theatre piece that he and his family present were clearly within the basic ideas of the show. Oscar Brown's theatre piece *In De Beginnin* has a religious base as does *Different Drummers.*

The criteria for choosing the "bits" that were included in the program—the songs and the pieces of conversation directly focused on the ideas underlying the show—*are* those very ideas. The function of the continuity is to link the various elements within the parameters of the underlying concepts to which the series addresses itself and, at the same time, to provide interesting comment and inviting introductions.

In this episode of *Different Drummers,* several modes of recordings are used. Not only are there people on camera, live, but there are tapes (VTR), cards, and slides.

Sometimes the show for which continuity must be written is of a special kind. It may be a kind of actuality, but an actuality that is invented or contrived. Yet, the same basic premises apply. For a public show before a large audience, for example an awards presentation,* the program will probably be arranged by the producer (TV) and the committee for the event in consultation with each other. There will have to be enough time for preparation so that all the stars who are to participate will have been spoken with and their agreements to perform confirmed. (This may include special releases through their agents.) Then, the musical elements and tapings from other productions, if there are to be any, will have to be selected and releases for them obtained. Finally, whatever will be performed live—or taped beforehand, so that to the TV audience it will appear live—will be selected and clearances obtained.

It is at this point that a writer will be called upon to write the continuity. After all, she or he can't write anything until all that has been listed above has finally been decided upon and confirmed. Even then there may be last minute changes. Perhaps certain clearances don't arrive in time, and something else has to be written into the script as replacement. Perhaps one of the performers becomes ill, and a replacement

---

*A presentation show like the Motion Picture Academy Awards, for example.

has to be found. But, whatever the vagaries of chance, the writer will still have to conform to the basic idea of continuity: it has to be "of a piece," that is, it must adhere to the integrity of the fundamental ideas of the show; it must be interesting and enticing; and, for live actors to say, it must provide the kinds of words that will be comfortable for them.

When writers are dealing with a series, such as *Different Drummers*, they know who will be delivering their lines and know the manner of that delivery. Therefore, they can write with that voice and that delivery in their mental ears. It's a little more difficult when they are less familiar with the speakers who will be required to say their words, and, in a special event program they can be sure that the performers will change their lines to fit their own way of speaking. Yet, they can still provide some kinds of personal quality associated with the performer.

Even if you should live in a small town, there might be kinds of events that your local TV station could conceive of as a special program. It does not take much stretching of the imagination to see how the process for preparing and writing an awards program could be adapted.

Talk Shows

The actual writing of scripts for industrial or educational television programs is done in the same way, and with the same understandings, as the writing of industrial or educational films. There are less of them aired on television because some films deal with subject matter that simply wouldn't appeal to a television audience, which obviously cannot be so selectively specialized. Such films include sales training films, sales promotion films, dealer training films, and the like.

On the other hand, there are certain kinds of non-fictional programs that do lend themselves to television. These would be in those subject areas that used to be the territory of radio talk shows—travel, sports, special interests such as photography, needlework, cooking, and so on. In television, these kinds of programs have to have a visual base, with a narrative or conversation complementing whatever the viewer is looking at. Some things can be filmed on the spot and thus are a special kind of actuality show—sewing, hobbies, or cooking, for example. Others, like fishing, hiking, travel, and similar subjects, need to be filmed first so that the pictures can be presented on the television screen while the narrator or the traveler tells the audience about the material.

All I have said before about narration applies to programs of these various kinds. If the visuals are interesting and informative themselves, there is no great reason for a lot of talk. Let viewers enjoy what they can see. In any case, whatever is said by the narrator should not duplicate what is happening in pictures. The narration should *complement* what is being seen so that the experience of the audience will be richer and more interesting.

When film for subjects such as these is used on television, the filmed material may be presented without any recorded narration or music on the sound track, because the narrator may be talking "live" while the picture is being projected. This is no reason to avoid preparation or to encourage the speaker to ad lib if he or she is not good at it. It is far wiser to write a good interesting narration and learn how to read it, in the same way that I have suggested radio narrations be read.

Because of the need for visuals, any kind of program on television is vastly more expensive than a similar program on radio. A travel program on radio, for example, might use only recordings of ethnic music (which may well have been purchased at a local record shop) and a talk prepared from research at the library. In television, someone will have had to go to the country being described to take the motion pictures that are being shown, and to this expense must be added the cost of photographic equipment, the film and processing, and so on. By the same token, it is an unfortunate truth that anyone who gives a travel "talk" on television must also either have enough money to have hired a photographic team or have learned the required photographic skills himself.

There is, as you well know, a style of show called a "talk show." This, however, differs greatly from a radio talk because the talk is really extemporaneous, although on some of the more serious talk shows the participants may do their homework and come prepared with notes, data, quotations, and the like. Unfortunately, this kind of show often puts a premium on the wrong qualities of the talkers, all of whom will probably lack that one prerequisite of having written down what they are going to say. This I have called a "missing prerequisite," for what they do say is not always what they wanted to say, or what they may have in some way prepared themselves to say.

The conversation is often led to other emphases or to other topics by the host—who is clearly the modern descendant of the interlocutor of the old minstrel shows of the nineteenth century and in equal control of the proceedings.

4 Documentary

First, let us understand what we mean by documentary. It is not simply that a film or a radio or television program that is non-fiction is therefore documentary. No useful service is performed by using two different terms to say the same thing. John Grierson, the "father" of English language documentary films, first used the word *documentary* when he reviewed Robert Flaherty's film *Moana* for the *New York Sun*, February 8, 1926. He later defined the term as meaning "the creative treatment of actuality," but he also said that the definition was an awkward one.* It is, perhaps, the result of its "awkwardness" that the meaning of the word has become so cloudy.

When Lewis Jacobs prepared his collection of writings about documentary, he wrote in the Preface: "I have not included those documentaries [sic!] commonly classified as industrials, educationals, art and architecture, training films, and other types of sponsored films primarily aimed at instructing, improving public relations, or increasing sales. I have selected only those films which seem to me to best illuminate the artistic and social concerns of their times and which had the most influence in advancing the genre."†

My own definition of documentary films and, by extension, documentary radio and television is narrower and more rigorous. To me a documentary film, TV show, or radio program must deal with some human social relationships. It deals with relationships between people and people, people and their environment, people and their work, or any combination of those relationships.‡ The essential task of the documentarian has remained, "to capture 'fragments of actuality' and combine them meaningfully. It remains, as Grierson put it, 'the creative treatment of actuality.' Such formulations stress two functions: (1) recording (of images and sounds) and (2) interpretation.

---

*Paul Rotha, *Documentary Film* (London: Faber and Faber, 1936), p. 68.
†Lewis Jacobs, *The Documentary Tradition*, 2d ed. (New York: W. W. Norton, 1979).
‡I have discussed many definitions of documentary film in the first chapter of my book *About Documentary: Anthropology on Film* (Dayton, O: Pflaum Publishing, 1974, distributed by International Book, Chicago).

"To be sure, some documentarists claim to be 'objective'—a term that seems to renounce an interpretive role. The claim may be strategic, but is surely meaningless. The documentarist, like any communicator in any medium, makes endless choices. He selects topics, people, vistas, angles, lenses, juxtapositions, sounds, words. Each selection is an expression of his point of view, whether he is aware of it or not, whether he acknowledges it or not.

"Even behind the first step, selection of a topic, there is a motive. Someone feels there is something about the topic that needs clarification, and that if one can document aspects of it (the whole truth is legal fiction), the work will yield something useful in comprehension, or agreement or action.

"The documentarist has a passion for what he *finds* in images and sounds—which always seem to him more meaningful than anything he can *invent*. It is in selecting and arranging his findings that he expresses himself; these choices are, in effect, comments. And whether he adopts the stance of observer, or chronicler, or whatever, he cannot escape his subjectivity. He presents his version of the world."*

Historical Development

Documentary presentations are by no means recent in origin. It may not be stretching things too far to suggest that Homer's *Iliad* might be considered documentary since its creative treatment of actuality was sufficiently reliable for Schliemann to use it as a guide to discover the ruins of the ancient city of Troy. A thousand or more years after Homer the *Anglo-Saxon Chronicle* was begun. Written in Old English, it was a history of Britain told in annual entries. The first entry is dated 60 B.C. and the most recent is dated 1154 A.D., the year that Henry II, the fifth Norman king of England, began his reign. The *Chronicle* has been described as having "the twofold interest of historic fact and of graphic narrative."†

Four hundred years after the last annal of the *Anglo-Saxon Chronicle*, Thomas Deloney was born in London in 1543. For most of his life he was a silk weaver at Northwich and also a pedlar selling what he could on the roads of East Anglia, those counties of Southeast England that border the North Sea. Towards the end of his life he turned to serious writing, and he has left us novels that are of considerable value today because of the picture they give of the people of his time and region living

---

*Erik Barnouw, *Documentary* (London, Oxford, New York: Oxford University Press, 1974), pp. 287-288. I also discuss the question of objectivity in *About Documentary*, chapters 5 and 6. My views coincide with those of Barnouw.

†A. J. Wyatt, *The Threshold of Anglo-Saxon* (Cambridge: The University Press, 1929), p. 9.

their normal lives and going about their daily work. Perhaps the novel that demonstrates most clearly the point we make here is "The Pleasant Historie of . . . Jack Of Newbery." It bore a subtitle that informed the reader that the books tells, among other things, "how he set continually five hundred poor people at work, to the great benefit of the Commonwealth." The book describes, in fact, one of the first textile factories. It appeared in 1597, during the lifetime of Shakespeare and the reign of the first Queen Elizabeth.*

In 1861 Henry Mayhew published the first volume of his *London Labour and the London Poor*. This was to be a four-volume investigation of all those who could be included in the terms of the title. It was the author's hope that the total work would "form when complete, a cyclopaedia of the industry, the want, and the vice of the great Metropolis." This quotation from the Preface was followed by these words: "It is believed that the book is curious for many reasons.

"It surely may be considered curious as being the first attempt to publish the history of a people, from the lips of the people themselves— giving a literal description of their labour, their earnings, their trials, and their sufferings, in their own 'unvarnished' language; and to pourtray [sic] the condition of their homes and their families by personal observation of the places, and direct communion with the individuals.

"It may be considered curious also as being the first commission of inquiry into the state of the people, undertaken by a private individual, and the first 'blue book' ever published in twopenny numbers.

"It is curious, moreover, as supplying information concerning a large body of persons, of whom the public had less knowledge than of the most distant tribes of the earth—the government population returns not even numbering them among the inhabitants of the kingdom; and as adducing facts so extraordinary, that the traveller in the undiscovered country of the poor must, like Bruce, until his stories are corroborated by after investigators, be content to lie under the imputation of telling such tales, as travellers are generally supposed to delight in."†

There is clearly a point of view expressed by Mayhew as there was by Deloney in his novel. On the other hand, while Mayhew's work is not fictional, it is surely creative in the sense that it is the first such work ever attempted.

The tradition of documentary is rounded out by a modern work that might well be totally unexpected because it was not written for broadcast nor as a non-fiction work for publication. One of America's greatest poets, Stephen Vincent Benét, wrote a narrative poem describing his perception of the Civil War. It is a long work in which he used

---

*Deloney's short novel is to be found among other short novels in a collection entitled *Shorter Novels, vol. 1, Elizabethan and Jacobean*, Everyman Edition (London and Toronto: J. M. Dent & Sons; New York: E. P. Dutton, 1929).

† Henry Mayhew, *London Labour and the London Poor* (London: Griffin, Bohn, 1861).

very many different rhyming schemes and meters. He called it, simply, *John Brown's Body.*

Benét wrote a Note prefatory to the work in which he made these comments: "As this is a poem, not a history, it has seemed unnecessary to me to encumber it with notes, bibliography, and other historical apparatus. Nevertheless—besides such original sources as the Official Records, the series of articles in *Battles and Leaders of the Civil War,* and the letters, memoirs, and autobiographies of the various leaders involved—I would like to acknowledge my indebtedness to Channing's *The War for Southern Independence* and McMaster's *The United States Under Lincoln's Administration,* to Oswald Garrison Villard's *John Brown: A Biography Fifty Years After,* to the various Lives of Lincoln by Lord Charnwood, Carl Sandburg, and Ida Tarbell and the monumental work of Nicolay and Hay, to Nathaniel Wright Stephenson's *Abraham Lincoln: An Autobiography,* and, finally, my very particular debt to that remarkable firsthand account of life in the Army of the Potomac, *Four Brothers in Blue,* by Captain Robert Goldthwaite Carter, from which the stories of Fletcher the sharpshooter and the two brothers at Fredericksburg are taken.

"In dealing with known events I have tried to cleave to historical fact where such fact was ascertainable. On the other hand, for certain thoughts and feelings attributed to historical characters, and for the interpretation of those characters in the poem, I alone must be held responsible."*

These words of Benét are in complete conformity with the definition of documentary given by Grierson. The poem *John Brown's Body* is Stephen Vincent Benét's creative treatment of actuality. In the words of Barnouw, it is "his version of the world."

The last third of the nineteenth century saw the advent of investigative journalism of the kind that we know today. In a social environment that wanted to know more and more about the "real" world through journalism and through books such as the kind initiated by Mayhew, novelists also found a new direction. Instead of romance or melodrama, novelists wrote *realistic* novels. Realism appeared in Russia, for example, in the work of Dostoevski and in France in the work of Emile Zola. Indeed, Zola was himself a journalist and his novel *Germinal* that dealt with the work and living conditions of the coal-mine workers in northeastern France came out of his investigations of those conditions.

It must be noted that in whatever form documentary has occurred over the centuries and to whatever degree a work falls into what might be called the *genre* of documentary, the work arises from knowledge and research. It does not matter whether the person who makes the "creative treatment of actuality" lived through the experiences himself, as did Deloney in the Elizabethen textile factories, or did investigations in

---

*Stephen Vincent Benét, *John Brown's Body* (Garden City, N.Y.: Doubleday, Doran, 1929).

depth as did Mayhew or Zola, or, for that matter, Benét; and it does not matter if the research was oral as the work of Homer. The "creative treatment" is based on deep research.

Nowadays, in the twentieth century, in addition to novelists and poets like Benét and Dos Passos, documentarists work in radio and film and television. The foundation of documentary remains, however, experience and research.

Audio-Visual Documentaries

When documentaries first appeared on film and on radio, their nature was dependent upon the equipment and materials that were then available. We are talking of the decade of the 1920s. Sound films did not come into being until the end of that decade, and in any case all recording, whether for film or for radio, was made on equipment that was extremely bulky and extremely heavy. It was portable only in the sense, as we used to say at the time, that it wasn't nailed down.

Radio sound was recorded on sixteen-inch discs on a material that was described as "acetate." It was black, soft, and could not be played back more than a few times without losing a great deal of high fidelity. This meant that for immediate recordings to be played on the air, they had to be re-recorded on new discs that had not yet been played. If there were to be many copies of the disc, they would have been pressed and not re-recorded.

When film began to be available with sound on it, the recording was equally awkward and complicated. The sound was recorded on film by means of an optical recording camera, and an optical soundtrack was thus made. But an optical camera is not portable at all: it is too bulky and heavy. There were a few motion picture cameras designed that were said to be "single system," that is to say, they could record photographic images and soundtrack simultaneously. But this gave rise to many problems in editing, and in any case they were likely to provide sound that was less than excellent quality.

It was not until about 1950 that magnetic sound recording became generally available for both radio and film. This relieved radio from depending on the very cumbersome discs and relieved film of the need for recording sound on a film sound camera, an optical recorder. Magnetic sound recordings are what you use in your cassette recorder, for example. The only differences may be in the gauge, or width. A great deal of original recording is done on quarter-inch tape, that is, tape that is one quarter of an inch wide. After the original recording has been made, it can then be transferred to cassettes or to wider tape for use in editing films. Commercial announcements on radio nowadays are all on cassettes or on cartridges, which are similar. The wider tapes used for film sound are either 16mm, 35mm, or sometimes 17½mm.

Space travel, however, has been the single most important factor in the reduction of the size of recording equipment, and now it is possible to have small recorders that will fit in a jacket pocket. Now we have tiny machines, extremely portable, providing excellent sound quality.

Radio Documentaries

In the days before magnetic recording, radio documentaries were made as well as the equipment would allow, but there was very little flexibility. The bulk and weight of the recording devices were such that they were difficult, often impossible, to carry to different locations. For this reason radio documentaries were for the most part written to be recorded in the studio. They might have had a very full narration spoken by a variety of different voices. They might have been made up of re-enacted sequences linked by narration. The re-enactments may have been spoken in local or ethnic accents and dialects. In fact, radio documentaries could have been made up of prose or verse, or a mixture of both. They may have attempted to recreate a realistic quality, or they may have been impressionistic or even expressionistic. The *Tribute to Fighting France*, in chapter 1 of this book, for example, was called a documentary in those days (it was written and performed in 1944).

Nowadays we can take our extremely portable equipment to any location we wish, and by so doing, we can "take you there" as well. It is not astonishing that radio documentaries are therefore vastly different from those of the "old days." Nonetheless we must still start with some considerable knowledge gleaned from our research, and this research will include reading books and journals, magazines and newspapers, as well as preparatory visits to the places where we expect to do our recordings.

If we are recording happenings, we may also record our comments about them as we would if we were journalists. We may, on the other hand, record interviews with all kinds of people. In either case, all that we will have recorded will be the raw material from which we can construct our radio documentary.

At this point you may begin to realize that the process of making a radio documentary proceeds by stages. The first stage is the collection of bits and pieces of recorded happenings or interviews, and the second is the selection and compilation of those bits and pieces into a whole, with the individual bits linked by appropriate narrative. The narrative will of necessity be explanatory, describing the locations and the environments within which the recorded speakers find themselves. The narration may also provide color so that the listener can sense the quality of the environments. In no case, however, can the narration usefully duplicate what is evident in the recorded bits themselves. It is as useless to make such duplications as it is in a film to show a picture of a beach on the screen and to have the narrator say, "This is a beach."

The writer's job is quite evidently to provide the narrative links between the bits that are being compiled, but where does this job start? It may begin as soon as the production begins, for he or she may accompany the director on the recording sessions. The writer certainly will have to work with the director during the labor of selecting the material to be compiled, because otherwise useful and creative ideas that it is the writer's job to provide might very well be lost; on the other hand, the writer and director may be the same person.

Because of the way in which radio documentaries are made, other characteristics may be discerned. If the program includes happenings, that is to say, actuality occurrences, the foreknowledge that such occurrences will take place must be achieved by the director or producer so that a crew can be present to record what may take place. Since such actualities will occur whether the crew is there or not, it can be assumed that nobody in the crew will have any influence at all on what transpires. Thus, a great deal more than will eventually be used will have to be recorded, and this will require a much greater amount of labor properly to select the final bits and pieces. Further, whatever does take place may suggest other occurrences to be recorded, other interviews to seek out, other locations to visit. Therefore the radio documentarist becomes willy-nilly an investigative reporter. This is even more true if the initial idea for the program is something that may have first emerged in a news story. Perhaps there has been a story about excessive overcrowding in the jails. The reporter (perhaps performing the role of director as well as writer) will go about investigating the story. Police officials, inmates, staffs of the department of corrections, members of the judiciary, members of the appropriate government bodies, all such people may need to be interviewed. Such investigation is not limited to events that are currently taking place. It may also deal with how things were a generation or more in the past.

It may be that the subject of the documentary requires that either the director or the writer be a specialist in some field of knowledge. The specialty may be ethnology or ethnography, for example, or it may be sociology. Perhaps it may be a specialty in one of the natural sciences such as ornithology and the songs of birds, or any of a host of other areas of expertise. If neither the director nor the writer is such a specialist and if the production requires a specialist anyway, then the services of a technical advisor may need to be engaged.

Charles Potter is a much-sought-after writer-director of radio documentaries in New York City. He has been generous enough to let us look at a couple of his scripts. The first of these deals with the massive unemployment of the 1930s, the Great Depression.

How Do You Spell Relief?

(teaser #1:) "During the 30's . . . .we want jobs!"
NARR: *How Do You Spell Relief?* The Unemployed Councils and the Workers'

Alliance organize the unemployed.* Part Two in a series of programs exploring the activities and achievements of militant women in the Great Depression.

(teaser #2:)   "When the crisis came . . . . fighting like anything."

NARR: 1929. After reaching an all-time high in June, the United States' production index began to decline. The roaring 20's had seen an unprecedented growth in business. National income had advanced by 50% in just seven years. But the new wealth was unevenly distributed. Gains in production were being made chiefly through mechanization—not through expansion of the labor force. The 20's had not been good years for radical political movements: a post-World War I red scare and many internal disputes had weakened the Left. New recruits were predominantly foreign-born and concentrated in big cities like New York. ANNA TAFFLER.

ANNA: "I was born in Russia. . . ."

NARR: Early in 1929, with the jobless figure over 400,000, the Communist Party and the Socialist Party had already begun to organize the unemployed. On Thursday, October 31st, the crisis arrived. With the collapse of the stock market, the boom came to a screeching halt. Like many other people, Anna soon found herself in trouble over the rent. Her son had been in the hospital.

ANNA: "I had no home to. . . . and I started in."

NARR: Within five months unemployment had increased 1000% to over 4 million. While only a few ruined speculators leaped to their death from Wall Street windows, the number of evictions in poor neighborhoods skyrocketed. Whole families were threatened and wives and mothers responded as they could. ANNA.

ANNA: "And this is how I started in. . . . of the U.C.'s."

NARR: Unemployment insurance did not exist. Relief derived almost entirely from charity: it was fragmented and inadequate. The Communist Party called demonstrations from coast to coast on March 6th 1930. 35,000 people attended the International Unemployment Day rally in New York City's Union Square. The event ended in a bloodbath, but the message was clear. ANNA TAFFLER.

ANNA: "After the March 6, 1930. . . . locality for itself."

NARR: On March 7th, 1930, President Hoover told the nation that the worst effects of the Crash on unemployment would be over in 60 days. Over the next 5 months 4,000 people were arrested at radical demonstrations. Communist Unemployment Councils and the Socialist Workers' Alliance brought pressure to bear directly on local relief bureaus. Funds for relief in 1929 had totalled 71 million dollars nationally. ANNA TAFFLER.

ANNA: "First when we came into being. . . .(UC's and WA). . . . complaints."

NARR: By the following March, unemployment had doubled again. In New York, where protest was strong—and Roosevelt Governor—local relief improved during these early years of the Depression. Mary Gale worked in a New York relief bureau at the time.

-----

*These two organizations are referred to as the U.C.'s and the W.A.

MARY: "I got a job. . . . organize them."

NARR: In 1932 the average grant to an unemployed person in New York City was 2 dollars and 39 cents a week. ANNA.

ANNA: "But their policy was. . . . going on."

NARR: ROSE KYRZAK.

ROSE: "We had some. . . . what they deserve."

NARR: With unemployment heading for a peak between 12 and 15 million, membership in radical organizations was also on the rise. Anna Taffler found her way from the YPSL* into the Communist Party through her involvement with the Unemployed Councils.

ANNA: "I was militant. . . . asked me to join."

NARR: Women were very effective in work within their traditional sphere. Turning closeness to family and community life into a strength, women often took the lead in the fight to protect tenants and homeowners, which became a key issue for the unemployed movement. ANNA.

ANNA: "I was asked to. . . . save hundreds of homes."

NARR: Rose Kryzak organized tenants in Sunnyside, a small Queens neighborhood.

ROSE: "It wasn't really a rent strike. . . . fighting back."

NARR: In 1932 the breadth and strength of protest was felt at the ballot box. Federal relief programs began in earnest after the inauguration of Roosevelt in 1933. By 1935 two billion dollars would be allocated to local aid for the jobless, for food and for housing. It would take continued militancy to see that the new programs were carried out. ROSE KRYZAK.

ROSE: "The CP was very helpful. . . . them very closely."

NARR: Attempts to organize a national unemployed movement began as early as 1933. In 1935 the Comintern directed Communists worldwide to form a 'Popular Front' with Socialist and liberal groups whom they had previously attacked. This cleared the way for a merger of the Unemployed Councils with the Socialist-led Workers' Alliance. ANNA TAFFLER.

ANNA: "At our planning meetings. . . . militant policy."

NARR: The Party also tried to reach out to activist women's groups which were becoming larger and more influential, especially in relief-related work. LILY EDEL.

LILY: "The 1936 election campaign. . . . our own party."

NARR: Within the left, however, few women reached leadership positions, even in the unemployed movement where they were very active. ROSE KRYZAK.

ROSE: "I wasn't a leader. . . . a lot of that."

NARR: So great were the problems to be faced at the outset of the crisis that no one considered this to be a problem. ANNA TAFFLER.

ANNA: "At that time. . . . our own platform."

NARR: Relief activity lost its local nature in 1935 as the New Deal drew the Workers' Alliance into lobbying activity on the Federal and state level. With the focus taken off of local protest, the women's role became less important, and their inequality within the movement never became an issue. ROSE KRYZAK.

---

*Young Peoples Socialist League.

ROSE:	"You see, I don't think. . . . different than a man."
NARR:	The woman's role in the struggle probably did come up around the dinner table. ANNA TAFFLER.
ANNA:	"My husband's idea. . . . limited."
NARR:	The unemployed movement depended heavily on family women. Yet it is difficult to imagine how Anna Taffler found the time to raise a son while organizing families all over Brooklyn.
ANNA:	"While I was dedicated. . . . to go!"
NARR:	MOLLIE GOLDSTEIN also had a son.
MOLLIE:	"Some time friends. . . . in those days."
NARR:	ROSE KRYZAK.
ROSE:	"I had round the clock help. . . . go out."
NARR:	ROSE is still active. How do her grandchildren feel about sharing her with the struggles of today?
ROSE:	"Oh, they know. . . . you know."
NARR:	Recalling how fiercely these women fought in the thirties, we can hardly fear for their commitment in the face of such tender criticism. What gave them the strength? Two months before her death at 82, ANNA summed it up:
ANNA:	"I'm active because. . . . not in with capitalism."
NARR:	You have been listening to "How Do You Spell Relief?," Part Two of *Grandma Was an Activist,* a radio series on radical women in the 1930's, produced for WBAI-FM and the Oral History of the American Left at New York University's Tamiment Institute Library. Oral historians for the series: Jon Bloom, Bea Lemisch and Ruth Prago. Project Directors: Paul and Mari Jo Buhle. Mix by Steven Ericson. Our special thanks to the many interviewees and contributors who made this series possible. *Grandma Was an Activist* was produced by Beth Friend and Charles Potter, Radio Arts Incorporated. Your narrator is Jill Eikenberry.
	Grandma Was an Activist was made possible by a grant from the New York Council for the Humanities.
	Be sure to listen to part three in this series, *On the Line: Radical Women in the Union Movement,* over this same station.

The term "teaser" occurs in the first line of the script you have just read. It means pretty much what it appears to mean. A teaser is something that happens at the beginning of a radio show (and equally at the begining of a film or TV program) before the introductory. It is some form of action, dropping the audience into the middle of things, so that the ritual of the opening titles doesn't kill their interest before the program starts.

The history of opening titles goes back to the days of legitimate theater when the title of the play and all the performance and production credits appeared on the printed program. This is a practice that began many decades ago and still continues in the theater. In the early days of radio a program would begin with the announcer introducing the title of the show and naming the actors and the author, and so on. This worked quite well so long as there were not many radio stations and there wasn't much choice of programs to listen to. As radio receivers became better and as the number of radio stations increased, members of the audience became "dial-twisters," searching for the program of greatest interest. In order to catch the interest of the listener, there grew up the practice of beginning with part of the story, *in medias res*, without lead-in, without introduction. If the story succeeded in keeping the attention of the listener for a while, no matter how brief, he or she would be more likely to stay with the show instead of twisting the dial. This practice of beginning with action is said to be a "teaser."

It would have been clear to those who worked on the broadcast of the preceding script that the lines in quotation marks represented bits of recorded interviews. In the middle of each such quotation the succession of periods (which is called an "ellipsis") represents the words that have not been reproduced in the script itself. The few words at the beginnings and ends of the quoted lines indicate the beginnings and ends of the portions of recordings that are to be included in the final form of the program.

The function of the narration, apart from identifying each of the speakers, is to provide the historical information necessary to understand the background and, perhaps, even some of the reasons behind the words of those who recount their memories. It does not have to be pointed out that the writer of the narration must have been completely aware of all of the recorded material in order to write the necessary explanatory words.

The next script is quite different in origin. It was one of a series of documentary programs that were the result of recording a workshop on community planning. In this sense the script is dealing with an actuality. The function of the narration in this case is to identify each speaker and to give the historical background to the workshop—much the same kind of function as the narration performed in the previous script. However, another aspect of the workshop discussions had to be dealt with. The participants in the workshop all had some level of common knowledge and experience that most of the audience did not share; therefore the narration had to provide some kind of foundation for understanding. The program is called *New Towns, Old Dreams*. This episode is the third in the series.

Coming Together: The Social Bond

Teaser—
FRIEDMAN: "It's a lot of fun. . . . especially for the kids."
Music: in and under.

NARRATOR: *New Towns, Old Dreams*, a workshop on community planning and new town building, recorded at the Institute on Man and Science in Rensselaerville, New York.
LINDA: "Originally most people. . . . keeps 'em there."
NARR: Part III, Coming Together: the social bond in intentional com-

munities; featuring residents of Corbett, New York; Springwood, Pennsylvania; and Reston, Virginia.

REHBURG: "What happens to those. . . . common philosophy?"

NARR: With commentary by Richard Rehberg, State University of New York at Binghamton, Joshua Friedman, publisher, editor and writer, Jane Schautz, Project Site Director with the Institute on Man and Science, and Ilene Kaplan, Union College, Schenectady, New York.

KAPLAN: "Social bonding. . . . to fall apart."

NARR: And an historical view by Thomas Bender, New York University and the New York Institute for the Humanities. *New Towns, Old Dreams* was funded by a grant from the New York Council for the Humanities and produced for broadcast by Radio Arts Incorporated. (*beat*) Professor Bender.

Music: fade under and out.

BENDER: "One of the great dangers. . . . conflict and time."

NARR: Reuben Merrill, Corbett, New York.

REUBEN: "A lot of our families. . . . in a three year period."

NARR: Corbett is not a new town in the strict sense. A company town in existence since 1912, Corbett was put up for sale in 1976 when the single local industry went bankrupt. The Institute on Man and Science bought the town in 1977 and undertook to help the residents become the managers and eventually the owners of their community. Today, the Institute is almost entirely clear of ownership in Corbett, although a close advisory relationship continues to exist. Thomas Bender.

BENDER: "What one wants. . . . the Institute on Man and Science."

NARR: The Institute on Man and Science is an independent educational and research center which has taken a special interest in the improvement of community life. Springwood, Pennsylvania, is an owner-planned, owner-built new town project launched by the Institute in 1979. Ken Moore hopes to live there one day.

KENNY: "We started out. . . . didn't realize that."

BENDER: "It is often assumed. . . . and they left."

NARR: The population of Corbet stands today at about 150. A relatively small number of families, 15%, have actually left the town, either willingly or through exclusion by other signers of the new town compact.

REUBEN: "Sure, we had some. . . . new tricks."

NARR: Thomas Bender cites early New England towns like Dedham, Massachusetts, as having set a precedent for such expulsions in highly intentional communities in America.

BENDER: "In their covenant. . . . can no longer isolate themselves."

NARR: Still, intentional communities appear to have some specific weaknesses which threaten their continuity today as in the past. Joshua Friedman grew up in the 40's and early 50's in a planned community: Roosevelt, New Jersey.

FRIEDMAN: "Most of these communities. . . . to get out of it."

BENDER: "Even within. . . . flexibility of response."

REHBERG::   "In Corbett. . . . deviation."

NARR:	(*soft*) Professor Rehberg.
REHBERG:	"I don't think. . . . belief system."
NARR:	It has taken a lot of hard work on the part of future Springwood residents to get where they are today: a community center and a prototype house stand on a prepared village site. But, according to Ken Moore, commitment and participation do vary.
KENNY:	"We also have some members. . . . get what they want."
FRIEDMAN:	"You have to have meetings. . . . their neighbors."
NARR:	(*sotto voce*) Joshua Friedman.
FRIEDMAN:	"It's important. . . . enclave sensation."
KAPLAN:	"We discussed. . . . keeping them apart."
NARR:	In two earlier programs we heard workshop participants talk about goals in intentional communities and about the structures which some of them have adopted. Such discussions naturally converge when one talks about social ties in these communities. The cluster-associations in the Virginia community of Reston are a case in point. Thomas Burgess is the Executive Director of the Reston Homeowners' Association and a resident of one of the clusters.
BURGESS:	"Cluster associations. . . . umbrella association."
NARR:	Ilene Kaplan.
KAPLAN:	"What I think. . . . of the community."
NARR:	Reuben Merrill, Corbett.
REUBEN:	"The social business. . . . family unit."
NARR:	Linda Nicholl, Springwood.
LINDA:	"It's really tough. . . . doesn't know."
KENNY:	"We've even. . . . it's not ours."
NARR:	Ken Moore, Springwood.
KENNY:	"I don't think anybody. . . . compel with."
NARR:	Jane Schautz, IMS site director at Springwood.
JANE:	"Let us be clear. . . . perception."
NARR:	Disillusionment with the goals, or impatience with the process, have exacted the heaviest toll in both Springwood and Corbett. In Corbett, however, the experience seems to be best characterized by the tolerant mutualism of the majority who have decided to stick it out.
REUBEN:	"As I said before. . . . accomplished something."
NARR:	As for Springwood, which has yet to see its first resident houses—and back fences—go up, only time will tell.
BENDER:	"The notion of coming together. . . . and revitalize."

Music: in and under.

NARR:	You have been listening to *New Towns, Old Dreams*, a workshop on community planning and new town building recorded at the Institute on Man and Science on July 16, 17, and 18, 1982 by Jerry Finan, Stephen Madarasz and Charles Potter, with technical support from WAMC in Albany. (The song "Uniontown" was written and performed by David Roth.) This program was mixed by David Rapkin and directed by Charles Potter.
	New Towns, Old Dreams was produced for broadcast by Radio Arts Incorporated. The series was made possible by a grant from the New York Council for the Humanities. Information regarding this pro-

gram can be obtained by writing to Radio Arts at 838 West End Avenue, New York, New York 10025, or to the Institute on Man and Science, Rensselaerville, New York 12147.
This is (name of announcer).
Thank you for listening.

Music: out.

There are two mechanical elements to notice in these scripts. The first is that the lines are not numbered as they were in some of the scripts that appeared earlier in this book. That is because there will only be one person to rehearse: the announcer. He or she can be instructed to find the appropriate place by page number and the name of the speaker whose quotation is adjacent to the lines. The second observation is that stage directions are in parentheses and italicized because they were underlined in the original script.

Finally, you can be sure that in its final form the documentary was enriched by music and perhaps even sound effects. These were selected by the director, although there may have been some indications for them included by the writer.

At the risk of boring you it must be repeated, however, that radio documentaries are, in fact, compilations. It may be that the pre-recorded elements were recorded specifically for the program, or it may be that they have been found in an archive of recordings. No matter: the program is compiled and presented. On the other hand, this very fact makes it possible to use a large variety of materials in the compilation. In addition to music and sound effects, there can also be archival recordings such as the voice of Herbert Hoover speaking of unemployment in "How Do You Spell Relief?"

Once again, the variety of presentations is limited only by the imaginations of those who are making the documentary.

Documentaries for Film and Television

Film documentaries have been around for a very long time. Robert Flaherty's *Nanook of the North,* to which we referred in chapter 2, was made in 1920, and that is generally considered the first of the genre. Although the camera in those days was bulky and heavy and awkward, there was no sound on film so one only needed the camera. The subject matter of documentaries tended to be ethnological in the manner of *Nanook* partly because they were exotic subjects and caught the imaginations of audiences and, therefore, of sources of finance. However, because the equipment was not only difficult to manage but also required considerable skill in order to be used successfully, the early documentarists were film-makers rather than ethnologists.

Part of the reason for the weight and bulk of the equipment in those days was the use of 35mm film. Although 16mm film was available, it was said to be "sub-standard" and that was the term used of all gauges of film less than 35mm. This larger gauge of film also served the film-makers better because most films were shown in theaters. There were by no means as many 16mm projectors to be found in schools, churches, and meeting halls around the country as there are today. In any case, then as now it was possible to make copies of films by reduction; that is, films made in 35mm originally can provide the source of 16mm prints (copies).

Documentaries, however, were a different kind of film from the fiction films that were being shown everywhere, and they came to be made by a growing band of documentary specialists—documentary film-makers, or documentarians. They were all socially minded because their films dealt with various aspects of society—their own and those that were more distant and exotic.

Even the advent of sound-on-film didn't change anything because the early sound equipment was also bulky and heavy, and film and sound technicians were needed, not ethnologists who were able to take motion pictures and record sound with difficulty and inconsistent success.

Filmed documentaries were then and are now largely compilation films using a process similar to what has been described for radio documentaries. Indeed the compilation process in film production is neither new nor dead. There are what are called "stock shot libraries" from which can be bought footage of virtually any imaginable subject—hurricanes and floods, wars and riots, wheat fields and salmon fishing, football games and jai alai, subjects without end. Some films have never been shot, only compiled!! By that I mean that no footage was shot specifically for the film in production: it was made entirely from stock shots.*

Sometimes circumstances seem to lead to compilation documentary films. During World War II each of the Allied Nations made films from footage that had been shot by combat cameramen. Among the Allied Forces such footage was pooled, that is, each nation's film production service received duplicate negatives of everything that had been shot by all the other Allied Nations. (The same practice was undertaken by the German Nazis and the Italian Fascists.) Many, many films were made from this "library" footage, and Leyda includes many of them in his list in *Films Beget Films*.

What is the role of the writer in the production of compilation documentaries? There is a role for a writer although it often happens that the writer and the director are the same person, and, more often than not, the director is also the editor. In general, the process follows this pattern.

First, one must start with research, as much research as possible.

---

*You will find a surprisingly long list of films made by compilation in the Appendices to *Films Beget Films,* by Jay Leyda (New York: Hill & Wang, 1964). From this small book you will be able to learn a great deal about making compilation films.

Since compiling a film out of already existing footage begins with *selection,* it follows that more than what will be finally needed must be available. This applies, clearly, also to research, for it is on the basis of good research that film-makers can establish their criteria for selecting the film segments, the sequences, that will be presented in a film. A writer doesn't write a final script before the editing begins. Remember, the logic of a film is not verbal but visual. There must be a visual logic to lead the eyes of the audience and thus also their minds. This kind of logic is provided by an editor, but he or she does not come to the editing table with the visual logic established in advance. As the editor works with the rolls of film the documentary takes shape in his or her mind. It is very helpful if the writer works with the director-editor because input from a creative writer is valuable.

Much can be learned from Paul Rotha's account of making his great compilation feature, *The Life of Adolf Hitler,* as included by Leyda in his book.

Rotha explained: "My method of working . . . [began] . . . with an agreement on the basic theme and then the search for footage. This latter is really the first creative process and difficult to describe. It is so instinctive—and personal. You and your assistants collect footage from every available source. You sit and screen it for hours and days on end. And always you look for two things: first, footage of a *general* nature about various aspects of the subject; second, key shots which *symbolize* a specific point you want to make. For example, in the Hitler film I was always looking for shots which visually revealed some aspect of the Führer's psychology. These later I might use wholly out of context to make a specific point. Imagine my delight when I found a very short shot of Adolf drinking a cup of tea with his little finger stuck out like a middle-class English housewife. . . .

"I began screening in London, January 1960 and by September had got around 150,000 feet printed up in my cutting room. [This is measured in 35mm film. It represents 60,000 feet in 16mm film, or about 30 hours of screening time.—RE] Early in September 1960 we screened our accumulated 150,000 feet at the studio in Hamburg."

Leyda comments: "At this point the script had become more precisely defined, Robert Neumann and Helga Koppel had prepared an outline, in which many problems were left unresolved, while Rotha had stuck to his heavy examination schedule without looking for much shape."

"But as the film unrolled day by day for a week [Rotha continues] certain conceptions came into my mind conditioned *by what I saw.*"

"In the four weeks of December 1960 [Leyda again], Rotha wrote a working script himself—one column of an English draft narration in three voices, and a column of visuals suggested by what had already been found."

"[Rotha resumes] I decided to do two main things. First, conceive the overall film much like some *New Yorker* profiles, that is to say—to tell the story of Hitler and his times and the German people in a series of facets rather than in chronological order: a sequence on Hitler the Man, Hitler as a self-appointed Military Strategist, Hitler's mastery of propaganda techniques, etc. My second decision was to tell the story through three voices—History, Reason and Force, plus synchronized dialogue by principal characters, Hitler, Goebbels, etc. Later I dropped the Voice of Reason and found it could be embodied in the Voice of History. . . . Now at last we had something to make a rough assembly with. Our first cut ran some two and a half hours. [Eventually it finished at 100 minutes.] The next months you can imagine. Recut, recut, shifting whole sequences around, dropping some, thinking up new ones. Redrafting the narration continually. I wrote in all 15 versions of it."*

Until the end of World War II, by far the greater number of documentary films was made from "silent" footage, that is, footage that did not have synchronously recorded sound. We have already discussed the reasons. Music and sound effect chosen by the director-editor would be blended together in the sound track with whatever narration had been written.†

When documentaries were to be made from film shot specifically for the purpose, the process wasn't very much different. As a result of the research, which might include an exploratory visit to the locations in which the filming was to take place, a treatment might be prepared. A treatment is a kind of synopsis of what the writer-director envisions as the probable film in its final form. This treatment emphasizes the *treatment* of the subject in pictures and in sound. It is similar to a treatment for a fiction film as described in chapter 2. For a half-hour documentary the treatment might be as much as three typed pages, but it might well be less. However, the treatment is in no sense final. It is only a starting point. The film might vary a great deal from it because of what is finally shot and because of what might have been learned further during the shooting itself.

Perhaps the most valuable aspect of preparing a treatment is that it provides an opportunity for a film-maker to articulate his or her attitudes and points of view about the subject of the film. It is to be hoped that a film-maker will not begin with an attitude charged with predispositions and prejudices. The most fruitful beginning is with an open mind whose attitudes and perceptions emerge from the researches and experiences upon which the treatment is based.

Although hand cameras had been invented a great many years ago, it was World War II that provided a primary spur to the development of lighter, smaller, more efficient cameras, which could be used by combat cameramen. By about 1950 magnetic sound recording tape became available, as we have said, and the diminution of the size and weight of

---

*Leyda, *Films Beget Films*, pp. 94–96.
† An important exception was *Housing Problems* made in England in 1935 by Edgar Anstey and Sir Arthur Elton.

the cinematographic and sound recording equipment developed for the space age made another great difference in film production. Cumbersome equipment meant that a lot of people were necessary to run it. Lighter, portable, simpler equipment meant that fewer and fewer people were required, even to the point that much film could be made, both picture and sound, with only one person running the equipment. By their experience the earlier documentary film-makers became, if you will, lay anthropologists or ethnologists. With the new equipment professional ethnographers and anthropologists could become film-makers. Of the film-makers turned sociologist one example is Joris Ivens, whose first real documentary was made in the 1920s and who is still making documentary films; as ethnologist turned film-maker one can point to Jean Rouch, who has developed new ways of using film-making equipment and new genres of films.

The greatest problem facing those who make documentaries is finding the money with which to operate. Except in the Office of War Information in the United States during World War II, the Ministry of Information in Great Britain at the same period of time, and the continuing National Film Board of Canada (and its counterparts in other Commonwealth countries such as Australia, New Zealand, and India), it is almost impossible to find a steady job as a documentary film-maker. The people who are engaged in this pursuit must find their own sources of money. They may find a few people to provide large portions of the money needed, or they may find a large number of donors each of whom will provide a small portion. In order to raise the money needed for the next production two things are necessary: first, some kind of "track record" so that the investors or donors can have reassurance that the project will reach a successful conclusion; and second, some kind of presentation for the prospective donor so that he or she may learn something about the project. Such a presentation is called a "planning outline," or, more frequently, a "proposal."

James Martin, a senior member of the motion picture faculty of Columbia College (Chicago), organized and became the director of a large project funded by the National Endownment for the Humanities, called the Southeast Chicago Historical Project. One aspect of this was to be a film. Here is his proposal.

Valley of Immigrants, Mountain of Steel

This film will confront many issues and questions concerning industrial America, the changes it has undergone, and the kind of future it can expect. It is an examination of the condition of working class people in America, their problems, their values, and their survival. But most of all, it is an opportunity to dispel many misconceptions surrounding working class Americans, because this will be a view from the inside looking out. . . .

Southeast Chicago is the heart of America's major steel producing district. Someone once described it as a valley of immigrants surrounded by a mountain of steel. No matter where you walk, whether it's down 106th Street on the East Side or along Commercial Avenue in the business district, the symbols of heavy industry are visible. The smokestacks of U.S., Republic, and Wisconsin Steel tear holes in the grey sky. Gigantic drawbridges transport machines across valleys of fire, smoke, and slag. For eighty years it has been like this.

Among the community's 100,000 residents are enclaves of every major ethnic and racial group that settled in American industrial communities over the last century. They settled into pockets of intense national spirit which bred cooperation at first, rivalries later on, then cooperation based on common needs. All are bound together by the workplace—the harsh physical existence of high-temperature ovens and roaring furnaces. All share the economic uncertainties of industrial production. Within the common experience are also differentiated social, cultural, and religious experiences. From fragments of the Old World, new lives have been constructed; lives that preserve the distinct ethnic traditions of earlier generations.

The geography of Southeast Chicago is a mosaic. The steel mills themselves, with blocks of untouched land growing weeds, act as perimeters against the neighborhoods encroaching right up to the millgates. Density of industry, compactness of neighborhoods, yet unused land, natural divisions keeping out those who aren't in, and keeping in those who try to venture out. This landscape creates much more than a sense of provincialism. It creates a sense of community, strong national pride, peculiar affinities, distinctly different identities.

Drawbridges, dead-end streets, skyway overpasses, and the sluggish Calumet River—a Twentieth Century fiefdom. Grain elevators and shipping docks, rail lines and pipe lines, monuments to dead war heroes at busy intersections; there's a geometry to all this that isn't present anywhere else in Chicago. And the names of the neighborhoods: Slag Valley and Irondale; Millgate and the Bush. These are strong names. They have the clang of steel.

Historically, Southeast Chicago has existed like the colony of a great nation; politically exploited, wealth exported, its people foreign and unseen, their fates determined by distant corporate managers. The people of Southeast Chicago have worked steel and spent their lives in the grimy shadow of the mills for generations. While many have moved to the suburbs, ties to the community remain strong; family, work, and church form an unbreakable cord. For the older generations, Southeast Chicago is not a way station, but a staying place. These people know the privation, the injury and ill health, the struggle, the bleak mean neighborhoods more common to intensely industrial, dependent communities of an earlier time.

We will travel to Southeast Chicago and stand at the foot of United States Steel's southgate, see the narrow streets, the old men and women who sit on their porch steps to reminisce, and the corner taverns that still act as public forums. We will speak to the people of these neighborhoods, people who, in spite of the harshness of mill work and the economic uncertainties, won't surrender the spirit, the energy, and the traditions that tie them to the community.

Today, Southeast Chicagoans wrestle with a number of questions. For a community so dependent on a single industry as Southeast Chicago is dependent on steel, how will changes in that industry affect the community's future? What happens to a community so deeply rooted in the industrial era when that era has passed? What happens when the closing of even one mill can mean 3,500 jobs lost and the disappearance of millions of spending dollars? Eighty years is a long time for any community in an industrially active city to keep its neighborhood base constant. In light of plant shutdowns and higher unemployment, how can a community maintain its cohesion if many workers are forced to move away from the workplace? What do forces that disrupt the community's stability do to its commercial life, its ethnic and racial relationships, and to its primary neighborhood organizations like the churches, tavern cliques, and political associations?

A unique opportunity exists to address these questions. The people of Southeast Chicago are involved in a two-year National Endowment for the Humanities project, to document themselves through the use of oral and family history, union history, photography, and other media. The documentary we envision would use this material to create a historical perspective from which to examine the problems facing the community today. It is a film about working people in changing times. A film which can represent the issues as they are seen by the people who are living them.

This is a community where people work, live, and raise families. Therefore, our documentary exploration will look at three major aspects of Southeast Chicago and its people: *the Workplace; the Neighborhoods and Institutions;* and *Ethnic Ties and Family Life.* The natural rhythm and flow of life and events in each of these aspects is the means by which we depict life and address problems. For example, a union local meeting gives access to issues concerning work and unemployment. A historical event like the Memorial Day Massacre can give insight into how people felt now and then about unions and the right to organize. Interviews with people on the job will be informative as well as visually stimulating. Neighborhood and institutional events like block parties, feast days, street fairs, beauty pageants, and sports provide strong material from which to consider the forces threatening the stability of the neighborhoods and institutions. A Polish, Mexican, or Croatian wedding provides an exciting background to begin an examination of ethnic ties and family life. Residents like Ed Sadlowski, third generation steelworker and prominent trade unionist, will help articulate the issues. Views of third and fourth generation Mexican-Americans and Blacks will give added meaning to our understanding of working class Americans.

The foregoing sets out the basic point of view from which the film is expected to be made. It isn't an outline of the film; rather, it is a philosophy. A preliminary outline of the film itself is somewhat different.

Film Outline

The film is divided into three distinct segments of approximately 25-30 minutes. In the first sequence of the film we will deal with all four neighborhoods in much the same way as the book, however, the film will examine parallel subjects in each of the four neighborhoods* before moving on to the next historical consideration thereby contrasting each neighborhood.

---

*The outline for only three neighborhoods is included here.

EARLY SETTLEMENT, THE COMING OF STEEL, 1830-1900 (SEQUENCE I)

A. *South Chicago*

South Chicago was and still is the center of the Southeast Side of Chicago. The earliest commercial and industrial development in the area took place here. This sequence will deal with the development of a multi-ethnic, multi-racial "core" neighborhood which originally centered on the Calumet River and later on in South Works and other lakefront steel mills. Once the South Works opened in 1880, immigrants were drawn to the district in large numbers. First a settlement of Irish, German, Scandinavian, and other Western European workers, it soon developed into a community dominated by the so-called New Immigration from Eastern and Southern Europe. Polish, Croatian, Serbian, Slovak, and other church steeples joined those who had come before to challenge the smokestacks for dominance of the local skyline. These groups in turn were followed by even a newer migration of blacks and Hispanics. South Chicago affords an excellent opportunity to test the various theories of ethnicity that have been put forth in academic circles; such as the melting pot concept, Anglo-Conformity and other such theories concerning assimilation and acculturations.

The community's social history is a long one. It is perhaps the quintessential 19th Century industrial neighborhood. In a 1901 survey of the city's housing, South Chicago was ignored because it was felt that conditions were so bad as to be atypical. Local social life has always been tied to the steel industry. Strikes, layoffs, and union elections affect the entire neighborhood and are communal events. The sequence will deal with all of these as they relate to South Chicago's historical development. Some of these will be dealt with in greater detail in the second and third sequences under the subjects of Workplace and Ethnic Life. The following is a tentative outline of the narrative flow of the film, however, the order may vary as script consideration dictates:

1. The Pottawatomie Nation
2. Early White Settlement—A Fishing Village
3. Early Industrial Development
4. The Coming of Steel: 1880–1900
5. Brown Steel Company
6. South Works 1880–1900
7. The Creation of an Industrial Neighborhood, The Bush
8. The Meaning of Neighborhood in the Industrial-Walking City

B. *South Deering*

South Deering is an old industrial neighborhood located to the south of 95th Street and to the west of the Calumet River. In the 1850's the Illinois Central and the Rock Island Railoads crossed the area. Throughout the 1860's it remained a haven for hunters and fishermen. The initial spark that led to the area's industrial growth was Congress's decision in 1870 to improve the Calumet River's harbor. From that point on South Deering developed into a manufacturing and grain elevator center.

Like South Chicago, South Deering attracted various waves of immigrants, especially after the opening of Wisconsin Steel along Torrence Avenue in the 1900's. Chief among these were the Yugoslavs who in 1930 made up 48% of the foreign-born population. Unlike South Chicago, this steelworkers' community was composed primarily of one-story, single-family frame homes. The only major exception to this was and is the Trumbull Park Homes built by the Public Works Administration in 1937-1938. Later this housing project was the scene of racial fighting in the 1950's.

South Deering's history is one that portrays the effect of the federal government on local community life. From the beginning, Congress's decision to improve the harbor and later wartime industrial development, as well as the building of the Trumbull Park homes, are symbolic of this involvement.

The neighborhood is also a good example of a community hurt by the changes brought about by the so-called post-industrial era. The huge Wisconsin Steel plant's closing in 1980 left over 3,500 workers without jobs and had a devastating effect on the entire neighborhood. The history of South Deering is one of the rise and fall of a traditional northern industrial community.

1. Area Remains Virgin Prairie Until After Civil War
2. The Effect of Improvement of the Calumet River and Harbor
3. The Development of the Calumet River and Dock Company
4. Early Industry
5. Irondale, 1875–1900
6. John Brown Iron and Steel Co., established at 109th & Calumet River in 1875: First Steel Mill in Southeast Chicago
7. Small Workers' Community Established in the Northern Part of the District: In 1880, 926 Residents Lived Here.
8. In 1889 South Deering Becomes a Part of Chicago

C. *East Side*

Like other Southeast Side neighborhoods the East Side can trace the growth to the industrial and commercial development of the Calumet Region. As late as 1872 there were perhaps six families living in the community area. These were engaged primarily in fishing, hunting, and farming. The opening of Silicon Steel Company's rolling mills along the Calumet River initiated the settlement of the northern part of the area.

The 1880's saw considerable economic growth. Original settlers were predominantly German, Swedish, and Irish in nationality. As the century came to a close Southern and Eastern Europeans were attracted to the community.

Residential settlement tended to move southward from 95th Street. In the 1920's residential construction took place mostly east of Ewing Avenue. The city's construction of Calumet Park increased the desirability of this area. The park was built on landfill created by the dumping of slag into Lake Michigan.

The 1920's also saw more industrial development as Republic Steel, Youngstown Sheet and Tube Company, and the Chicago Shipbuilding Company opened plants. This led to further population growth. By 1930 the Germans, Swedes, Italians, and Yugoslavs were the leading nationalites in the neighborhood.

The Great Depression hit the community hard. In fact, the 1930's saw a decline in the population of the area. The East Side was in some respects a suburb of South Chicago, and it received as residents those who were able to afford better housing. When the economic collapse hit, these lost their homes and left the neighborhood.

The war boom, however, saw the East Side grow again. From 1940 to

1950 the district's population rose by 31%. Once again the area was the beneficiary of a migration of steelworkers from the older neighborhoods. This trend has continued throughout the post-war period. In 1960 the Yugoslavs, Poles, Italians, and Swedes were the leading foreign-born nationalities. Today large numbers of Hispanics are joining the other nationalities on the East Side.

The East Side is a good example of an industrial urban area which also shows signs of being a middle class suburb. In 1945, 23% of Chicago's land area had still not seen construction. Much of the first round of suburbanization actually took place within Chicago's boundaries. This enabled the city to retain the middle class for a longer period than other cities with a smaller land area. It was because of this that Chicago received the sobriquet "the city that works." A study of the East Side allows a look at this "in-city" suburban development.

1. Michigan and Southern R.R. Extends its Tracks Through the Area in 1848
2. Early Steelers
3. Silicon Steel Opens Plant in Early 1870's
4. Michigan and Southern R.R. Opens Railroad Station at 100th & Ewing Avenue
5. Economic Expansion 1880 Onwards
6. Riverfront Development
7. Shipbuilding
8. Granaries

● ● ●

PHOTOGRAPHS & ILLUSTRATIONS

The bulk of the visual material used in the early settlement scenes will be photographs, maps, and illustrations drawn from the archives of the Southeast Chicago Historical Project. . . . Details.)

Examples of Photographs & Illustrations for Sequence I

- Early Surveys and Maps
- Drawings of Pottawatomie Settlements
- Glassplate Photographic Surveys of Lake Michigan
- View of South Works—1880
- Housing—85th & Houston—1880
- Housing—87th & Baltimore—1885
- McGovern Women Family Portrait
- Berg Family Portrait—1890
- Photograph of German Church—South Chicago
- Surveys Showing Reason to Center Chicago on Calumet River Rather than Chicago River
- Early Picture of Ice House on Lake Wolf—1895

Clearly there is a difference between the proposal and the first film outline. What follows is the first part of an outline of sequence titles, if you will, made much later in the production process and after a quantity of film had been shot.

Film Outline—Southeast Chicago: A Family Album

SEQUENCE I: "They Came to Work Steel"

Essentially the immigrant experience based on historic photographs, film footage, interviews and oral histories. All of this material is available to the project. We will move in a non-linear fashion from past to present and back again.

1. Fade up on a large banner held by high school students in a contemporary marching band. There is only the sound of a drum roll as the camera moves around the band and over past the drummer to a flag pole. Up the flag pole to an American Flag waving in a stiff breeze. The national anthem is played as the superimposed title *Southeast Chicago: A Family Album* appears along with other opening credits. As the anthem ends we dissolve to . . .

2. The interior at U.S. Steel's South Works around the turn-of-the-century. In this series of photographs we see the mill and shots of the area and early housing before it was developed. The voice of a 70-year-old, retired steel worker and other workers describe working conditions and how they or their parents or siblings came to work steel. The narration explains how South Chicago was the entry point for immigrants, and which ethnic group came first, etc. We end on a picture of the paymaster's office with a sign in 5 languages. Dissolve to . . .

3. Retired steelworker pointing to where he worked, two of his fingers are missing. We go with him on a short tour of the mill, it is in color now but still looks the same.

Thru 40—Shots of Mill

41. Final shot in mill of a huge ladle pouring steel, cut to series of photos of East Side in 1912. The Camera comes to rest on a shot in which several buildings are seen. Dissolve to . . .

42. Same shot as seen from Chicago Skyway. An East Sider is pointing out view from the Chicago Skyway, high above the East Side after a few words. Cut to . . .

43. West shot from lake looking up Calumet River from Lake Michigan we see heavy industry, all around ships with foreign flags at mooring. Voices over talk about our port. Dissolve to . . .

44. Black and white engravings showing the time when Pottawatomies lived there. Voice over talks about early history of Calumet Region.

This is a brief example of the beginning of the film. The first sequence continues moving through the four neighborhoods, setting the tone, and establishing the geography and history of the areas. In this sequence we want to establish the industrial nature of the community as well as the multi-ethnic, multi-racial base of the community. The family nature of the community will also be established. Newer immigrant groups to the area will also be presented in this sequence.

• Artist's Conception of South Deering
• Irondale—Brown's Mill
• Photograph of 1st House on East Side
• Mrs. Reese, Owner of Hegewisch
• Maps of All Four Neighborhoods

II. SECOND SEQUENCE

Parallel development of all four neighborhoods as the community of Southeast Chicago from 1900 thru World War II.

    A. *South Chicago*
        1. Residential Maturity 1900–1917
            a. A City Within a City
            b. Commercial Development
            c. Transportation
            d. Local Politics
            e. Ethnic Change
        2. Years of Strife 1916–1920
            a. World War I—The Effect on Both the Ethnic and Larger Community
            b. Racial Conflict—1919 Race Riot
            c. Labor Strife—1919 Steel Strike
        3. 1920's
            a. Further Growth
            b. The Effect of Further Migration to South Chicago
            c. Juvenile Delinquency and the Immigrant Family
        4. The Great Depression and the 1930's
            a. Economic Life
            b. The Chicago Area Project and the Movement for Neighborhood Improvement (Burgess, Alinsky, Rev. Lange, Bubacz)
            c. Labor—SWOC–CIO
                1. Organizational Drive
                2. CIO Impact on Local Life
        5. South Chicago and World War II
            a. Steel and the War Effort
            b. Women and Steel
            c. War and the Community

• • •

Once the major part of what has to be filmed has been shot, it is assembled in the rough order in which it is expected to appear in the final version. This stage of production is called, as you might expect, the first assembly. When the assembly is screened, it is possible to perceive a kind of rough shape. It is also possible to recognize certain blanks, *lacunae*, that need yet to be filmed. These may not have been evident before seeing the assembly. The few pages that follow are part of the script of the film about Southeast Chicago written at the time of the assembly. Please note that the words in parentheses are either visual instructions to the editor or notes of already shot film. The asterisks (*) indicate that the scene described has been shot and is already in the editing room. You will see that the indicated sequences present pretty much what has been written in previous stages of the scripting, but in this stage there is no discussion of philosophy nor of the attitudes to be expressed in the film, only the description of the visuals. The visuals are often indicated as "sync sound" shots, that is, shots or sequences that have been filmed with the speech recorded simultaneously.

Assembled Footage

1. Montage set geographic contemporary boundaries   (to be shot)
2. Open credits over Labor Day Parade*
   Few comments by Ald. Vrdolyak at podium   (shots of faces)
3. Commercial Avenue shots of people*—South Chicago has always been the heart of the four neighborhoods   (shots of faces)

    (dissolve to)

4. Pottawatomie Indians
   (use V.O. Fitzgibbon talking about Pottawatomie Tribes)
   (Archive stills)
5. Early mill shots—1880   (Brownsmill   Southworks   Aerial shots   Pre-1900 shots)   Information use subtitles   (Archives)
6. Immigrants   (montage   archives)
7. Interviews with various people re: how they got there:*
   Fitzgibbons
   Cordero
   Sadlowski & Father
   Buocchio
   Bork
   Solomon
   Mendelsohn
   Others
8. Mexican Independence Day Parade, check for interviews*
9. Martinez women interview*
10. Possible interview w/Buoscio and others—relating each immigrant experience.
10a. Minnie Lightfoot interview?
11. Photo montage on historical development of 4 neighborhoods. These should move us to present.
    South Chicago
    East Side
    South Deering
    Hegewisch   (Archives)

One aspect of this kind of film-making, in which no dialogue has been written before filming (as it would have been if we were making a fiction film, a story film) is that we are still, in a very real sense, making a compilation film. Sequences are filmed because they cover parts of the total subject, and these are parts that will help to build the complete structure. The structure itself is completed in the editing process. Although the film that is being shot is specifically for the documentary that is being made, it is, nevertheless, to be put on a shelf in the editing room, to be selected or rejected, for the assembly and the final editing.

During the filming not only is the dialogue of the interviews recorded, but also the speeches of important people at public meetings and gatherings. Likewise other sounds are recorded—the sounds of picnics and parties, of fireworks and cheering. These are the sounds that occur in the places in which the filming is done. Not surprisingly, these are called "indigenous sound" and will be available for use in the edited film, perhaps as sound effects. Some of the speeches in the interviews may also be used as narrative over scenes other than the interviews themselves. This capability of recording such sounds as we have described has changed the nature of documentaries as compared to those that were made before the end of World War II.

As was pointed out earlier, finding the money that is needed to make a documentary is not always easy. There are a few foundations, a very few government organizations like the National Endowments, and a few opportunities from educational television. The stages of scripting that will be set out next are for a documentary made by Gordon Quinn and Jerry Blumenthal for their company Kartemquin Films, Ltd. It was made for public television. The first piece of writing that is presented here is the proposal that was given to public television in the search for their sponsorhip.

The Last Pullman Car

On March 7, 1979, the Ten O'Clock News in Chicago carried a story announcing that the Pullman Standard works in Chicago and northern Indiana would be closing. Pullman, the first modern corporation, the first with an industrial assembly-line (even before Ford), the first with a company town. . .was giving up producing the railroad passenger cars on which its corporate fortune and world-wide fame had been built.

The plant's closing would mean not only job-loss, but the disruption of an entire community. The workers at the plant were stunned. It was not something they expected to be learning about from a TV anchorman. What about the energy crisis and the compelling national need for mass-transit, they asked? Pullman was the last American-owned corporation building mass-transit railroad cars. How, in the face of recent "Buy-American" legislation, could Pullman pass up the opportunity to build passenger cars that Amtrak was committed to buy?

Recovering from their initial shock, the new leadership of USWA Local #1834 (called the Eugene V. Debs local, in memory of his role in the historic 1894 strike at Pullman) began a campaign that would lead them to investigate not only their own historical roots, but also those of the corporation for which they work, and the history of the abandonment of mass-transit in America. As they became aware of the epidemic of plant closings around the country, they began to link up with other "Save Our Jobs" committees—in Youngstown, at Wisconsin Steel and at Dodge Main.

Local #1834 saw the situation at Pullman as a particularly dramatic example of a shut-down which was against the national interest, and it led them to question the traditional American attitude that corporate decision-making and the "free marketplace" can really deliver what America needs. They saw that their struggle could be as historically significant to the future of the country as was the first Pullman strike in 1894.

•   •   •

Our film will intercut three stories: (1) the efforts of Local #1834 to form new alliances and take their message to the nation; (2) the 1894 strike at Pullman and how it became a national struggle centered in Chicago; and (3) the history of mass-transit in America and its dismantling.

In most documentaries, historical material is used to ruminate on the past, to evoke nostalgia, sometimes even to "extract" a lesson for the audience. Our film will treat its historical material differently. It will be seen from the point of view of the Local #1834 members who are seeking out a history that matters to them, at the same time that they are making their own history. We work from the premise that to understand the past you must frame it with the present.

The story of the 1894 strike, which began over arbitrary wage-cuts in the plant coupled with rent raises in George Pullman's paternalistic industrial community, has never been told on film. When the striking workers were joined by Debs' American Railway Union, a violent national conflict with the Railroad Companies' General Manager Association was set in motion. Subsequent to the strike, President Cleveland, Governor Altgeld, and Jane Addams were among those involved in investigations which greatly influenced the labor reform movement all the way into the 1930's, and helped change American attitudes toward the relationship between industry, labor and government. There are rich archival sources on the Pullman struggle, mostly in the Chicago area. We would use stills, music, voice-overs and a sparse narration for this historical material, which would in turn be juxtaposed to Local #1834's present-day struggle to reach out for national support in the new ideological battleground of the mass media.

In our treatment of mass-transit we will also intercut the past and the present, to reveal new meanings, and to suggest new strategies for America's technological and political development. Our history will not be academic. As the membership of Local #1834 look around their community they see that most workers cannot reach Pullman except by automobile. (There was once an effective network of streetcars and trains). This will lead us to examine the decline of public transportation all around America—for example, in the Los Angeles area where General Motors bought up the intra-urban rail system, dismantled it, and then replaced part of it with less efficient and polluting G.M. buses. The rest was left to the automobile, on government subsidized expressways. In this way we will begin to understand the consequences of the Pullman Corporation's decision to concentrate its investments in petrochemicals and other high profit areas rather than public transportation.

In the present, the film will focus primarily on the activities of the membership of Local #1834. Their search for new allies and for ways of reaching the nation has taken them to Bill Moyers' Journal, to the Phil Donahue Show, to seminars on plant closings held for European unionists with similar problems, and to Wall Street to protest at the celebration of the Pullman Centennial. (On Wall Street they encountered the police in a scene similar to the one in "Harlan County, USA.") At a recent State AFL–CIO conference they tacked onto a "Buy-American" proposal a clause that if no other way could be found to keep the Pullman works open, the federal government should nationalize it. This unprecedented demand passed almost unanimously. Their yellow T-shirts with the slogan "Keep Mass-Transit Rolling—Save Our Jobs" can often be seen on picket lines of other locals, where they lend support and tell their story. We will follow the yellow T-shirts, and we will try to capture the frustration of being denied time on a local news show, as well as the exuberance of addressing thousands at an anti-nuke rally.

Local #1834 is now preparing to negotiate a new contract in the face of the recent closing of two other Pullman plants—by the Wheelabrator-Frye Conglomerate, who recently bought the Pullman corporation. The Local's best hope now is that the Conglomerate will sell their plant to a partnership of Kawasaki and Thrall (an American corporation). The federal government also supports this move, but as of February 1981, the Conglomerate's intentions are far from clear.

We are proposing a 60-minute documentary that will examine the issues raised by the struggles of Local #1834. Along with them, we want to know what forces in our past have left us standing contemplating the absurd possibility of the last Pullman car pulling out of the station.

This proposal sets out clearly the foundation and the purpose of the documentary, and it also sets out the proposed contents and structures. There can be no doubts and few questions in the minds of prospective sponsors about what the film-makers expect to do, what they want to say, and how they expect to say it. The proposal was successful, and the film is now completed.

Once the production began, the same kind of work had to be undertaken as was done on the Southeast Chicago Historical Project. A great deal of archival footage had to be unearthed and a great number of archival still photographs. With some idea of this material in mind, a more detailed treatment could be written. Here are four pages of the beginning of that treatment, which, because it is so detailed, is very long. During production it was called the "monster treatment."

Opening Montage

VISUAL	AUDIO

Chicago 1981 (title)

TV NEWS: Normal transit service will continue through tomorrow; after that, it's anybody's guess. . .

Headlines:
Mayor Byrne says no to Governor
Thompson's bailout scheme

CTA gets another jolt
Dunkirk near for Mass Transit
Fare hikes—Service cuts
Ridership down 11 million in September

TV NEWS: Interview clips.
1st WOMAN: There goes my lunch money
2nd WOMAN: The trains are dirty, they smell, they're slower, and now they cost more
MAN: I'm not gonna take the train—I'll drive!

Chicago 1980 (title)

TV NEWS: Pullman is getting out of the passenger car business after 100 years.

1st PULLMAN WORKER: Something's wrong—the country needs mass transit and we build it.
2nd WORKER: Pullman doesn't care about the working people—just about making billions—they're sinking all of their money into petroleum.
3rd WORKER: The job situation is very bad; everything is being taken away from us.
4th WORKER: Can America really do this? All we need is good management. We built streetcars and El cars for the city of Chicago.

Traffic jam on the expressway as . . . the elevated streaks by.

Chicago—long a city synonomous with transportation.

Exterior shots: Pullman, Wisconsin Steel plant shutdown, picket lines of workers.

People waiting for trains and buses. Crowd on a snowswept El platform.

But today, two groups of Chicagoans who depend vitally upon mass transportation—the workers who build it and the citizens who ride it—are finding themselves out in the cold.

Headlines and TV newsclips:
Youngstown mill closes
Unemployment highest since Depression (long lines at unemployment office)

SEPTA in crisis
Birmingham Transit shutdown
Amtrak cutbacks
Four more stations may close: CTA

The story is familiar in most of America's older industrial cities. The good jobs and working conditions, achieved after nearly a century of bitter struggle, are slipping away. And integrated public transit systems, responsive to the needs of riders rather than speculators and investors, are more elusive than ever.

Bustling train station
Abandoned station being demolished
French, Japanese high-speed trains
Pix of railroads
Pix of highways

LA freeway and smog
Lines at the gas pump
Abandoned industrial areas

Early maps of Midwest
Early photos of elevateds
Demographic and industrial charts
Rail footage; early transit, Chicago
Steel rail fabrication
Pullman factory stills
Pullman strike 1894
1881 transit boycott litho
CIO handbill
Public transit league headlines demanding municipal ownership
Pullman 1981 picket line
State Street 1981 picketers blocking buses to protest fare hikes

Company signs beside empty parking lot.
Newsclips of CTA crisis

1981 (title)

PULLMAN WORKER: I represent the workers of Pullman Standard, the last American owned corporation building railroad passenger cars. This country needs legislation when a company can just close its doors without regard to the needs of the workers or the needs of the community.

WOMAN AT A CTA HEARING: I want to know how you think I am supposed to get to work. Since the 131 bus was taken off, I've been late to work five times, and I'm still getting up at 5:30. I waited 50 minutes this morning for the Madison bus and I had to explain it to my boss.

Rail transportation in America, once our greatest asset, is dying, and mass transit is in chaos. World leadership in railroad technology has shifted to Japan and Europe as America turned from rail to rubber.

At the heart of our problems with jobs, energy, and the environment are the decisions America makes on how to move its people.

There is no better place than Chicago to see how transportation affects the location, growth, and political economy of our cities.

Chicago was the nation's rail center and a major manufacturer of rail equipment. And like other cities, its growth was largely shaped by its mass transit system.

Chicago has a rich history of organized protest by workers and riders —people seeking control over their jobs and control over their transit system. People seeking decent, steady work, and convenient, affordable transportation.

And, today, Chicago's largest railroad car-building company—the Pullman Company—and the city's transit system—the Chicago Transit Authority—are collapsing.

The struggles of the workers who build our transportation, and of the riders who use it, began before the turn of the century. This is where we must begin if we are to understand the origin of some of today's most critical urban problems.

Chicago, 1894 (title)

Stills of early skyscraper construction

Animated map of railroads as they arrive in Chicago.

Pictorial materials of opening of the West, founding of new cities, the expansion and rearrangement of an industrial nation.

Brief montage of stills and sounds, linking the railroads to other primary Chicago industries . . . pigs and cattle arrive by train, as does lumber, grain, and textiles.

Chicago, 1894—the fastest growing city in North America—the center for the industrial boom of the Midwest and transportation link between East and West. Chicago, center for 26 railroads, the nexus of the largest accumulation of capital in American history as railroads absorb nearly half of the nation's investment capital. Chicago, the center of American railroad growth and culture. . .

Immigrants arriving in Chicago by train.

Stills of Packingtown slums and riverside shanties.

Children doing needlework.

Housewives scrounging for firewood in the railroad yards.

. . . and Chicago, crowded tenements for hundreds of thousands of immigrants who come to work in the jungle of stockyards, lumber mills, textile factories, and railroad yards.

Organizational, fraternal signs for German, Italian, Polish, Jewish, Irish groups.

Children in garment factories, women doing sewing in tenement room.

A crowded labor market . . . and . . .

Lithos from 1877 upheaval and Haymarket period strikes.

Hunger march down Prairie Avenue.

an erratic capital market with severe cyclical depressions—in 1877, and again in 1886, large violent strikes sweep the city as thousands of hungry people demand relief from wage cuts and layoffs.

Knights of Labor banner

American Federation of Labor convention

Anti-anarchist headline

IWW Banner

Photo of George Pullman

Chicago, the nation's largest and most turbulent center for unionism of many political persuasions.

Chicago, home of the Pullman Company—already the premier builder of railroad passenger cars in America. . .

Carpenters assemble car frame

Lithos of fabricating activities: glass

Pullman's company was a prototype of the modern multinational corpowindows, car wheels, fabric curtains, to finished car beside factory

Pullman ticket window in train station, photo of Pullman porter greeting passenger, Pullman conductor taking ticket, passenger asleep in berth.

Stills contrasting slums to Pullman town's wide streets, brick rowhouses.

Workers entering the plant

Cut to walking tour given by Professor William Adelman through Pullman (tour group includes present-day Pullman workers) explaining how the town included no taverns, no meeting halls, how rent and utilities were deducted from paychecks. Adelman describes the relatively high quality of most of the worker housing—reducing absenteeism due to illness.

Headlines of Pullman layoffs, car orders declining, unrest brewing

Adelman tells how bad conditions became in the town with food shortages and evictions.

ARU pamphlet

Photos of Debs speaking

Headlines of earlier strike losses by blacksmiths, painters, carpenters

ARU pamphlets—unite!!

ration—with assembly line production techniques and an integrated monopoly structure, both vertically. . .

and horizontally.

To avoid the unrest of Chicago, Pullman erected a company town south of the city.

The company town was a logical extension of the company's desire to control all aspects of production—including the workers.

Many people mistook Pullman's experiment in paternalism for philanthropy. Their illusions were shattered in the depression of 1893 and 1894. In the worst depression of the 19th century, Pullman laid off hundreds of workers and cut wages. After rent and utilities were deducted from their pay, some workers had but pennies to show for a week's work.

The Pullman workers went on strike under the banner of the new American Railway Union—led by the dynamic Eugene Debs, pioneering labor leader who sought to mold a new power for working people by organizing all the crafts together. The Pullman workers had painfully learned that one craft alone could not match Pullman's power.

Here was a new way for labor—industrial unionism.

Once again the process of refining the assembled footage began. After the process had gone far enough, it was possible to write a rough narrative. This will make it easier to see how the film was taking shape. Here are the first few pages of the rough narration.

OPENER
Car Pullout/Layoff inter
Title: THE LAST PULLMAN CAR

NARRATION:

1. For three years, the workers at Pullman Standard had lived with the threat of their plant closing.
2. For three years, their union local, USWA #1834, had worked to bring to national attention that the last American owned company building mass transit and railroad passenger cars was about to close.
3. But now, as they are getting the attention of the press and of their international union, it appears to be too late.

SYNC OF MEETING CBS NEWS STORY—TERRY ANZUR (PULLMAN PLANT CLOSING)

4. News reports like this are by now familiar—in Pittsburgh, Youngstown, Detroit, Los Angeles. The story of one local's struggle to survive at Pullman represents the stories of many locals across the country.
5. When they took office in 1979, the newly elected officers of Local 1834 knew they would have to do more than file grievances and bargain for a new contract. Without jobs, wages and working conditions would mean nothing. So the local launched a campaign to save their plant, and fight for the future of their industry.

LUGAR

6. They march to the local office of recently elected Indiana Senator John Lugar to protest his vote against mass transit funding.

BRAC/SOLIDARITY DAY II

7. The Local carries its banner in support of fellow unionists and rail car riders who are protesting cuts in mass transit and passenger rail service. These are the consumers for the products that Pullman builds. (Song/ Student)

WISCONSIN STEEL AT LOCAL 1834 OFFICE

8. In their office, the Local plans a rally with workers from Wisconsin Steel, a neighboring plant closed without warning.
   1) "That's what unions should fight for for the future"
   2) "March on Washington and open books"

RALLY

9. At the rally Calumet area politicians and union leaders express concern. But they can offer little concrete help to the workers and their communities faced with job loss and plant closings.

YOUNGSTOWN

10. Local 1834 travels to a conference in Youngstown, Ohio, where plant closings have devastated a whole city. Proposals range from seeking new legislation requiring corporations to give early warning of plant closings,

to the democratic social control of capital investment decisions. People
want to find a way to challenge the corporation's right to make decisions
that can close down their way of life.

Sync: ". . . city grew around industry. . ."
　　John—"We may have to own the jobs"

[IN PLANT]

1834 UNION MEETING—John: Need for plant closing legislation

(cam. roll #132, sound out, cam. roll #35 call for nat'l. coalition) or
(John, cam. roll 63 #9. "We need plant closing legislation" and cam. roll 64
　#20, sound out.)

11. Their demonstrations have brought little response from Pullman or the
government. The Local's new strategy is to turn to other union and community groups to get laws passed to protect jobs.

BUS TO SPRINGFIELD

12. Local 1834 members and unemployed Wisconsin Steelworkers leave for
the State Capitol to join the Illinois Public Action Coalition for a day of
lobbying. They plan to meet with the Governor to seek help for the unemployed and to lobby their state representatives to vote for a recently
introduced plant closing bill. The law would require corporations to give
one-year notice of plant closings and also to pay into a fund to offset the
impact on communities.

13. They hope their example will spark the state and national AFL–CIO to
seek new legislation to protect workers from corporate decisions.

MARCH TO CAPITOL

14A. IPAC is a coalition of citizen action groups representing women, minorities, seniors and environmentalists. Their hope is to form a united
front with labor around issues of jobs, mass transit, equal rights, social
security, plant closings and unemployment.
Although the state AFL–CIO did not endorse their lobby day, they are
getting the support of a few hard hit Locals, like Pullman.

ossibly put
alanoff
etween the
wo state reps.

LOBBY INTERLUDE

14B. (In Plant) Work continues on the Amtrak order as more workers are laid
off.

ossibly use
ritish trade
nion.

(Layoff Footage)
(meeting—John under
talking about the laid off.)

The Local tries to
keep the laid off
workers involved.

LOOKING FOR WORK PIECE

(add piece from roll 91)

AFL–CIO LABOR LOBBY DAY

15. Three weeks after IPAC's, the Illinois Federation of Labor calls its own
lobby day in Springfield. An IBEW Local has chartered an Amtrak train.
Local 1834 joins the mass demonstration.
The AFL–CIO is here to oppose pending legislation that would reduce
unemployment compensation, weaken health and safety regulations, and
reinstate the anti-union right-to-work law. 20,000 workers have come to
defend labor's past accomplishments.

(Att. They brought 20,000 workers to defend the basic rights that unions have won.)

After the rally, the governor invites everyone to his house for beer. Local 1834's leadership stays behind to try again to convince the governor of the need to prevent the closing of passenger car plants.

LOBBY DAY ASSESSMENT INTRO (1834 UNION MEETING)

16A. The two Springfield lobby days did help defeat anti-labor legislation. But 1834's main concern, the plant closing legislation bill, died in committee.

LOBBY DAY ASSESSMENT INTRO (1834 UNION MEETING) cont.

16B. A national movement demanding a voice in corporate investment decisions and against plant closings has failed to emerge. The national AFL–CIO leadership is beginning to respond to the crisis, but it finds itself on the defensive.

SOLIDARITY DAY

17A. On September 19, 1981, the AFL–CIO called a demonstration in Washington to protest the Reagan Administration's anti-labor policies. Labor was joined by women, minorities, and senior citizens. They all felt past gains were being eroded.

17B. Workers from across the country found themselves confronted with layoffs, runaway shops, plant closings, and the worst unemployment since the 1930's, particularly in older unionized industries like auto, steel, and rail.

The Reagan administration is perceived as hostile, and corporations are using the economic crisis as an excuse to confront unions with sophisticated union-busting consulting firms; decertification elections; and demands for contract concessions, not only in wages and working conditions, but in seniority, grievance procedures, and job classification— hard won rights that the unions feel are necessary for their survival.

Sync: Piece by AFL–CIO leader about not turning back the clock

Local 1834's union, the United Steel Workers of America, has lost one fourth of its members since 1980, most of it from plant closings. (get accurate statistics)

STRIKE—1981

18. A brief strike in the spring of 1981 brought home to Local 1834 that the fight for their jobs would take more than defending their union and its past gains.

With only a few months of work left on Pullman's final order, the union was prepared to make major concessions (including a 1 year wage freeze) to encourage Pullman's new owner, Wheelabrator-Frye, to stay in the passenger-car business. But on the last day of negotiations, the company came in with new demands which the union found unacceptable. The company refused to extend the old contract, and the union felt forced to call a strike. Being forced on strike is similar to the situation other plants find themselves in as corporations take advantage of the recession to try and break unions.

City of Chicago labor police have been called in to patrol the picket line. The strike is settled after 3 days and the Local holds a meeting.

AFTER STRIKE MEETING

19. Defending the contract would be a hollow victory if the union could not save the jobs.

    In its 40 years of struggle with the company, the union had never had to face the possibility of Pullman getting out of the passenger car business. When Pullman workers first tried to organize they had no contract—no say in wages, seniority, safety conditions, or work rules. But they did have jobs. And Pullman was building a passenger car monopoly.

20. 19th century monopolies and trusts sought to maximize their profits by controlling the entire market and thus its prices. Many controlled the production process from raw materials through manufacturer, sales, and service.

21. In 1894, the Railroads were the most powerful monopolies. Subsidized by government land grants and franchises, the railroads were able to absorb much of the wealth being created by America's booming industries, and kept the economy expanding. By the turn of the century, half of the investment capital in America was going to the railroads.

22. They were linking western goods to eastern markets, creating new cities and were the backbone of the Industrial Revolution.

23. George Pullman built his first car in 1859. He then constructed a huge plant south of Chicago and began building his monopoly.

24. In order to control the cost of his materials, he built his own lumberyards, brickyards, wheelworks, paintworks, and glassworks.

25. He controlled the day to day operation of the cars by leasing them to the railroads. The passengers were served by Pullman employees and bought their sleeping car tickets from the Pullman Co.

26. When the 1894 strike occurred, Pullman was totally committed to the rail car industry. He had even built a company town to house his workers. Today, everything has changed.

27. A group of present-day Pullman workers, in an attempt to understand what happened since Pullman's time, tour the company town and factory with labor history professor Bill Adelman.

    SYNC

28. ADELMAN: So his theory was that he would create a perfect environment with the workers all hand-picked.

    SYNC

29. ADELMAN: He was very particular about who he allowed to work for him. . . . All hand-picked, basically Anglo-Saxon Protestants, a few Germans, Scandinavian carpenters, no Irish, by the way, he would not hire Irish under any circumstances, because he considered the Irish too intemperate, too belligerent, and too pro-union. So they were not allowed to be workers in Pullman city.

    JIM: He wouldn't hire any Irish at that time. What about blacks?

    ADELMAN: Blacks were only supposed to be sleeping car porters. The idea was that in the Pullman car, you were supposed to have the Old South. You were supposed to have wonderful meals, people serving you, and the idea—black people serving you.

    ADELMAN: In 1893 and 1894 he reduced everybody's wages 24 to 54 percent without any reductions in what they had to pay for rent, for the company houses, for the water bill, or their gas bills. There's a story of just prior to the Pullman Strike, one worker was working about 70 hours a

week, and by the time that Pullman had deducted fees for his rent, the
water bill, the gas bill, and all the other fees of the town, he took home just
three or four cents.

30.   The strike which followed grew into a major conflict between Eugene V.
Debs' newly formed American Railway Union and the railroad monopolies.

In a film such as this, in which so much of the narration will be
spoken by the narrator, a kind of *vox ex machina,* the narration will be
refined as the picture editing goes through its stages of further and
further refinement. In order not to destroy the pace of the motion picture
sequences, some paragraphs of narration may have to be abbreviated
while some may need a small amount of lengthening. The narration
must be written so that it can be spaced out over the pictures. Finally,
both narration and motion picture images will be of such consonant and
harmonious lengths, and the narrative will be so fully complementary of
the pictures, that the words of the narrator can be recorded. It must be
emphasized again that the narration is weakened if it only duplicates
what can be seen on the screen. The function of the narration is to
explain, provide collateral information, supply additional color, and in
every way possible *complement* the pictures on the screen. In their own
way, this is also the function of sound effects and music—if, indeed,
there is music to give emotional impact or sound effects to give a sense of
immediacy.

Although the work of the writer of documentary films is no less
important than the work of the writer of any other kind of film, his or her
work is not the starting point of the film as it is for educational, advertising, or fiction films. The writer of the documentary film begins with
preparing the proposal and perhaps a preliminary treatment, but then he
or she must wait until the production has progressed so that scripting can
reflect what has been achieved in photography or what is possible to
achieve. The final re-write takes place as the editing is simultaneously
completed. In other types of films, the writer's work is generally finished
before photography begins.

Film, Video, and Investigative Reporting

You have seen stages in the scripting of two different documentary
films, the first made for the Southeast Chicago Historical Project, the
second about the closing of the Pullman plant. The first film was made to
be a film: there was no broadcast release arranged for by the time of its
completion. The Pullman film, on the other hand, was sponsored by and
made for release on public television. Further, although one of the documentaries was made for television, it was made on film and not on
videotape. For a variety of technical reasons most longer films are made

as motion pictures. Shorter pieces, especially television commercials, are frequently made on videotape. Videotape is cheaper and faster for making TV commercials.

On the other hand, almost all television news nowadays is recorded on videotape and not on film. This means that libraries of historically valuable visual material are being created, and thus, much videotape material is available as sources for stock shots to be included in other films.

As a writer it makes no difference to you if the final documentary is to be on film or on videotape other than being a valuable factor to be considered when assessing the nature of the audience for whom you are writing.*

Both the documentary scripts we have been discussing demonstrate the necessity of great amounts of research. Reporters for the media also do research, but we call it by a specific name: investigative reporting. The results of the work of the investigative reporter for television is almost invariably recorded on videotape. The process of making a well-researched report, a story, as the result of investigative reporting, is very much the same as the process of making any other documentary. There is research, recording sound and picture, assembling the material, editing it, and writing whatever has to be written for the explanatory and linking narration. However, do not think that, just because you are not dealing with fiction, you will not find an opportunity to be creative in writing documentaries. On the contrary, it is because there is so much room for creativity that so many documentaries have become classics.

Structure

In documentary films the need for structure is just as great as it is in any other kind of film. Structure is the internal logic of the work, whatever the work may be, and it is what makes it possible for the audience to find a sense of involvement in what is being expressed. Film, like music, dance, and theater, exposes itself as time passes. The passage of time is required for the work to be experienced. It is not surprising, therefore, that structural forms of music can be transmuted into similar forms in film. Similarly, the forms of poetry can also be transposed.

One form that is common, in many ways, in both poetry and music is the rondeau, or rondo. A rondeau is a verse in stanzas and with lines or phrases repeated, perhaps in some unexpected order, throughout the work. In music a rondo is a composition in which the music returns to a musical idea, generally the first one in the piece, and that musical idea is repeated periodically.

---

*This aspect is discussed in Robert Edmonds, *The Sights and Sounds of Cinema and Television* (New York: Teachers College Press, 1982), chapters 22 and 23.

One of the most famous of all American documentaries is called *The River*, made in 1937 by Pare Lorentz for the U.S. Farm Security Administration. *The River* deals with the Mississippi and its tributary rivers and the first part of the film (approximately half) is presented in the form of a rondeau. The film returns to scenes of the succession of tributaries, from tiny rivulets and creeks to the great river, the rains and trees, the mountains and the towns. And the narrative is written in verse that is also in the form of a rondeau. Here is a portion of that narration by Pare Lorentz.

From as far West as Idaho,
Down from the glacier peaks of the Rockies—
From as far East as New York,
Down from the turkey ridges of the Alleghenies
Down from Minnesota, twenty five hundred miles,
The Mississippi River runs to the Gulf.
Carrying every drop of water, that flows down two-thirds of the continent,
Carrying every brook and rill, rivulet and creek,
Carrying all the rivers that run down two-thirds the continent,
The Mississippi runs to the Gulf of Mexico.
Down the Yellowstone, the Milk, the White and Cheyenne;
The Cannonball, the Musselshell, the James and the Sioux;
Down the Judith, the Grand, the Osage, and the Platte,
The Skunk, the Salt, the Black, and Minnesota;
Down the Rock, the Illinois, and the Kankakee,
The Allegheny, the Monongahela, Kanawha, and Muskingum;
Down the Miami, the Wabash, the Licking and the Green,
The Cumberland, the Kentucky, and the Tennessee;
Down the Ouchita, the Wichita, the Red, and Yazoo—
Down the Missouri three thousand miles from the Rockies;
Down the Ohio a thousand miles from the Alleghenies;
Down the Arkansas fifteen hundred miles from the Great Divide;
Down the Red, a thousand miles from Texas;
Down the great Valley, twenty-five hundred miles from Minnesota,
Carrying every rivulet and brook, creek and rill,
Carrying all the rivers that run down two-thirds the continent—
The Mississippi runs to the Gulf.
New Orleans to Baton Rouge,
Baton Rouge to Natchez.
Natchez to Vicksburg,
Vicksburg to Memphis,
Memphis to Cairo—
We built a dyke a thousand miles long.
Men and mules, mules and mud;
Mules and mud a thousand miles up the Mississippi.
A century before we bought the great Western River,
   the Spanish and the French built dykes to keep the Mississippi
   out of New Orleans at flood stage.
In forty years we continued the levee the entire length
   of the great alluvial Delta,

That mud plain that extends from the Gulf of Mexico
   clear to the mouth of the Ohio.
The ancient valley built up for centuries by the old river
   spilling her floods across the bottom of the continent—
A mud delta of forty thousand square miles.
Men and mules, mules and mud—
New Orleans to Baton Rouge,
Natchez to Vicksburg,
Memphis to Cairo—
A thousand miles up the river.
And we made cotton king!
We rolled a million bales down the river for Liverpool and Leeds . . .
1860: we rolled four million bales down the river;
Rolled them off Alabama,
Rolled them down the river!
We fought a war.
We fought a war and kept the west bank
   of the river free of slavery forever.
But we left the old South impoverished and stricken.
Doubly stricken, because, beyond the tragedy of war,
   already the frenzied century had taken toll of the land.
We mined the soil for cotton until it would yield no more,
   and then moved west.
We fought a war, but there was a double tragedy—
   the tragedy of land twice impoverished.
Black spruce and Norway pine,
Douglas fir and Red cedar,
Scarlet oak and Shagbark hickory,
Hemlock and aspen—
There was lumber in the North.
The war impoverished the old South, the railroads killed the steamboats,
But there was lumber in the North.
Heads up!
Lumber on the upper river.
Heads up!
Lumber enough to cover all Europe.
Down from Minnesota and Wisconsin,
Down from St. Paul;
Down to St. Louis and St. Joe—
Lumber for the new continent of the West.
Lumber for the new mills.
There was lumber in the North and coal in the hills.
Iron and coal down the Monongahela.
Iron and coal down the Allegheny.
Iron and coal down the Ohio.
Down to Pittsburgh,
Down to Wheeling,
Iron and coal for the steel mills, for the railroads driving
West and South, for the new cities of the Great Valley—
We built new machinery and cleared new land in the West.
Ten million bales down to the Gulf—

Cotton for the spools of England and France.
Fifteen million bales down to the Gulf—
Cotton for the spools of Italy and Germany.
We built a hundred cities and a thousand towns:
St. Paul and Minneapolis,
Davenport and Keokuk,
Moline and Quincy,
Cincinnati and St. Louis,
Omaha and Kansas City . . .
Across to the Rockies and down from Minnesota,
Twenty-five hundred miles to New Orleans,
We built a new continent.
Black spruce and Norway pine,
Douglas fir and Red cedar,
Scarlet oak and Shagbark hickory.
We built a hundred cities and a thousand towns—
But at what a cost!
We cut the top off the Alleghenies and sent it down the river.
We cut the top off Minnesota and sent it down the river.
We cut the top off Wisconsin and sent it down the river.
We left the mountains and the hills slashed and burned,
And moved on.
The water comes downhill, spring and fall;
Down from the cut-over mountains,
Down from the plowed-off slopes,
Down every brook and rill, rivulet and creek,
Carrying every drop of water that flows down two-thirds the continent.

Certainly, documentary is non-fiction, but it can be, nonetheless, creative—as creative as any other kind of work. After all, Grierson, who first used the term, meant what he said: documentary is "the creative presentation of actuality."

Multi-Image and Multimedia Presentations

Multi-image is just what its name implies. It is a kind of presentation in which there are some, or many, images on a screen at the same time. The screen is generally much wider than the screen we are used to seeing for motion pictures, and the images are all in the same medium, that is to say, they are all slides or they may be all motion pictures.

Multimedia means, of course, that more than one medium is used. The images may be slides together with motion pictures, and there may be other media as well, for example, live action. The projected images, whether slides or film, will appear on the screen, and if there is live action, it will be on a stage in front of the screen. In such a case, the screen may be translucent and the images projected from behind so that the action taking place in front will not cast shadows on the screen images. There may also be video images, each projected from a videotape and made visible on individual monitors (and of course a video image from one tape can be fed to many monitors simultaneously), or the various images may be on a giant video screen. There is almost no limit to the possibilities.

The images of both multi-image and multimedia presentations need not fall on top of each other on the screen. On the contrary, they are projected from several or many projectors, and each projector may direct its images to its own area of the screen.

Preparation of Presentations

The aspect ratio of an image on the screen is the proportion that may be established between the width of the image and its height. The aspect ratio of film is 4:3. For both multi-image and multimedia the aspect ratio of each image can be changed at the will of the director and the art director for two reasons: first, so that many images can fit on the available screen area, and second and most important, so that there can be the greatest development of visual dynamics in the total presentation.

The aspect ratios of projected images can be changed very easily. For motion pictures, the borders of the image can be changed in three ways.

A mask can be placed behind the lens of the camera so that the image recorded on the film is within a border of the desired shape. If the shape of the frame is to change after the shot has been filmed it can be achieved in what is called an optical printer, a machine that will make copies of the shot within whatever border is desired. A third way to modify the aspect ratio of the image is to put a mask behind the lens of the projector just as we can put one behind the lens of the camera. Film-makers have been modifying the aspect ratios of motion pictures since at least 1913, and in that year multi-image in motion pictures also appeared.*

If ten images are to appear on the screen at the same time, even if they are in different areas of the screen, then it is clear that there must be ten projectors, for each image is projected by its own projector. The means of controlling the projectors and the refinements of those controls have been developing very rapidly. For this reason I will simply discuss the principles of the controls available.

The basic requirement is some mechanism that will start the motion picture projector when it is needed and turn it off when it is no longer needed. If the projector is a slide projector, the mechanism must so control it that the slide is projected for as long as necessary, then turn off the slide projector. At the same time, the projector must be instructed to advance from one slide to the next as rapidly as the presentation requires. Further, projectors are so devised that the controlling mechanism can make the images fade in or fade out. These fades can be used also as dissolves if two projectors are directed at the same space on the screen.

Finally, the sound track, which may have been recorded on one or more tapes, must also be controlled by the same kind of mechanism so that the pictures and the sounds—voice, music, sound effects—will be synchronized. The plurality of sound tracks may also serve if the sound is to be presented stereophonically.

All the projectors and sound reproducers are controlled by a computer tape that has been programmed by a special technician so that pictures and sounds will appear exactly as the director and the art director have devised.

In actual fact, the only thing of primary importance to you as a writer of either multi-image or multimedia presentations is to be fully aware that you are writing for the director and the art director. It is they who know all the ins and outs of these strange new hybrids, because it is they who, through their experience, can invent marvellous effects. Through their efforts, your script will have gone through extraordinary changes by the time the presentation confronts the audience. It is possible, for example, to ask for zooms, in or out, even in a slide presentation, because the apparent movement can be accomplished by a rapid succession of different slides, each of which has a view of the subject increasingly

---

*For a fuller discussion of aspect ratios, see Edmonds, *Sights and Sounds of Cinema and Television*, pp. 22, 193–195.

nearer or farther from it. The zoom can also be generated by mechanically moving a zoom lens that has replaced the normal lens on the projector. This will change the size of the image instead of appearing to move closer to the subject or farther from it while keeping a constant image size. It is possible to superimpose lettering over the images, whether they be motion pictures or slides, and lines can be added or removed successively. Images can be distorted by means of computer animation, either for slides or moving pictures, and all sorts of wondrous effects can be achieved. However, it is clear that this is completely the realm of the director and art director. They will make it happen. In the same way they will compose the sound track for music (original or library), sound effects (specially recorded or library), and voice or voices.

Almost without exception, multi-image and multimedia presentations are made with specific audiences in mind. These audiences are almost never mass audiences, in the sense that the auditors are gathered in large numbers for simultaneous viewing as they would in large theaters, in drive-ins, or on television. Most of the multi-image and multimedia presentations are to audiences who have gathered together for a particular purpose. It may be that the audience is made up of salesmen of an individual company or of an individual industry, or it may be viewers who are being enticed to travel to certain places or to have certain kinds of vacations. The most important aspect of these presentations, perhaps, is that, because of the relative bombardment of the audience by the stimuli, both auditory and visual, the result is much more likely to be motivational than informational. That is not to say that information cannot be presented, but the nature of the human animal is such that, in the face of many stimuli, it responds sensorially rather than intellectually.

There is a corollary to this. It is that, because of the many auditory and visual stimuli and the resultant motivational drive of these presentations, it is wiser to concentrate on only a few intellectual ideas, only a few pieces of "hard" information. If there are too many images, individual images won't be remembered: they will instead be merged with all the others, and we come away not so much with clear bits of information but rather with general feelings about what we will have seen, general feelings, responses, attitudes.

As for any writing for a specialized audience, your job as writer begins by learning as much as you can about the audience. Of course you will need to have whatever printed material you can obtain that will give you information about the subject of the presentation, but you must know about the audience. What size will it be, and in what kind of hall will it take place? Is this to be an individual presentation or will it be part of a larger program for a longer meeting? At what time of day will it take place? (Audiences are not equally attentive in the morning, the afternoon, and the evening.) Is the presentation to be part of a business meeting or part of a vacation meeting? There are many questions that you will learn to ask in order to complete the job successfully.

Your script will, of course, organize the materials because you will be writing the narration or the dialogue and the succession of these words is the organization of the subject matter. With the narration you will at least suggest the kinds of visuals that you are asking for to emphasize and give dynamic to your words. The script itself will not clearly distinguish between multi-image and multimedia. Scripts for both kinds of presentations seem to look alike. This is because it may not be until the director and the art director will have the script in their hands and begin to work on it that the final determination of the mode of presentation will be made. Because of the tremendous flexibility in the use of sophisticated equipment, the variety of multi-image and multimedia presentations is limited only by the imaginations of those who are producing them.

Multi-Image and Multimedia Scripts

As we have already noted, scripts for multi-image and multimedia presentations may have little if any scene descriptions. Or writers may give considerable attention to what has been described, or they may disregard it entirely. In the case of the following script the writer clearly expected to function at least as co-director, and so the directions are given in considerable detail. The client is a pharmaceutical manufacturer, MSD AGVET, a division of Merck & Co., Inc., and the product was developed for the care of horses.

EQVALAN . . . In a Class by Itself

VISUAL	AUDIO
Computer generated animation fades up on the center screen. The left and right screens remain in darkness. We see unfolding before us—through graphic animation—the evolution of the horse from the Dawn Horse, *Eohippus*, through the *Mesohippus, Merychippus, Pliohippus*, and ending with the modern horse, *Equus caballus*. Simultaneously, in the four corners of the center screen, animated type and graphics trace the horse's evolution in four ways: • a clock working continuously from 50,000,000 years; • scientific species names identifying the various developments of the horse;	MUSIC: Open with a large and encompassing symphonic piece such as Strauss' *Thus Spoke Zarathustra*. NARRATOR: In the beginning . . . the horse.

- a world map showing the migrating pattern of species development from North America to Asia and Europe and back to North America;
- and the continuous flashing of horse parasite species names.

The animated *Equus caballus* on the center screen freezes and holds.

The type and graphic data in the four corners cuts off. The *Equus caballus* dissolves into a full color, live action wild horse, running alone in a field. We follow this horse until it joins its herd. Then, the right and left screens fill with slides of a herd as the center screen continues with live action footage. On the three screens we see the birth of a foal, the death of the old leader, socialization of the young colts and fillies, mating, play, and territorial prerogatives. The slides of the wild horses on the right and left screens fade out; the live action horse on the center screen freezes in position.

Through a match dissolve, the wild horse becomes an ancient Greek sculpture. On the left and right screens we fade in slides of horses and how they've been used by man for thousands of years. This historical survey of man and his horse will depict—through art and photographs—the use of horses in the military; as beasts of burden; for transportation; and as objects of adulation.

The left and right slides fade out and leave a photograph on the center screen of a cowboy working his cattle herd. Then, this frozen image comes to life as we begin four distinct sequences showing the ways man uses horses today. Through slides and live action we build a sequence of the cowboy working the range.

Next, we build—through slides and live action—a horse-show sequence featuring the hussars from the Royal Windsor Horse Show.

MUSIC: *Opening theme continues.*

SOUND EFFECTS: *Natural sounds from a wild herd of horses keyed to the visuals.*

NARRATOR: And wherever we find horses . . . we find their parasites.

MUSIC: *Opening theme continues.*

NARRATOR: For 6,000,000 years . . . the horse and its parasites.

MUSIC: *Opening melody continues under voice-over interviews.*

VOICE OVER INTERVIEW #1: Out here on the range, when you've got to cover a couple of thousand acres, and find those strays, I depend on my horse. Without him . . . I'd be nowhere.

VOICE OVER INTERVIEW #2: I've been participating in the Royal Windsor Horse Show for more years than I'd care to remember. Why do I do it? I guess you would say that

In the next sequence, we are at the racetrack for a major stakes race. We follow the horses around the track.

it's a matter of pride in my own ability to train them. And then too, there's the thrill and excitement of just being here . . . with the Queen.

VOICE OVER INTERVIEW #3: You could say it's the money . . . but really that's only half of it. I love to win. The competition. The challenges. Seeing a yearling grow to full size . . . watching a two year old's first victory. . . I like to race because I like horses.

In this final sequence we go to a local horse club on a Sunday afternoon. The riders mount up and go out for a leisurely ride.

VOICE OVER INTERVIEW #4: Actually, I got my first horse when I was ten . . . a little pinto yearling. I've been hooked ever since. Last year I started jumping . . . we have a little course the club set up . . . and I really love the feeling, you know, when you're mid-air and flying over the hurdle. It's great. Just great!

The screen divides into four equal segments showing these four horses: the cowboy; the Hussars; the race horse; and the pleasure horse. Each screen freezes, one after another, stopping its horse in mid-action; catching a calf; closing ranks; crossing the finish line; and clearing a hurdle.

NARRATOR: Veterinarians know that the major obstacle to a happy and healthy horse is nothing but another animal . . . the parasite. Horses play host to over 150 different internal and external parasites. As a result they suffer from a variety of debilitating diseases. Diseases which affect their ability to convert feed, to maintain body weight, to reach their true genetic potential: on the ranch; in the show arena; on the racetrack; and even on a Sunday afternoon ride in the country.

Full screen panorama of healthy horse. Super animated art of the *Strongylus vulgaris* over horse. Slow fade to black.

Veterinarians also know, all too well, that parasites, especially the *Strongylus vulgaris,* can kill a horse. Stop it dead in its tracks.

Dissolves of archive material showing an historical overview of parasitic control in horses.

That's why, for 6,000 years, man has valiantly tried to destroy the parasites which afflict his horses. Various techniques were developed; but all used the same principle: poison the parasite without poisoning the horse. It was pretty much a hit or miss affair.

We have only reproduced a portion of the script, but it will suffice, I'm sure, to demonstrate what a relatively detailed multimedia script looks like. That it is multimedia and not multi-image will be clear to you if you read the scene description carefully. You will see that much of what is called for will have to be photographed on motion picture film. On the other hand, there are many images that must, just as obviously, be slides. If one or two of the terms that have been used in the descriptions aren't quite clear to you, don't worry about it. You may be encouraged by the script that follows. In it there is not a single scene description. There is only the audio portion of the presentation, and the writer has left it to the director and the art director to work out the visuals. It's the first portion of a presentation that introduced some live action scenes on a stage, and there was a closing presentation that we do not reproduce here. The total production was presented at a sales meeting, as will be seen from the first line of the narration.

Creativity . . . The Key to Life—Part I/Opener

NARRATIVE

SFX: *Sounds of knocking, pounding, doorknob rattling*

NARRATOR V.O: Opening the door to sales would be easy if all we had to do was present the facts.

(*sounds continue . . . more desperate . . . but not include scratching, coded taps, etc.*)

NARRATOR: But it takes more than "hard tell" or "hard yell" to be a success at sales.

What is it?

SFX: *sound of key turning in lock*

Creativity

(*music up and under*)

imagination brought to bear on the practical

a quality of mind. . .

a flip of a mental switch that allows the mind to roam freely

in and around. . .

over and under. . .

inside and out. . .

to seek a fit that's original.

. . . more than inspiration

. . . beyond luck

(*music changes pace*)

So what's creativity all about?

Those who are creative—and they excel

in every field—say it takes
desire
and effort of will. . .
liberally mixed with the right combination of shoe leather and scholarship
a healthy dose of judgment and intuition
letting the subconscious do the work
after the facts are assembled.
It's invention. . .
when facts come together in new combinations. . .
to light up life!
When teamed with persistence, too, it is
a quality of mind. . .
the conviction that what has been invented has value and should be used.
Without that conviction, creativity could
never get off the ground.
Persistence overcomes the natural human resistance to the new idea. . .
the fresh approach. . .
the unique plan
. . . the innovative design
It sells the thought . . . and keeps it sold.
There are no bounds to creativity. It's
self-perpetuating. . .
in music. . .
art. . .
drama. . .
literature. . .
business. . .
life.
Creativity is the key to life. . .
forging permanent bonds between the
known. . .
and the new.
SFX: (*musical triangle sound*)
(*Music tempo up*)
In selling, creativity elicits that certain
emotional something that makes our
product preferred.
It's a mental path traveled every day to
its rich, fulfilling reward. . .
winning.
(*Music up tempo*)
You are winners.
You are creative . . . masters of the art of
creative selling.
Viewing each prospect in unique light. . .
reflecting the radiance of creativity with

each success.
Persisting when you meet rejection.
For you . . . the winners . . . creativity IS
the key to life.

Although no scenes are described in the foregoing script, the narrative is laid out in such a way that the director and the art director can write in what they plan for the visuals. The style of this narrative is that of a sales pitch instead of being didactic, and it is fairly high pressure. The content is clearly intended to be motivational rather than instructive. It might be a useful suggestion to propose that you read the narration carefully and try to invent appropriate and stimulating visuals to make an impressive presentation. You won't be able to achieve much in a very short time. After all, the director and the art director are highly paid people who spend many hours developing the visuals for presentations like this.

To demonstrate what I have been saying, look at the four pages that follow. They are the beginning of a script for a multimedia show developed for a chemical coatings manufacturer. It is also an "opener" like the previous script. Note that the descriptions of visuals and sound are in capital letters instead of italicized (underlined), as in the previous script. Either way is acceptable; what matters is that everything is clear, legible, and quickly comprehensible. The scene descriptions have been developed by the director and art director and written on the working script by hand.

If you don't have to write any scene descriptions when you write a script for a multimedia or multi-image presentation, then, obviously, you must think like a writer of radio. You will be writing the voice portion of the presentation. It need not be written for only one voice. In fact, even if it might appear from your script that one person could very well say what you have written, the director may elect to use more than one voice if he or she thinks doing so will enhance the vigor of the presentation. Of course, you can indicate sound effects as you imagine them; but, once again, don't be surprised if your suggestions are totally ignored. That is just as likely as is their being followed.

But one aspect must be borne in mind. Because there are many images on the screen—changing perhaps rhythmically, perhaps not; perhaps changing symmetrically, perhaps not—there is no linear logic to be discerned from the visuals. That kind of logic lies in the words you write. You could read and make sense out of the three scripts we have presented without any thought of visualization or without any further sound. The logic is in the narration. Nevertheless after the show has been completed, there is even a new kind of logic in its total form. There is a perfectly sensible logic in a human skeleton, but there is a different, more moving logic when the skeleton is covered with living and breathing flesh.

SHERWIN-WILLIAMS CHEMICAL COATINGS DIVISION
"Meeting Tomorrow's Challenges Today" (opener)

VISUAL	AUDIO
SCREENS COME ALIVE WITH SPECIAL EFFECTS THAT SUGGEST THE MYSTERY AND EXCITEMENT AND CHALLENGE THAT IS TOMORROW (E.G. SHAPES, FORMS, COLORS, OUTLINES OF NEW MODES OF TRAVEL AND ENERGY AND LIVING, ETC.).	SFX: OPEN WITH A CRESCENDOING ELECTRONIC CHORD
THESE EFFECTS PLAY WITHOUT COMMENT ABOUT 30 MOOD-SETTING SECONDS THEN CONTINUE WITH THE NARRATIVE	SFX: UNDER
Objects dropping in and out of a cloud pattern. Perhaps starting with a waveform signal to a TV pic flying out of screen. An X-rayed calculator falls into the horizon. A prism or ice cube whizzes by.	NARRATOR (A RICH VOICE WHOSE DRAMATIC QUALITIES ARE MUTED BY A QUIET ALMOST CONVERSATIONAL APPROACH THAT TALKS WITH RATHER THAN AT THE AUDIENCE) Tomorrow -- it's there just up ahead. Waiting for us. Calling for us. Triggering changes whose challenges call for response.
Technology advances. The cloud pattern symbolizes the vistas of our consciousness. We are aware of new frontiers by a revolving falling magical window which reveals our future + our past. This universe has no up or down + no dimension. Objects + elements fly away and to us. All of this over a mirrored bottom which reflects this moment.	But, then, that's not new. Tomorrow has always been a time of change and challenge. What's new is the way our response to it must come sooner...faster...better than ever before. Meeting tomorrow's challenge today -- that's the call. A call Sherwin-Williams has been answering for over 115 proud pacesetting years...!

VISUAL

Build of Sherwin Williams Paint Cans in a matrix which then flies off into infinity. Then Blue diaphragm closes up on Scene Quad dissolves to Logo

SCREENS CUT TO ON-LOCATION ACTION
SHOTS OF THE CHEMICAL COATINGS
DIVISION WITH THE FOCUS ON SKILLED
DEDICATED PROFESSIONALS AT WORK
DESIGNING, TESTING, AND MANUFACTURING
SUPERIOR PRODUCTS FOR BUSINESS AND
INDUSTRY

Quad dissolve from Logo Business Machines. Blue diaphragm opens to reveal any photos of Plastics + processes, Manufacturing.

AS THE ACTION CONTINUES, WE LAYER
OVER IT A SPECIAL EFFECTS TREAT-
MENT OF THE SHERWIN-WILLIAMS LOGO
OF THE GLOBE. THIS EFFECT LASTS
ONLY A FEW SECONDS TO PUNCTUATE
THE NARRATIVE AT THIS POINT

Zoom of Logo

Flash Logo over changing industrial Pictures.

AUDIO

The result has been the nation's leading paint and accessories manufacturer with today's premiere network of retail stores and wholesale outlets!

SFX: MUSIC UP TO FULL A FEW TRANSITIONAL
      SECONDS AS THE SCREENS PLAY WITHOUT
      COMMENT

SFX: UNDER

And not only in the consumer world!

In the industrial world too, for ever since the early Twenties Sherwin-Williams has 'covered the earth' in the commercial as well as the home market.

We call this our Chemical Coatings Division; our customers call it one of the most product-effective cost-efficient things that ever happened to them. . .

SFX: MUSIC UP A FEW TRANSITIONAL SECONDS
      THEN UNDER

VISUAL	AUDIO
	Sherwin-Williams' Chemical Coatings Division operates with high-technology market outreach into six specific areas. Six custom-designed business units serving:
	Industrial plastics. . .
	Rail and off-road industry. . .
	Coil coating for both residential and commercial buildings. . .
	Forest products. . .
Quad dissolves	General products. . .
	And, of course, one of today's most important and dynamically changing fields: Transportation.
SCREENS CUT TO A SYMBOLIC TREATMENT OF OUR CONTEMPORARY SOCIETY ALIVE WITH SOCIO-ECONOMIC CHANGES CREATING NEW DEMANDS AND DICTATING NEW RESPONSES FROM OUR INDUSTRY	SFX: MUSIC UP AGAIN TO FULL A FEW TRANSITIONAL SECONDS AS THE SCREENS PLAY WITHOUT COMMENT
Quick cuts. Hi con-Pic's + Posterized crowds. Last Pic floats back and dissolves to clouds w/ Grd into infinity.	SFX: UNDER
	The Eighties!
	A decade packed with more change per cubic inch of humanity than any other decade in history. And what's true in general is surely true of the chemical

VISUAL	AUDIO
Continue floating until we hit with EPA + OPEC Glow then Wipes ———————>	coatings field in particular where two sets of letters tell much of today's story: EPA and OPEC.

on + off <———
Screens — Pic's of   wipes
Environment + industry

Industrial Process Photos done in wipes across. One building on the other. Showing Products being dipped or Sprayed or pressed + just industrial environments. Coil Coatings, QC processes, people on the production Line.

Diaphragm from last Pic to clouds to Quads to diaphragm to clouds with Grid.

On one hand the Environmental Protection Agency has imposed tough clean-air requirements on all chemical coating products. . .on the other, the OPEC nations have imposed an equally tough cost-of-energy requirement.

Together they mean that as industries like automotive turn increasingly to plastic parts, it is no longer enough to simply find the nicest-looking-highest quality-at-the-lowest-cost chemical coatings. The inexorable crunch of both environmental and energy factors now demand coatings that meet every requirement every time -- from product quality to esthetic quality, from environment saving to energy saving, from efficiency of application to efficiency of labor.

But then no one needs to tell _you_ what's needed; what _you_ want to know is how the needs can be best met.

6

Filmstrips and Sound Slidefilms

Fifty to seventy-five years ago one of the more common genteel, yet exotic, pastimes was to attend lectures given by travellers who returned from distant lands with photographs of the strange and beautiful sights to be found there. Travellers would have a lecture tour arranged, and at each lecture they would project on a screen the photographs that had been taken and accompany them with a talk. The photographs might be ordinary kinds of photos printed on heavy paper, or they may have been on glass slides. The projectors were either what are called nowadays opaque projectors (for projecting paper photos or other illustrations from books or magazines) and what were called in those days magic lanterns; that is, slide projectors, which were bulkier than the slide projectors of today, although they worked on exactly the same principles. Both these kinds of projectors had to be located at the back of the room where a projectionist operated them. The lecturers stood up front on a dais. They would give their talk and describe the pictures on the screen, and when they were ready for the next slide to be projected, they would snap a little metal cricket (always to be found in Christmas stockings), a noisemaker that cost very little and made a brisk snapping sound that would indicate to the projectionist that the picture must be changed.

There was another pastime of the latter part of the nineteenth and the first quarter of the twentieth century that was enjoyed by individuals, one at a time. You may have seen a stereopticon in an antique or curio shop or, perhaps, on a shelf at your grandmother's home. It was a little machine that had two small lenses side by side and a place cut out for your nose so that you could place the contraption close to your eyes. A few inches farther away was a little rack that could be moved closer or farther from your eyes and into which you placed a card with two photographs on it. The photos looked almost identical and, in fact, were almost identical, except that each was taken through a lens so placed that the distance between the lenses was the same as the average distance between human eyes—what is called *interocular distance*. In the stereopticon the viewer saw an image that appeared to be three-dimensional. On the back of each card was a sentence or two or three that gave appropriate information about the scene that had been photographed.

A series of photographs, each with its own caption, such as could have been seen in a stereopticon program, still exists, but in a new and different form. No longer having the appearance of three dimensions, these collections of photographs have been enriched by the addition of artwork. They are no longer photos printed on paper cards; they have been rephotographed on successive frames of 35mm film. They are no longer limited to black-and-white but appear nowadays in color. The captions can appear as separate frames, which may occur between photographic or artwork frames, or they can appear as *supers*, that is, as lettering superimposed over the lower (or any other) portion of the picture.

As you probably know, 35mm film has the same format whether it is used for motion pictures or for 35mm strips of still photography. The film itself is 35mm wide and just inside each margin is a row of perforations. These perforations serve as the means whereby a mechanism in the camera or projector can be engaged in order to move the film a frame at a time. A *frame* in 35mm is the name given to each individual picture (or its equivalent) or to a piece of film that has a certain size. If you were to draw a line across the film, from margin to margin, joining two opposite perforations, and were then to draw a similar line four perforations away, you would have enclosed one frame.*

Filmstrips are lengths of 35mm film bearing a succession of picture frames. Usually, for a filmstrip that will last about 10 minutes, there will be 35 or 40 frames. *Title frames,* the frames on which there are captions without pictures, are additional to this number. Of course, there is a great deal of elasticity in the amount of time required to project a filmstrip. Teachers or lecturers or salespersons can proceed at any rate of speed that suits their convenience, so long as the audience can follow the presentation. They can keep one frame on the screen for as long as needed if a series of questions or a discussion should arise from it. However, as indicated, the usual length of a filmstrip that is expected to last about ten minutes would be about 35 frames.

The function of a writer in the preparation of a filmstrip is two-fold. Before a filmstrip is made, research has to be done just as it would for any kind of non-fiction film. From the research a description of each of the individual picture frames is written. This includes descriptions of all frames that need to be done as artwork rather than photography, and the required content of each artwork frame needs to be described in considerable detail. The titles (or captions) are written as though final, but the second part of the writer's job takes place after the photography and the artwork have been completed, for then the titles have to be rewritten in final form to take care of any modifications that the final pictures may demand.

Classroom filmstrips are usually prepared in sets. Each set deals with a specific subject area, and each filmstrip in the set deals with a relatively narrow portion of the subject area. For example, if there were a set of

---

*This is one-half the size of a transparency photographed by a 35mm still camera. Such a transparency is 35mm wide and 8 perforations long.

filmstrips about Iceland, one strip might deal with the climate (both summer and winter), one with the natural wildlife to be found in Iceland, one with the volcanic origin and condition of the country, one with the existence of the hot water springs and the ways in which the water is put to use, one with the fishing industry, one with the people, one with the history of the country, one with travel and tourism, and one with the language, literature, and the arts. There could be, perhaps, eight possible filmstrips and, if all eight were made, they might well appear in two sets, one of which would deal with the nature of the country geographically and physically, and one with the social science aspects of Iceland.

It is clear that a filmstrip is really a didactic tool, whether it is designed for use in a school classroom or in a sales meeting. It has great use as a sales training tool because of new techniques of preparing photographs and artwork. An explanation of how a part of a piece of machinery works is possible by means of *exploded* drawings or photographs, for example. An exploded photo or drawing is one in which all the parts are separated one from another but in the correct spatial relationship to each other. Thus, the block, crankshaft, and pistons of an internal combustion engine as in a car can be set out in such a way that their relative positions can easily be seen. If such a frame of artwork were made, it could be repeated so that each successive repetition would bear an arrow in a different place—pointing in one frame to the block, in another to the crankshaft, in another to the pistons—so that specific instructional or explanatory titles could be used with heightened clarity and emphasis.

If the descendant of the old stereopticon show is the filmstrip, the descendant of the illustrated lecture is the sound slidefilm. The physical format of the pictures and other illustrations in a slidefilm is the same as the format for filmstrips. The pictures are on successive frames of a length of 35mm film. The great difference between a filmstrip and a slidefilm is in the use of sound. Obviously, if there is a recorded narration or other kind of lecture, you don't need to have explanatory titles either between pictorial frames or supered over them. On the other hand, because there is sound, the dynamic of impact shifts. The attention is caught by that which moves and changes, and the more the change, the more the attention is held. Since it is the sound that "moves" in a sound slidefilm, it is the sound that maintains the attention of the viewer even more than do the pictures. Thus, while a motion picture is a series of visual sequences complemented by its sound track, a sound slidefilm is a sound track that is illustrated with photographs or other graphics.

For this reason, the sound track of a slidefilm is of paramount importance. It should be made with great care and forethought and developed with as much creativity as possible. What medium does it most closely approximate? Radio! It is in radio that the most care is taken to develop the creative and dynamic use of sound, and it is in the sound slidefilm that similar energies and efforts are required. If you think of a sound slidefilm as an illustrated radio show, you will find the correct focus on the medium more clearly.

How do the pictures change to proceed in time with the sound track? There are two kinds of sound slide projectors. One is manual, which means that the transportation of the film, a frame at a time, is done by hand by a projectionist. To give the projectionist the right cues at the right times, sound tracks used to have some kind of sound placed on them at those places where the picture had to be changed. Bells, gongs, or beeps, were used. They made it easy for a projectionist to keep pace with the sound track, but they were very interruptive of the sound itself.

Later technology developed newer techniques, and automatic slide-film projectors were invented. These are machines that respond to *inaudible* sound signals that are recorded on the sound track. The signals are inaudible because they are at very high frequencies, pitches that are beyond the capability of the human ear to hear—something like a special dog whistle. Because the signals are above the frequencies heard by the human ear, they are called *supersonic*. The projector mechanism is activated by the supersonic signal and automatically transports the strip of film one frame for each such signal. The sound track is recorded either on a regular phonograph disc or on a magnetic recording tape. This automatic technique of projection does not interrupt the sound with extraneous signals and thus permits the creative use of sound to be unalloyed.

The job of the writer of sound slidefilms begins with research, and the script is developed after the research is completed. The format will look quite like a film script. There will be two columns: the left hand column will carry descriptions of the visuals and the right hand column will be the audio script, complete with narration, dialogue (if any), music, and sound effects. In contrast to the method of writing motion pictures, however, the sound slidefilm requires that the *right hand* column be written first —not all of it, perhaps, but a number of frames at a time, at least. One must think as if he or she were really writing a radio script; and the radio script must be written before one can think of illustrating it. Instead of listing numbered scenes, as in a film script, each frame is numbered.

Because the individual who presents a sound slidefilm does not provide the lecture personally—it's on the sound track, of course—he or she has no control over the length of time the presentation will take. That is inexorably built into the program itself. It has been found that for a sound slidefilm of 15 minutes duration, the usual number of frames will be about 90. The running speed, therefore, is about six frames a minute— about twice as fast as the rate for filmstrips. The increased speed is necessary because of the greater intensity of the more creative sound track that is one salient element of the sound slidefilm.

In movies members of the audience will identify, or sympathize, with the characters on the screen because they move and speak and appear to be alive and real. In neither the filmstrip nor the sound slidefilm do the characters move and speak. Therefore, the filmstrip or the sound slidefilm is far less successful in modifying attitudes. They work best to demonstrate a thing or a process. An attempt is often made to overcome this "disability" of the sound slidefilm by developing a sound presentation that includes full dialogue with sound effects and music and illustrating these with pictures of characters in the appropriate situations somewhat in the manner of comic strips; but this usually results in a rather distant approximation of real attitude building. As I have already indicated, the most productive use of these two media that use still photographs or graphics is in demonstration, explanation, or some other form of didactic process.

7 Commercial Announcements and Storyboards

A storyboard is a kind of script that is written with pictures as well as with words. Its function is to provide some kind of visualization so that others who have to participate in the production will have a clearer comprehension of the visual intent of the script. Sometimes a storyboard is not prepared at the time of the scriptwriting, but later, after the modifications required by the director have been incorporated.

Generally storyboards are not made for live-action films. Very few directors work with them for such films; an exception was Alfred Hitchcock, who made complete storyboards for each of his features. (It should be noted that he started in films in the early 1920s as a scriptwriter and art director.) Clearly, a storyboard can be most useful if the material to be photographed is completely under control. If it isn't, then the storyboard will be a piece of fiction that has no bearing on the finished film. For this reason, a storyboard kind of script preparation is almost always used for animation films, since the drawings, the photographs, or the puppets that will be photographed are completely under the control of the animator and the director.

Often a storyboard is prepared because some of the people who are to be involved in the production of a film are not really capable of thinking in pictures. How can this happen? Very easily if a film is to be used for advertising, because some of the people who may have obligations or interests in the film's use may have little experience in film production. This would be true, probably, when a script has to be presented to an advertising manager of a manufacturer or dealer, for example. Such a person might have a lot of experience in print and other advertising media but little or none in film. It might also be true in some advertising agencies, although nowadays people in advertising agencies are all fairly skilled in film. It didn't use to be so. In the early days of television advertising, the people in the agencies who were in charge of TV advertising were those who had become highly skilled in radio, not in film, and film is a very different kind of medium.

Storyboards are still used for preparing television commercials, however, even if they are live action, so that there will be some clearly understood consensus of the images that are to be achieved in the film and to meet the rigorous time limitations.

A storyboard can be almost minimally sketchy, or it can be what is called *finished art*, that is, fully drawn and fully colored pictures. A simplified, sketchy kind of storyboard may be drawn in black-and-white pencil, or ink, or even in black-and-white wash. A colored board can be done in pastel chalks, in transparent watercolors, or tempera.

Simple Black and White Storyboards

A simple storyboard is presented on pages 178–179; it was drawn for a television commercial for OLD LEGEND Furniture Polish. This is an imaginary product so I am not treading on the feet of any real advertiser. The commercial in this case would be 30 seconds in running time. (On television this means that there can be 30 seconds of picture but no more than 28 seconds of sound. If there were more sound, part of it would probably be lost because of the need of the broadcasting people to switch from the projector on which the commercial is playing to another on which there may be another commercial or a movie, or to the live studio or to the network for whatever may have to follow.) On this storyboard you will see that underneath each picture—called *frames*—there is written a part of the narration—it could be dialogue—that is to be spoken. In this way one can indicate what part of the speech is to take place during which part of the picture. You will also see that each frame in the storyboard is not necessarily indicative of a separate shot. The first frame is one shot, frame 2 is another, and frame 3 begins a third; but frame 4 could be achieved by simply "pulling back" from frame 3 by means of a dolly or a zoom lens; and frames 5 and 6 could simply be continuing bits of action in frame 4. Thus, in terms of the classic definition of a shot ("a piece of film that has no discontinuity in time or place"), frames 3, 4, 5, and 6 are all one shot!

Before the scenes are actually photographed, the director, the cameraman, the producer, and the client's representative sit down together and agree on the way of handling each shot and on the kinds of transitions that will be undertaken to get from one shot to the next. (The phrase *to get from one shot to the next* refers to the pictorial progression or the pictorial logic.) Corrections in the storyboard may be necessary because of changes made during these pre-production conferences. In a simple black-and-white storyboard such as the one shown here, you'll find a couple of corrections of this kind in the text under the pictures.

It is clear that the storyboard can be adhered to during the actual filming only if there is total control of the scenery, the people, and the action. To the degree that control is diminished, to that degree will one approximate or stray from the storyboard.

Full Color Presentation Storyboards

Fully drawn and colored storyboards are prepared for animation films to achieve total control of everything that will appear in each scene in the film, because color is such an important part of animation, totally integral, and an essential element in the characterizations of the "performers." Colored boards are also prepared for presentations, and a presentation is something that every scriptwriter must know about intimately.

When writers have an idea for a film they would like to make or to write—and get paid for!—they have to make some kind of presentation to some source of money to underwrite or sponsor the film. They may go to someone who will put up the money and hope to get it back with a profit through releasing the film to paying audiences, or they may go to a client for whom the film will provide, hopefully, some valuable service. For a film that will be exhibited to paying audiences, a script and some names of performers, marquee names, are needed. The story and its own possibilities, which are much greater if it has been a successful novel or play and can therefore bring a great deal of prepaid publicity with it, or the attraction of name performers who have agreed to play in the film, are what you need to raise money. In addition, very often, some kind of track record in writing or film-making is essential. If you have no track record, then you may have to have a contract for the release of the as-yet-unmade film, and that's pretty hard to get! Thus, far more often than not, you will go to a sponsor, when you are not yet an established film-maker, to seek his underwriting the cost of the film, which will then belong to him and which he will use for his own publicity, advertising, or public relations.

It is one of the peculiarities of the business that while television commercials are prepared by advertising agencies, industrial films of almost every kind are not. There are two reasons for this. In the first place, TV commercials are actually written and produced by an agency, which will hire a production house to make the films; therefore they are economically attractive to an agency. In the second place, an agency will handle the distribution of the commercials by buying time on the various stations across the country and by making sure that prints of the commercials are at the right station at the right time. Longer industrial films, however, which will not be written or made by an agency and will be utilized by the sales or public relations department of the sponsoring company, present no financial attraction to an advertising agency, and they are almost invariably handled directly by the sponsor. Sponsors require a pretty vigorous presentation to induce them to spend thousands of dollars, and for this reason a pretty extensive and costly presentation has to be made.

The second set of storyboards was made for such a presentation. There is a small town in Illinois called Union where the Illinois Railroad Museum is located. The storyboards are part of a presentation by means of which it was hoped to raise the money for a film explaining and publi-

(SUPER: Old Legend furniture polish presents: "Henry VIII")
1. (slow dolly in)

"Hello, I'm Ann Boelyn, ... and that ...
2.

.. ARE REALLY ROUGH ....
5.

on my furniture ....
6.

and leaves a deep shine like
9. a hard wax finish ...

So try old Legend on your
10.   wood work ..

cizing this museum. For this reason, the storyboards are very full and lush. Although the boards are painted in full color, they are printed here in black-and-white.

The first two boards in the set—numbers 1 and 2—are for the opening sequence of the film; the last three, numbers 3, 4 and 5, are for the final sequence. In between these two sets of boards is one called a *concept board*. This board indicates the major topics to be presented in the body of the film. As in the simple storyboard for the TV commercial, each frame consists of a picture with some words in a box below it. In this storyboard, however, there is no narrative or dialogue. Although not reproduced here, the text below each picture is set out in two colors, red and black. Red is generally used to indicate the camera angle and the camera movement, while black generally indicates the subject that is to be photographed and the accompanying sounds.

Once again, each frame does not necessarily represent a different discrete shot. It may, but it may also indicate a position *during* the movement within a shot, as in frames 2 and 3 on board 1, or in frames 4 and 5 on the same board. In this presentational storyboard, the transitions suggested by the creator of the boards are indicated in the text for each frame. To avoid confusion, each frame is numbered, even though the boards are also numbered. Because the first two boards deal with one part of the film and boards 3, 4 and 5 deal with a totally different and unrelated part of the film, the frames in the last three boards are numbered in a new sequence beginning with 1 in the upper left corner of board 3. The concept board also has its own sequence of numbers. Thus the numbers of the boards themselves indicate the order in which they are to be set up, and the numbers of the frames indicate the order of the progression of images.

There is no doubt that this fully painted set of boards evokes a strong response. The artwork is excellent, and as it is presented as finished art and in full color, it cannot fail to generate interest and a clear understanding of the flow of images and ideas.

You will have no difficulty identifying the characteristics of the different camera angles discussed earlier in chapter 2 for the images in the storyboards will aid your visualization of them. Frame 2 on board 1, for example, is a high angle shot because the camera is above the subject and looks down upon it; it is also a close-up. On the same board, frame 6 is a low angle shot. Frames 7 and 8 on the next board are extreme close-ups. On board 3 there is a new term, *macro close-up*. Macro simply means large; it is the opposite of micro. Frames 2 and 4, therefore, are very large, or very close, close-ups. On the next board, in frame 8, the term *3/4 shot* means a shot that is half-way between a front shot and a side view, half-way between full-face and profile. Depending upon what one is looking at, the terms *3/4 shot* or *half profile* or *3/4 front view* or *3/4 rear view* can be used. Remember, the terms are not exact but only indicate as clearly as possible just what is meant.

Because the terms are, in a sense, inexact (although as specific as

#1

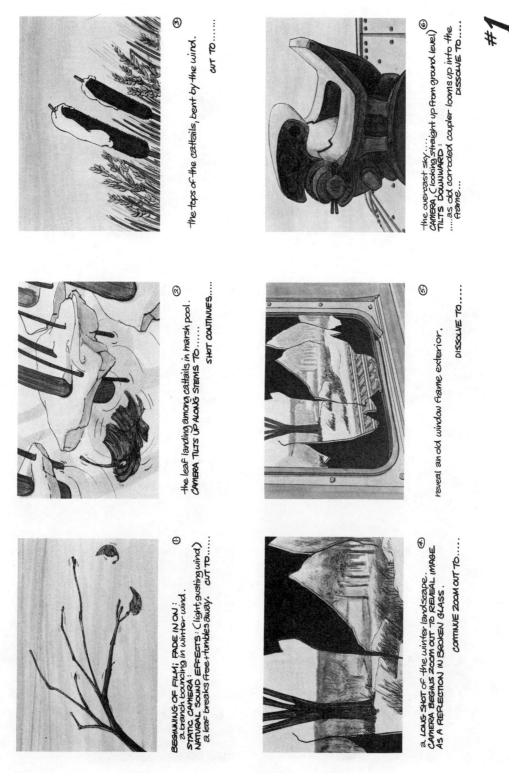

③ the tops of the cattails, bent by the wind.

CUT TO.......

⑥ the overcast sky......
CAMERA, (looking straight up from ground level)
TILTS DOWNWARD:
.....as old corroded coupler looms up into the frame.....

DISSOLVE TO......

② the leaf landing among cattails in marsh pool.
CAMERA TILTS UP ALONG STEMS TO......

SHOT CONTINUES.....

⑤ reveal an old window frame exterior.

DISSOLVE TO......

① BEGINNING OF FILM; FADE IN ON:
a branch bouncing in winter wind.
STATIC CAMERA:
NATURAL SOUND EFFECTS: (light, gusting wind)
a leaf breaks free + tumbles away.   CUT TO......

④ a LONG SHOT of the winter landscape...
CAMERA BEGINS ZOOM OUT TO REVEAL IMAGE
AS A REFLECTION IN BROKEN GLASS.

CONTINUE ZOOM OUT TO.....

#2

⑩ a LONG SHOT of a trolley skeleton. STATIC CAM. SOUND EFFECTS: natural, then a few moments after start of shot — a rythmic, metallic bang-ing is heard faintly in the distance. CAMERA BEGINS 180° PAN AFTER FIRST FEW BANGS, AND......

⑫ Member of ILLINOIS RAILROAD MUSEUM repairing old boiler of locomotive. CAMERA DOLLYS IN FOR CLOSE-UP OF WORKMAN AND HAMMER STRIKING WELD. —— END OF FILM'S FIRST SCENE ——

⑨ an old pressure guage — OUT OF FOCUS. CAMERA RACKS FOCUS to bring image into SHARP DEFINITION. CUT TO......

⑪ CAMERA NARROWS IN ON SOURCE OF BANGING-SOUND, PAUSES, DOLLIES IN ON LOCOMOTIVE. SOUND EFFECTS: now banging is more clear, less hollow and ominous sounding. DOLLY IN TO FIND....

⑦ CAMERA DOLLYING ALONG OLD SPLINTERED TIE, HOLDS AS SPIKE OCCUPIES CENTER FRAME. line of locomotives in background, SOFT FOCUS. CUT TO......

⑧ DOLLIES ALONG, OVER, UNDER AND THROUGH PARTIALLY RESTORED CARS + ENGINES — "SEARCHING" FOR THE SOURCE OF THE SOUND...... SOUND EFFECTS: banging becomes nearer + nearer.... CONTINUE DOLLY TO......

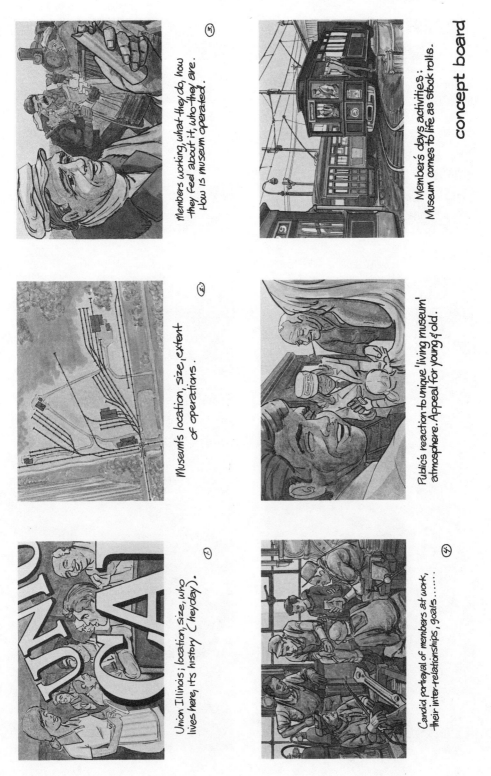

concept board

(1) Members working, what they do, how they feel about it, who they are. How is museum operated.

Member's days activities: Museum comes to life as stock rolls.

(2) Museum's location, size, extent of operations.

Public's reaction to unique "living museum" atmosphere. Appeal for young & old.

(3) Union Illinois; location, size, who lives here, its history (heyday).

(4) Candid portrayal of members at work, their inter-relationships, goals ......

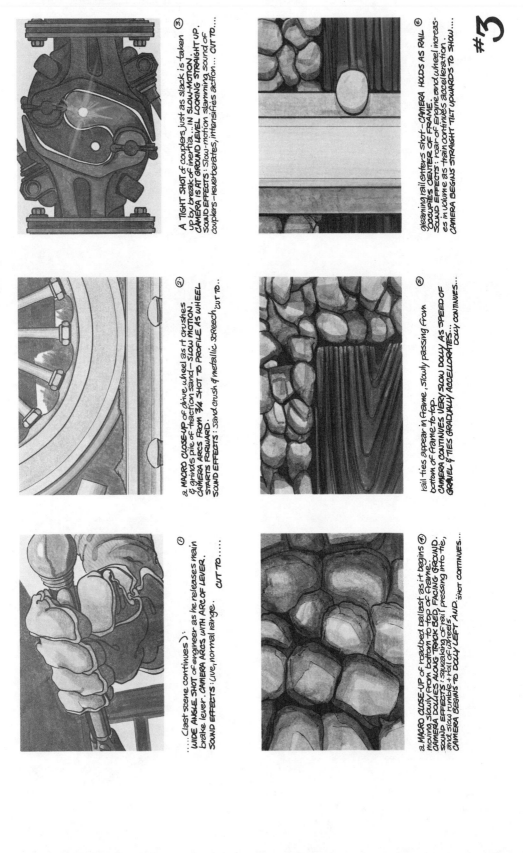

③
A TIGHT SHOT of couplers just as slack is taken up by break of inertia... IN SLOW-MOTION. CAMERA IS AT GROUND LEVEL, LOOKING STRAIGHT UP. SOUND EFFECTS: Slow-motion slamming sound of couplers—reverberates, intensifies action... CUT TO...

⑥
gleaming rail enters shot—CAMERA HOLDS AS RAIL OCCUPIES CENTER OF FRAME. SOUND EFFECTS: roar of engine and wheel increases in volume as train continues acceleration. CAMERA BEGINS STRAIGHT TILT UPWARDS TO SHOW...

②
a MACRO CLOSE-UP of drive wheel as it crushes & grinds pile of traction sand—SLOW MOTION. CAMERA ARCS FROM ¾ SHOT TO PROFILE AS WHEEL STARTS FORWARD. SOUND EFFECTS: sand crush & metallic screech CUT TO...

⑤
rail ties appear in frame, slowly passing from bottom of frame to top. CAMERA CONTINUES VERY SLOW DOLLY AS SPEED OF GRAVEL & TIES GRADUALLY ACCELERATES... DOLLY CONTINUES...

①
(last scene continues):
.....CLOSE SHOT of engineer as he releases main brake lever. CAMERA ARCS WITH ARC OF LEVER. SOUND EFFECTS: Live, normal range.   CUT TO......

④
a MACRO CLOSE-UP of roadbed ballast as it begins moving slowly from bottom to top of frame. CAMERA DOLLIES ALONG TRACK BED, FACING GROUND. SOUND EFFECTS: squealing of rail pressing into tie, and slow rumble + roll of wheels. CAMERA BEGINS TO DOLLY LEFT AND... shot continues...

#3

#4

⑨ the engineer leaning out cab at controls.
SOUND EFFECTS: Full range of locomotive sounds.
CAMERA HOLDS, THEN BEGINS ZOOM OUT TO SHOW A....

⑩ a WIDE ANGLE shot of engineer's hand as it grabs
then pulls whistle chain.
SOUND EFFECTS: quieter sounds of cab interior.
CUT TO.....

⑤ a 3/4 SHOT of complete drive system.
SOUND EFFECTS: whining of drive system.
CAMERA HOLDS MOMENTARILY, THEN TILTS UP TO.......

⑪ HOLDS IN A POSITION LEVEL WITH RIM OF
STACK OVERLOOKING LENGTH OF TRAIN.
SOUND EFFECTS: Full range of engine noise,
emphasis on stack roaring.   CUT TO....

⑦ a MACRO CLOSE-UP of front guide wheel-Flange
slams inside of rail.— CAMERA HOLDS.
SOUND EFFECTS: Roar & banging of wheel Flange.
Train continues to accelerate.
CAMERA BEGINS ARC TO RIGHT w/ SLIGHT CRANE UP TO......

⑧ a 3/4 WIDE ANGLE shot of entire locomotive.
SOUND EFFECTS: Fullest & loudest range of entire
engine roar, train has reached Flat-out speed.
CAMERA HOLDS, THEN BEGINS ARC BACK LEFT AND......

(15)
as tunnel exit approaches.
SOUND EFFECTS: chugging sound slowly begins to
fade-out as "tunnel racket" continues, and,
slowly intensifies its rumble.   SHOT CONTINUES.....

(18)
—the modern train streams out and into distance.
CAMERA HOLDS AS CREDITS ARE OPTICALLY PRINTED
OVER THIS FINAL SHOT.
SOUND EFFECTS: natural range; train fades off.
————— FADE-OUT; END OF PICTURE —————

(14)
WIDE ANGLE GLIMPSE of tunnel entrance just as
train zooms into the darkness. CAMERA IS NOW
MOUNTED ON TOP OF LIGHT BOX AIMED FORWARD.
SOUND EFFECTS: now hollow shriek of whistle
cuts out and its echoe mixes w/ tunnel racket.
                                        SHOT CONTINUES.....

(17)
—the CAMERA JARS TO ABRUPT HALT, NOW SUSPENDED
FROM TOP OF TUNNEL EXIT,
as a modern diesel-electric locomotive shoots
out of tunnel underneath the camera.
SOUND EFFECTS: (normal diesel) horn fades w/ distance.
                                        CAMERA HOLDS AS.....

(13)
LOW WIDE ANGLE of whistle just as it blows.
SOUND EFFECTS: Piercing howls of steam whistle.
(an instant after the whistle blast begins,
a shadow cuts across whistle and smoke.
                                        CUT TO.....

(16)
AS CAMERA CLOSES IN ON EXIT OF TUNNEL.
SOUND EFFECTS: as tunnel rumble peaks—
SUDDENLY AIR HORN OF DIESEL ENGINE BLARES OUT!!
                                        AND......

#5

they can be!), don't be disturbed if the artist who makes a storyboard occasionally uses a term that is really not the correct technical one, even when such technical terms are available. For example, in frame 12 on board 2, the last line of the legend is: END OF FILM'S FIRST SCENE. This really should be: END OF FILM'S FIRST SEQUENCE, but those who really know what is meant don't worry about the error because they *do* know what is meant; those who don't know, won't catch it! In the same way, an artist uses the word *arc* when talking of a camera movement because that's the way he *sees* the action. More technically experienced film-makers would use the word *pan*.

There is one further term that might confuse you. In frame 8 on board 2 is the phrase *racks focus*. This means that the focus of the camera is changed while the camera is running, so that the viewer actually sees the change of focus. It is fairly common nowadays to change focus from something close to the camera to something farther away, or vice versa. When both things (or people) are not in focus at the same time, a *selective focus*, has been used, that is, one element of the composition on which to focus has been selected at the "expense" of something else. The focus can, of course, be changed to direct the spectator's attention from one thing to another. This, also, is called *racking focus*.

In frame 7 on the same board, the instruction *soft focus* means essentially the same thing; while we watch, the scene goes out of focus. While out-of-focus we then cut (although dissolve might be a better transition) to the out-of-focus beginning of the shot indicated in the next frame.

As I have said, all the terms are simply to make as clear as possible how the finished production will appear. I reiterate that all scripts are only blueprints from which the final productions will be built. Storyboards are special kinds of blueprints or special kinds of clarifications of such blueprints. Neither the script nor the storyboard is the final result, no matter how well they may look. It's the show that counts!

Local Commercials

Local commercial spots, however, may have to be produced locally to save money. They may or may not be shot on motion picture film; the alternative is a series of still photographs. But such spots still have to be written, and because they are locally produced, they have to be written locally. This is where a writer, as an employee of the TV station, comes in. It will be very difficult to make such local commercials interesting and exciting or enticing, yet, if they do not have these characteristics, they won't really do a selling job. You can see such advertising spots in a different environment and on a large screen if you ever visit a local movie theatre or drive-in in a small town or in the countryside. This kind of isolation from the medium where you expect to see TV commercials, will, perhaps, draw your attention to the qualities—or lack of them—that are needed in good local TV spots.

If you refer back to the Christmas cake commercials in the discussion of radio in chapter 1 and keep in mind the pictorial expense of making television commercials, your imagination will soon lead you to another trick that is used to cut economic corners. Beginning with the basic concept of a one-minute commercial, an ingenious and creative writer will be able to "lift" some visual scenes from longer commercials, perhaps rearrange them slightly, and then, using a slightly modified narrative, provide a commercial of 30 seconds running time, or even 20 seconds, without needing to shoot a single new piece of photography. Such shorter television commercials are actually called *lifts;* one talks of a one-minute commercial with a 30-second and a 20-second lift.

You can never forget the limitations of your budget when you are writing for film or television, for, more often than not, it is through foundering on the rocks of budget that your barge of beautiful words and ideas will break up.

It goes without saying that storyboards are of inestimable value in clarifying for all concerned—verbalists and visualists alike—precisely what is intended in the longer spots and the lifts to be taken from them.

Here are two television commercials, each designed to run 30 seconds. There is no original photography. Each spot uses slides, which may have been photographic or artwork, to provide the visuals. Each spot is identified by its own series number and carries the date of its videotape recording.

Plywood Minnesota	**PL-4-274-B**
Fall Sale—Panels and	**10/18/77**
Wallpaper	

30" TV Spot—Oct. 31 through Nov. 19

SLIDE B1—TITLE:
  Save on panels and
  wall papers
  PLYWOOD MINNESOTA
  FALL SALE!

ANNCR: (VO) If you want to panel or wallpaper a room in time for the holidays, do it now . . . during Plywood Minnesota's warehouse-wide annual Fall Sale!

SLIDE B2—PANEL SCENE AND SUPER
  Reg. $7.92
  Vinyl Panels
  Now only $5.92

First quality vinyl panels—regularly $7.92—are sale-priced at only $5.92 per four-by-eight foot panel!

SLIDE B3—WALLPAPER SCENE AND SUPER
  Reg. $3.99 per single roll
  Vinyl coated Wallpaper
  Now only $2.89
  (Save $2.20 per double roll!)

And pre-pasted, pre-trimmed vinyl wallpapers—regularly $3.99 per single roll—are now only $2.89 per double roll!

SLIDE B4—TITLE:
PLYWOOD MINNESOTA
FALL SALE
(Ends Nov. 19)

Now, during Plywood Minnesota's Fall Sale!

**Plywood Minnesota
Fall Sale—Fuego**

PL-4-274-C
10/18/77

30″ TV Spot—Oct. 31 through Nov. 19

SLIDE C1—CU BURNING FIRE-PLACE WITH TITLE:
Your fireplace is robbing your home of heat!

ANNCR: (VO) Your nice cozy fireplace is actually *robbing your home of heat* . . . right up the chimney.

SLIDE C2—FUEGO FIREPLACE

But now you can stop the heat loss. Install a Fuego* Fireplace Converter—the amazing steel insert that directs heat *into* your home—not up the chimney.

SLIDE C3—ILLUSTRATION
WITH ARROWS
SLIDE C4—FUEGO FIREPLACE

Ten pounds of firewood produces half the heat of the average household furnace running a full hour!

Tempered glass doors provide beauty and safety.

SLIDE C5—SUPER TITLE:
$25 rebate during
PLYWOOD MINNESOTA
Fall Sale!

Get a Fuego during Plywood Minnesota's Fall Sale . . . ending Nov. 19 . . . and you get a $25 rebate to buy firewood.

The slides are also identified by number because, over months and even years, a large library of such visuals can be built up for a client by an advertising agency. Thus, commercials can be assembled from an existing library. Such a collection of visuals need not be limited to slides; it may also include *film clips* (short pieces of film) and short *videoclips* (short pieces of videotape) such as were used in the script for *Different Drummers,* in chapter 3.

The nature of these two commercial spots, with their rather driving insistence, is said to be *hard sell*; such a spot might also be called *a pitch*.

---

*Pronounced *Fway*-go.

8

Writers' Jobs and
Writers' Markets

As a general rule, the only full-time staff jobs for writers of scripts for any of the media I have discussed will be in radio or television stations, in advertising agencies, or, occasionally, in in-plant production units.

There are no full-time staff jobs for writers of dramatic scripts in any of the media I have been talking about, whether radio, television, or film.

Recognizing that there may be occasional exceptions to these two generalizations—exceptions that prove the rule—I can now discuss the possibilities of becoming a professional writer of audio-visual scripts.

Radio

Drama

Radio drama proliferated during the 30 years from 1920 to 1950, the years when radio suffered no competition from television. Since television's intrusion into virtually every home, radio drama has come upon hard times. Nevertheless, CBS has, as noted earlier in this book, reintroduced radio drama with a series of nightly hour-long mystery plays. It has apparently been successful in building and keeping an audience over its first couple of years, for the same network has begun to present a young people's adventure series as well. It might appear that the prognosis for the re-emergence of radio drama is favorable.

It may be that some of the radio stations that are owned and operated by universities and colleges also present a possibility for writers of radio dramas, although this would not be a lucrative market.

In countries where the government provides radio broadcasting, as in Canada, Australia, New Zealand, and the United Kingdom, there is a market for radio drama. I have already drawn attention to a couple of dramas commissioned by the BBC in the United Kingdom. A writer need have no fear of government interference in the kind of broadcasts that are presented in these countries. It just doesn't happen. Instead, the programmers in the various networks in these Commonwealth countries do reflect their respective social environments and select what they broadcast in such terms.

These markets pay for scripts at respectable professional levels. The Writers Guild in the United States, for example, has a reciprocal agreement with its counterpart in the United Kingdom, so that you can be sure your work will be protected there as well as it is here, and, similarly, paid for at legitimate rates.

Dramatic radio scripts are bought by the heads of the radio drama department in each of the government networks. Their addresses may be found in appropriate trade publications, such as *Broadcasting Magazine,* or from the respective embassies or consulates. Do not telephone; it is better to write. It might be wise, especially if you are not a citizen of the country to whose network you are submitting your work, to write a letter of inquiry first and to accompany it with some kind of list of credits, if you have one. When you write your introductory letter, you would do well to ask what length of program is best suited to the corporation's or network's needs, so that you can compose your drama to be most salable.

For writers in the United States who are dealing with contemporary topics, it seems logical to suppose that Canada might present a more ready market because of its proximity and its probable awareness of the subject matter with which you are dealing. Also, because of proximity and familiarity, the current daily language spoken in our two countries contains no phrases or idioms that might sound strange.

There are, however, many dialectal differences between English as spoken in the United Kingdom or Australia or New Zealand and English as spoken in North America. These dialectal differences tend to disappear entirely in plays that are historical and especially in plays that are in verse. Educated English diction remains a shared treasure in all these countries, even though it may be pronounced somewhat differently from the way it would be pronounced in the United States. (After all, even in this country, there are regional pronunciations that differ from one another greatly.)

For those of you who are comfortable writing for children, the Commonwealth networks always provide programs for this segment of the audience.

Talks

Radio stations in small towns (where they do not have to face head-on the competition of the network broadcasts), FM stations (which, because of their small geographic coverage, are somewhat similar to small town stations), and university stations seem to be the only extant markets for radio talks by "personalities." Personalities are people who, by reason of some special current or past activity, bring to their audiences something of interest. They may be regular weekly or even daily broadcasters, or they may be one-time special programs. Occasionally they are employed not so much because of their interesting activities as because of a strong and entertaining, or even abrasive, personality that colors whatever they may say. Are you a writer-broadcaster of a radio talk? The activities that may generate interest are travel, sports and recreation, child care, interior decorating; cooking, or literary, dramatic, or music criticism, among many others.

Talks programs are regularly included in the schedules of the major stations in the networks of the Commonwealth countries, though they are less popular here in the United States.

Compensation in this country will be in proportion to the capability of the station to pay and the importance of the name of the "talker." If this kind of program is congenial to you, you will have to negotiate your own compensation in all probability.

Advertising and Spot Announcements

Spot announcements are almost always done by staff writers, which means that there are full-time jobs in the industry. The large commercial stations in the larger metropolitan areas are more difficult to enter, but it is not too difficult to begin at one of the many smaller stations that are located all over the country. The pay may not be astronomical, but there is a great opportunity to learn one's craft, and very little damage results from the usual beginner's mistakes.

On local stations there is a considerable amount of advertising to write. National advertisers prepare their radio commercial announcements—their spots—in the big metropolitan centers because that is where the advertising agencies operate and where those agencies can find the recording facilities and talent that are best suited to producing the best possible recordings of the spots they have written. Such spots are supplied to local radio stations on audio tape, so there is no writing of spots for national advertisers in local stations.

But there are many local advertisers who are persuaded by the people who sell time on local radio stations that this is an important advertising medium. These local advertisers—automobile dealers, ice cream parlors and restaurants, entertainment of all sorts, shops with sales, and so on—have a continuing need for writers of commercial announcements. Local advertisements of this kind almost never go through an advertising agency; the amounts of money are usually too small to pay for the services of an agency and advertisers don't want to dilute their dollars by buying those services anyway.

Continuity

Most programs of recorded music do not have written continuity. The music is introduced by disc jockeys who, though they may have done their homework and researched the music they are presenting, nevertheless ad lib all their remarks. As they become more and more expert, they may develop recognizable personalities and become "names."

There are some special kinds of programs broadcast over small local radio stations that provide opportunities for radio writers. Occasionally there are programs of live music performers, and continuity has to be written for them. If the station broadcasts classical music, musical continuity will also be used, and this continuity may be written or ad libbed from notes. The choice will depend on the competence and fame of the announcer.

News

In local radio stations, just as in the large metropolitan stations, there are several kinds of news that are broadcast. The first is "piped in" from the network, if the station is part of a news network. In such a case, international and national news, perhaps national sports, will be broadcast by national news announcers and commentators, and a local station will "take the feed" from the network and broadcast it locally.

On the other hand, international and national news as well as sports and even feature stories will come to a station on what is called *the news wire*. This is the teletype service to which the station subscribes. Individual stories are taken from this supply source and read on the air by a news announcer.

Finally, there is the kind of news that you may be able to write yourself! Probably you will have a better chance if you have had some kind of experience in journalism, even if only in high school or college. You might begin as a local radio news reporter. You would have to dig up the local news yourself—police, city hall, fire, sports—and write the news stories. This would give you a very special and important kind of experience.

This kind of news reporting can be the beginning of investigative reporting, digging into the stories that are in the general news and discovering their backgrounds and even, perhaps, their importance to the community. This kind of in-depth news reporting leads also to the skills of feature news writing.

Getting a Job

To get a job in a radio station, you should have a portfolio of what you have already written, even though it may have been for entirely different media. Don't try to pretend you can write for radio if you haven't done so. Simply make it clear that you can write and want to get into radio. On a small station you may well find that you are asked to write all kinds of things—continuity, commercial announcements for local advertisers, community announcements, and even local news. Grab every opportunity.

As you gain experience in radio writing, you will also learn about how radio stations are operated and how people "graduate" up the ladder to larger stations and to more important and better paying jobs. Keep carbon copies of what you think are your best pieces, and, when the opportunity presents itself, obtain audio tapes of broadcasts of your better things. This will provide an invaluable portfolio to exhibit when you are applying for some kind of promotion, either with the employer for whom you may already be working or with a different radio station.

As you might suppose, major stations in the major cities can be expected to hire members of the Writers Guild. Membership is open so you will have no trouble joining if the station wants to hire you. The Guild establishes minimum pay scales and working conditions for your protection. In the smaller stations throughout the country, you will probably have to work out your own salvation and do your own negotiating.

Motion Pictures

Dramatic Features

Most film features are made with the hope, if not the expectation, that they will receive television broadcast after their theatrical release. On the other hand, there are a considerable number of feature length films that are made specially for television that may, in their turn, receive theatrical release.

I have already talked in chapter 2 about the stages through which a feature script grows—the synopsis or story idea, the treatment, the screenplay or scenario, and the shooting script. (The shooting script of a feature is really a detailed organization of the screenplay.)

Generally, a synopsis will not be accepted from a writer who is new to a producer, nor will a treatment nor screenplay. For many years the Hollywood studios have refused to accept stories from anyone other than writers they know or from writers whose work is submitted by agents. If any stories come to them from other sources, they are usually sent back to the writer unopened. This is simply to protect the studios from plagiarism suits. After all, there aren't very many new story situations; there are only large numbers of variations. (The very successful Broadway comedy *Boy Meets Girl* arises out of this phenomenon.) Until this self-protective rule was established, the studios found themselves involved in such suits. Most of them were either won outright by the studios or were settled out of court for small sums of money, but the nuisance was still very disturbing. The studios' protection is to return all manuscripts that come in from unknown writers, or arrive unsolicited, without even opening their envelopes.

An established literary agent, however, carries a quality of reliability on which the studios, or the independent producers, can count. So it has developed that, as a general rule, stories a writer hopes to sell to film studios or to television studios or networks will have a better chance by far if they are handled by a literary agent. There are several advantages.

The agent knows the people who can buy stories so the submission goes to the right person in the first instance. The agent knows the requirements of the Writers Guild of America, Inc., with which all the major film studios and independent producers, as well as television studios and networks, have contracts. And lastly, the agent knows what kind of people or what kind of producer is likely to buy what kind of story. On the other hand, if producers, whether film or television, receive a submission from a reputable agent they are far more likely to read it because they know that this reputable agent really thinks that the story may very well interest them.

Feature motion pictures are very often adapted from successful novels. This is not for any literary or cinematic reason; it is simply because the film can have a relatively free ride on the publicity that has been generated for, and by, the novel and its success. This practice has gone on for a very long time and has given rise to a kind of sub-profession called *screen writing* or *scenario writing.* Sometimes you will see on the credits of a film that the screenplay was written by so-and-so from a novel or play by so-and-so. This means that the screenplay was written by a scenarist who knows the craft of writing for motion pictures.

If you have written a novel that has sold very well and which your agent, or your publisher, can sell to a producer, you are on the way to films with a head start. Likewise, if you have written a play that has had some kind of success and can be sold to a film producer (or TV producer) by an agent or by the theatrical producer, you are in luck. (It should be clarified here that very often an author's contract, or a playwright's contract, spells out the right of the publisher or the producer to sell the work to the movies or to TV.) Clearly, if you have a successful novel or play in your pocket, you also have a lawyer or an agent (or both) to protect your interest, no matter who has the rights to sell it to additional media.

If your work is sold to film or television, and if you have anything to do with the preparation of the scenario, you will have to become a member of Writers Guild of America, Inc., which is in business to protect you. While novelists and playwrights have the option to join the Authors League or the Dramatists League, virtually all film producers and actually all television producers of any size at all have contracts with the Writers Guild of America, Inc., that *require* that all material be written by members of the Guild. This does have advantages, however, that might at first escape your notice. First of all, the Guild has reciprocal agreements with its counterpart in Britain so you are protected should your work be bought (or shown on TV) by some station in the British Isles or Commonwealth countries. This is important because writers' contracts specify what are called *residual rights,* that is, payment of additional sums when, as and if, a work is broadcast again, or rerun in some other ways. Such protection is invaluable.

Such protection is also available if you should write directly for the British Broadcasting Corporation, for example, or for independent television in Great Britain. These markets are far more likely to read and perhaps buy a dramatic screenplay because of the difference in the organization of the television industry in that country and in the USA. If you have an agent in the USA, he will be able to have an arrangement with a British agent or with agents in other countries and will be able to find out what people in distant lands might be interested in. It's to the agent's interest to help you, because he receives an over-ride commission on everything a foreign agent sells.

On the other hand, each of the major foreign broadcasting companies maintains an office in the USA. If you are a serious writer and have a script to submit for consideration, you should be able to find out from such an office the name and address of the person or office to which a submission might be made.

Getting a Job

If you are in a town or city that possesses, or is near to, an educational television channel or a university television station, there is an outside possibility of finding a market for your material in such an outlet. Your proximity makes it possible to ask for an appointment with the program director, or the director of dramatic programs, so that you can explore with that person the possibilities of selling your work. Your writing must differ, however, if you are aiming at this market, from the writing that you might do directly for film. Educational television channels of all kinds suffer from relative poverty no matter where they are found. You must cut your suit to match your cloth. You must write for an inexpensive production. Watch the dramatic shows that are broadcast on such channels. They are usually filmed or taped during production at a similar station somewhere else in the USA and reflect the tightly limited budgets available.

While it must have become obvious that writing a feature film as a *beginning* writer, as a way of *breaking into* the profession, is not warmly recommended, nevertheless you may have have an absolutely overpowering urge to disregard the warnings. What, then, can you do?

The first possibility, and probably the hardest to achieve, is to find someone who likes your script so very much that he or she, too, cannot overcome the desire to realize it as a film. Who might that someone be? Not someone in New York or the West Coast, in all probability, because they, too, would want to have had an introduction from someone on whom they have learned to rely. If you live in such a place, you may know someone yourself who would accept you on your recognizances. On the other hand, if you come from a smaller town, maybe you can put together a group of investors who would then search for a producer and a director. It's not likely to succeed, unfortunately, because without a good knowledge of film financing and film production, you and your friends can go broke very quickly and have nothing to show for it.

Much more productive is to search in the various listings of authors' agents* to find those who deal in scenarios and screenplays (motion picture properties) and who will read unsolicited manuscripts. Remember, not all agents will do so.

I regret to repeat the warning that breaking into the feature film writers' markets as a beginner does not, as a rule, present a healthy prognosis.

Non-Theatrical Films

As we have seen, there is a whole film industry engaged in making what are called non-theatrical films: television commercials, documentaries, public information films, films for schools, and industrial films of all kinds. This part of the industry is so large that there are perhaps a thousand such producers listed in various telephone books throughout the United States, maybe more. Even beyond this very large, but relatively hidden, industry, are the very considerable numbers of in-plant production units. These are film and videotape production units that are developed within, and for the use of, large companies.

Films that are used in the schools are called classroom or instructional films. Most people who have attended primary and secondary schools since World War II have had to watch many of these films, and some older students of the public school systems have seen educational films (as they used to be called) since the 1920s. For a long time classroom films were made to match exactly the topics found in the curricula of the schools. This meant that such films didn't stray very far from the material found in textbooks. As the years went by, however, teachers, students, and parents learned that films could do at least three things that neither a textbook nor a teacher could do. They could bring into the classroom something that a teacher couldn't bring—a trip down the Seine or a visit to the salt flats of Yugoslavia or Spain. They could make easily visible to every member of the class things that had previously been seen by only a few at a time, things like microscopic views of cells and insects or demonstrations of processes done in what is called *animation*, artwork or puppetry that moves on the screen. Finally, it was found that motion pictures could draw attention to similarities and make associations that could not be made nearly so well by any other means; this, in turn, led to the development of new approaches to interest, excitement, and motivation.

The importance of films and related audio-visual tools is indicated by the fact that for many years since World War II all governments in the Western world have given some form of support to school systems to help them acquire and use these means of instruction. This support is still continuing.

I mentioned in-plant production units earlier. These are the film pro-

---

*Lists of reputable agents can be obtained from Writers Guild East, Inc., New York City, and from Writers Guild West, Inc., Los Angeles.

duction units, which may also work in videotape, organized in and for certain large companies: banks, hospitals, insurance companies, automotive companies, aircraft manufacturers, and so on. Some of the larger in-plant production units employ writers on staff, although, more often than not, film writers who write for these units are writers of other materials for the companies as well. They probably write manuals, brochures, prospectuses, and so on. You should also realize that the choice of whether your written material will be recorded on film or on videotape will not be made by you. This will be a choice made by the producer and will have to do with technical and budgetary problems and criteria that you would not be expected to be competent enough to judge. (By the same token, writers who write for film find that they are writing for producers who also produce tape and vice versa.)

A few federal government departments in the United States may have film writers, but, as in the in-plant units, they will probably be writing other kinds of things most of the time. In Canada, of course, The National Film Board of Canada makes films for government departments, as well as its own independent productions, and employs writers, although frequently the film-makers will write their own scripts.

In both the United States and Canada, the individual states and provinces have some production facilities for film and TV, usually for tourism, conservation, and the like; in some states, these functions may also be performed for the states by university film production units.

These university production units prepare many kinds of films and TV programs. They began, in some cases nearly half a century ago, as producers of films of football games, and they are probably still engaged in this activity. As time passed and the use of audio-visual tools developed, university film units have gone on to make films for many departments in the university. They make films for teaching, for recording growth and development, for recruitment, for soliciting alumni gifts, and a host of other purposes.

Getting a Job

How do you get a writing job in any of these kinds of units? In the article written by Dudley Nichols that I have already quoted in chapter 2, he points out that you can't easily get a job writing for the movies if you don't have experience, and you can't get experience if you don't write for the movies! What do you do?

If you can, of course, you go to a school or university that offers courses in screen writing. It doesn't matter if the courses do not provide college credits unless you are seeking a degree. Nor does it matter if the courses are in what is called the extension division of the institution. The function of the courses is to provide both instruction and the opportunity to write under some degree of discipline. Attendance at some college or university that also has a film production unit or an educational television station has another major advantage: it is more than likely that a close relationship will exist between your instructor and the production facilities. It is even probable that some of your more advanced writing assignments will be undertaken with the hope, even the expectation, of being produced. Therefore, if working in such a film production unit or television production facility is your goal—immediate or long term—this is a fine introduction.

If there is no opportunity of obtaining this kind of training and exercise, then you must proceed by a somewhat more devious route. What you must try to do is gain experience and knowledge of the medium and, at the same time, prepare a collection of your own writing that you can show to prospective clients to prove to them that you can do a job of screen writing for them. The devious route is thus to become friendly with a film director or producer and through that friendship insinuate yourself into every possible opportunity of working as an apprentice on a film production. In this way you will learn a great deal about how movies are made and what is required to write them. Perhaps you can develop an idea, a brief story outline, something like the outline that appears in chapter 2, *The Man Who Died Twice*. If you can interest a director or a producer in your story idea, perhaps you can persuade him or her to let you work on the development of the script itself—even if the actual script writing is done by someone else.

Once again, you should be advised that you stand a far better chance if you begin with a small film producer in a small town because your competition will be far less. Even in the major centers though, there are many producers who may be interested because the writers who are already established—and there really aren't that many!—may be busy, or the producers may want to try new talent.

You may have an idea for a classroom film you want to present to a producer of this kind of film. Remember what I said before—most distributors of classroom films will be happy to consider an idea for a film if it fits their understanding of the market demands and if it is concerned with a subject area they emphasize in their catalog. If such a distributor only distributes and does not produce films, he probably knows producers who would be interested in making your film if he tells them he is interested in its distribution. Obviously, this will open the door to the producer for you.

You can even develop your own industrial or commercial clients in another way. Perhaps you know of a company that could stand to benefit from a film. If you do some research concerning what it does, how it does it, and what its market (audience) is, you might be able to stimulate its interest in the idea of a film—especially if you have developed a film idea and further ideas of how such a film might be distributed to give the company greatest benefit. Once its interest is raised, then you have a great deal of ammunition with which to go to a film producer to work out a deal for production in which you have an interest both as salesperson and as writer or assistant writer.

Your interest, of course, is to sell your writing. To do this you have to earn some money to have the time to learn to write and to sell yourself to further clients. Everything you write is an addition to your portfolio. Everything you earn—and a sales commission ought to be ten percent of the price of the film—makes your existence that much easier. Incidentally, many writers of industrial films are also salespeople.

Whenever possible, try to obtain a copy of the films you write (they are called *prints*). In most cases they are too expensive for you to buy and too expensive for your client to give you one free. But you should have a paragraph in your letter of understanding with the producer, or in your writer's contract, stipulating that you can always have the opportunity of borrowing a print of the film to show to another prospective client. Such a print is still a further addition to your portfolio.

It goes without saying that as you become known by producers, and perhaps by the companies who are their clients, you are continuing to assure yourself further writing jobs. Additionally, you are building up a backlog of screen credits. Most important, perhaps, you continue to learn more and more about the craft of writing for films and about the care and treatment of all kinds of clients!

Industrial films, in contrast to national commercial spot announcements, are not usually handled through advertising agencies. The companies that sponsor industrial films or institutional films usually, indeed almost always, work directly with a film production company. For this reason, your dealings will be directly with the company and will not have to be buffered by the defences of advertising agencies.

Not only institutional films sponsored by large companies, but institutional films actually sponsored by large institutions, are marvelous opportunities for the non-fiction screen writer. Fraternal organizations such as Kiwanis, Rotary, Elks, sister organizations like the Order of the Eastern Star, community organizations that operate on a national scale (and therefore have enough money to sponsor films) like The Heart Association, and others, do sponsor institutional films. Organizations that direct their efforts to community or national problems such as drug and alcoholism addiction foundations, mental health organizations, and many other like groups are also involved in the production of institutional films. Organizations such as these are so actively engaged in sponsoring films for public education that they frequently have in their employ a person whose sole duties are to develop and supervise the productions and distribution of such films. Once again, if you have a film idea, these are people to whom you should present yourself. You'd be surprised to discover how many community funds across the nation have sponsored films that are designed to aid in raising money!

If you are beginning to write free lance, you have a difficult problem in learning just how much you should expect to be paid for writing an industrial script. It may not make much sense to you to be told that probably the average pay for writing an industrial film would be from five percent to seven and one-half percent of the total production price to the client. It may not sound like much, but if you realize that a film may well cost about $2,000–$3,000 a minute, then the fee for writing a 15-minute film could run from $1,500 to $2,250. To this, of course, would be added all expenses that the writer might have to meet if he must travel for research or to purchase special materials, even if he has to take some people out to lunch to obtain further information, although the latter kind of expense may have to be negotiated or may be included by the writer in his or her fee simply to make the proposition clean and easy.

The fees just mentioned apply to experienced writers who can command appropriate payment for industrial screen writing. These fees might be appropriate for relatively major clients and for relatively major producers. If you are a beginner at writing and if your client is a small producer who is making films for smaller clients, it stands to reason that there will be justification for far smaller fees.

Fees for writing educational films are generally less than those for industrial films. If you should be writing for one of the more established producers, or for one of the more established distributors, you might find it helpful to ask what the fee ought to be. They will tell you, and you can rely on what they say. Payment to producers of classroom films is determined very differently from payment to producers of industrial films. Industrial films are almost always made for clients who will exhibit them to selected audiences at their own expense. They will expect that the cost of production and of exhibition are to be born by their companies as part of their sales, or training, or promotional expenditures.

Classroom films, on the other hand, are distributed to schools and school systems by *selling* copies of the films to those schools and systems. The distributor pays royalties to the producer, in much the same way that a publisher pays royalties to a writer of books. Producers of industrial films are paid immediately upon delivery of the finished films,* and payment will include all their costs and profit. They do not have to wait for payment beyond the usual time every supplier waits to be paid by customers. Producers of classroom films must be paid out of royalties, which probably will not even begin to come in for a year or so. They may very well make a larger profit after four or five years on their films than producers of industrial films, but they have to wait four or five years. This delay means that they have to pay for that money as though they had borrowed it, and this payment, if reckoned into the costs of production, reduces the profit. Partly for this reason, and partly because the possible returns are much less than the price of producing industrial films, classroom films are made at much lower budgets, generally. The fees for writing classroom films, therefore, are often much less in dollars than the fees for writing industrial films, even though the percentage of the total budget may be much the same.

---

*Actually, they receive "progress payments," e.g., one-third of the agreed production price on signing the contract, one-third on completion of major photography, and the final third on delivery of the first satisfactory copy.

Filmstrips and Sound Slidefilms

I have described earlier (chapter 6) what these media are and how they are constructed. Most often, producers of industrial or educational films also produce industrial or educational filmstrips and sound slidefilms. Distributors of educational films very frequently also distribute educational filmstrips and sound slidefilms. Therefore, all I have said about screen writing for these producers and distributors applies equally to the writing of filmstrips and sound slidefilms. It will, of course, continue to be your responsibility to gain control of your competencies and to direct them so that the best possible scripts for their purposes will find their way to producers' desks.

Television

What I have said about jobs in radio also applies to jobs in TV. Look carefully at the programs on the television broadcasts you watch, and you will see what kinds of programs are actually in existence. Analyze them. There are always news and sports programs, for example, and everything I have said about news and sports radio programs applies also to the same kinds of programs on television. You'll discover, too, lots of other programs that are broadcast regularly.

I have already stressed the far greater expense of preparing video material compared with the cost of preparing audio (radio) material. This serves, to some degree, to limit what jobs may be available for writers on local TV stations. It also limits the actual numbers of television stations.

Talk Shows and Comedy

But special commentators and personalities are still broadcast; they deliver what are essentially radio talks that are illustrated by still photographs, drawings, and, occasionally, film footage that is acquired from some library of film footage. (These are called libraries of *stock footage*.) Most often, if the subject matter is an event that has taken place locally, it will have been filmed by a camera person employed by the station itself, and the speaker—whether news announcer or specialty speaker—will need to learn how to write for the visuals. (Remember what I said earlier about complementary writing.)

You will notice that on your available television airways the talk shows and the game shows seem to be what they purport to be—unrehearsed. For shows like these, the only writing that may ever have to be done is some introductory or concluding continuity, which will be repeated every time the show is on the air. Even these unrehearsed programs, unless they are initiated locally, are probably supplied to your local station in the form of videotape copies or film copies.

In the same category, perhaps, fall the special programs of comedy–talk shows, such as the late night shows, which are introduced by a relatively brief bit of comedy patter, jokes, or other routines, and then continue with guests. Comedy material and the writers thereof form a tiny little world all their own. One begins by writing gags. Perhaps the most open door to this world is writing for night club comics, small names to start with. A comic may pay a few dollars—and you may be surprised how few!—for a gag. But, if you can sell her or him a number of them, she or he will come to rely on you, and you may have created a job for yourself. If your stuff is good, you will rise as he or she rises. On the other hand, if, for some reason, your stuff is better than the comic, you will have a portfolio of material to show to a bigger name. Some important comedy actors, writers, and directors had their beginnings this way.

While it may seem that this field of comedy writing is small—and it is—the insatiable maw of television uses up as much as can be written. There is always room for good gag writing and good writing of comedy routines.

Drama

What has been said about the difficulties of breaking into the profession of writing feature films applies also to television drama. But before discussing the difficulties, let's just see what kinds of television drama actually do exist.

I have talked about serials—soap operas, for example—and about series—the suspense, mystery, and police series and all the possible variants on these modes. There are comedy series, some of which are called family comedies and some of which aren't for the *whole* family.

In the United States there is virtually no such thing as a dramatic television program that is not sponsored, that is, which is not paid for by some kind of commercial advertising client. For a variety of reasons, there is no such thing as a quarter-hour dramatic program, and there are very few half-hour shows, other than comedies. Almost all television programs are in series in which at least one character, the star, is a constant. In such a program, the character of the star's part has been set, and you can't change it, nor can you change the kind of problem that serves as the crux of the drama nor the manner of the main character's extrication from the problem. These, too, have been set. You can modify them, but you can't really change them. Certainly it's unlikely if you are unknown. On the other hand, if you have a top-notch story that can somehow be fitted into the gross parameters of the program, all things are possible.

Soap operas and other serials are even more restricted. Their patterns are set, as we have discovered, and, unless you are already an established writer, there is really very little chance that you will be admitted into the circle.

Getting a Job

Apart from these difficulties, the degree to which the doors of the producers are closed to the neophyte is the same as for writers of feature films. Listen to Edward Adler: "Develop some material in which you have confidence. Get other people to read it, and if they agree with you that it is up to professional standards, it is time to find an agent. Do not send unsolicited material to studios or producers. I say this on a personal level and as an officer of the Writers Guild of America. Do not send unsolicited material unless you send it to agents who have readers, who accept unsolicited material. . . . Wait, hopefully, for some response. It will get read, and if there's anything in it, you will be contacted. You'll just have to trust a particular agent to respond to you and to help define to you where the markets are. . . . On the basis of the script you wrote they may recommend you. It's not so true with theatrical motion pictures—features—but it's true in television. The need for writers is enormous. The need for scripts is enormous. As you know, the machine is a cosmic vacuum cleaner. It just sucks up material. . . ."*

Thus, there is a strange paradox: there is a continuing need for writers, yet the producers and even the agents resist reading the work of new, unknowns. Here's how it works, in the words of Adler: "Material is solicited by producers from writers by way of the agent. The (story) editors and the producers have certain agents they call on and certain writers they call on. If it's a producer out in Hollywood, he will use mainly West Coast writers who do episodic writing. A new writer can't get a hearing unless he's brought in by another writer who has written successfully for the show, or an agent they know. And it will be done in a step deal. They'll listen to what you have to say, and if you've got an interesting story and they think you can do it, they'll give you an outline to do first . . . that's step one. If they like the outline, they'll pick up the option, and you'll be commissioned to do a teleplay."

And what about treatments? Here is what Adler says: "Yes, there is a market for treatments if you market them in the same way you market a finished screen play. It's more salable. But many times a new writer comes in with an idea, a very good idea, and he's not trusted with executing it. They'll buy the idea, they'll buy the treatment, and they'll assign another screen writer to it. We have some new provisions in our contract (Writers Guild of America) now which protect the new writer. Producers must now give you the option of writing or rewriting your original material. They can hire somebody else, ultimately, but they must give you first refusal. If you think you have a good idea, I would put it down in an eight or ten-page synopsis, not a treatment . . ."

How do you protect your idea from being taken without your permission? Adler advises: "Everything must be registered. You don't send it to

---

*A Conversation with a New York Television Writer (Chicago: Columbia College Press, 1977). (The conversation took place at the College on March 18, 1977.)

Washington. Send it to the Writers Guild . . . and get your material registered. . . . The copyright, of course, is really stronger protection, but if the Writers Guild registers it, it will serve in any litigation as a copyright."

The Writers Guild of America, as explained, is a kind of trade union for writers. Adler says, "The Guild is divided up into several divisions. . . . There's a screen writers' division, a television writers' division. Documentary and news writers are represented, and there are also the people who do soap operas. They're all in separate categories, and each writer in every particular discipline has a different contract he's working under. Daytime soap operas are covered under one kind of contract for serial writers. And then the news and staff writers, desk assistants, are under another agreement. We have now included in the Writers Guild East, to our credit, the graphic artists of all the studios, and the three networks. I don't know what they have to do with writing. But they came to us for help. We had a jurisdictional vote, and decided to include them."

Let us suppose that you do get a contract to write for a series, what then? "According to the Writers Guild Minimum Basic Agreement, if I hire you to write (an episode of a one-hour series), you are obliged by contract to provide me with a one-hour script—a first draft, a second draft, and one polish. Now, usually by the time you finish with that polish, the script still has to be rewritten to accommodate all the production problems, not to mention the director's rewrite, the star's rewrite, whatever. Because when you write an episode for television, and you sit and watch what gets on the screen, and you say, 'It bears no resemblance to what I did,' it's not because of any malicious intent. It's simply that they can't shoot what you've written—because of money, budget, production problems, and so forth. The story editor is there to do the fixing, and it is one of the hardest jobs in the world because you mainly deal with writers, and you work a lot of times with your own friends. . . . Story editors are the producers' henchmen. They're usually writers—most of them are writers. . . . My belief, after all these years in the business, is that the writer's first and second drafts are the best you are ever going to get out of him because that's where the original juice lies. I think beyond two drafts, a writer rewriting his own material is in trouble, if he's writing for television."

And yet, in spite of all this, the returns are high. You can ask the Writers Guild of America for a list of Guild pay scales, which are, of course, minimum payments for scripts. Well-known and tried writers are usually paid much more than minimum scale.

Thus, the paradox—a door through which entry is extremely difficult, almost impossible, and yet, successful passage through it is rewarded with extreme generosity. That must be the view of the writer who has not yet "made it" and looks wistfully at the prospect.

The resolution of the paradox is not impatience. There will be no success if you present work that is not professional. Even if writing by fledgling writers should somehow reach story editors or the producers, these toughened professionals would not be fooled. Remember, the mark of the professional is the consistency of quality, and this cannot be replaced by brilliant flashes in the pan.

The resolution of the paradox is simply to achieve professional experience, through which control of craft and good understanding of the medium emerge.

Television devours material and is never satisfied. It is terribly difficult to find the right door to enter and terribly difficult to enter it. But— there is *always room at the top,* and the compensation would fully satisfy even Pooh-Bah, who said, "I'll do anything if the insult's large enough!"

9

Being Professional
and Being Creative

At the beginning of this book I gave my definition of a professional: a professional is someone who makes a living by exercising a skill or a craft, or, if not a full living, then at least a consistent income. This cannot be achieved by working only sporadically, whenever the whim strikes you.

Edward Adler is a busy and successful television writer in New York. During a conversation with students of Columbia College in Chicago he said this: "I write from 9:00 until about 2:00 every day, seven days a week. . . . I've been known to write an hour's script in two days. I've also written an hour's script in two months. I sometimes produce only one or two pages a day. Sometimes I do twelve pages of script a day."*

Adler added: ". . . keep writing. You'll make it if you're dedicated enough. A lot of guys, for one circumstance or another, don't persevere. But from personal experience, I would say that if you write half an hour a day, every day of the week, you're going to produce volumes of work, some of which is going to be very good, a small bit of which is going to be excellent. Thomas Mann, a novelist, has written shelves of material. There were some days when he went down and sat in his study and produced eleven words. But he wrote every day of his life."

To this I can add a memory of John Grierson, the founder of the British documentary film movement. During World War I Grierson served in the British Merchant Marine as a sailor. He, too, wrote every day. Each day, lying in his hammock, he would write for at least an hour. He wrote about everything and anything, even if it was about the bolt in the bulkhead before his head. He wrote for the discipline and for the practice. After the war was over, Grierson came to the University of Chicago for his graduate degree, and while there he was an art critic for British newspapers. He had developed the skills of the writer in his hammock while at sea, and these skills are amply demonstrated in the film essays written years later.†

So much for being professional. What about creativity?

---

*A Conversation with a New York Television Writer.

†Forsyth Hardy, ed., Grierson on Documentary (New York: Harcourt, Brace, 1947).

First understand that the basic prerequisite for any kind of creative productivity in any kind of medium is the greatest possible control of its tools and its materials. Great control is often referred to as virtuosity. This is one of the reasons that I emphasize the need to be professional, for the professional, simply by the continued use of the tools and materials of his or her medium, becomes a virtuoso.

What has to be added to virtuosity for writers to be creative? Creative writers develop new ways of seeing things about them, new perceptions of all their experiences. By means of their competence in the medium in which they are working, they can express these views and these perceptions. Further, because of their new ways of seeing and perceiving the world around them and new ways of relating to all their experiences, they also see the medium in which they are working in new ways. They have new perceptions of how they can work within it. The ability to develop these new ways of working can only arise because they have such complete control of their tools and their materials. These are the means by which creative work is achieved.

Regardless of what I may have said to the contrary, you should *never stop wanting to experiment,* nor should you ever avoid any opportunity to experiment, to "play," with unfamiliar equipment—but be sure you do it with the help of someone who can operate these unfamiliar pieces of hardware and can prevent them from suffering some irreparable damage.

You don't have to listen to what such an expert may tell you about the "right way" to use a machine. If we always relied only on "the right way" to use anything, there would never be any innovation, never any creativity.

There are lots of different kinds of machines: sound tape recorders and sound tape players, videotape recorders and videotape players, record players, slide projectors, movie projectors, and live microphones, among other things. And there is much more: not necessarily one screen, but several; not necessarily one speaker, but several. And there are special audio (sound) tapes that have special inaudible sounds on them that will turn on and turn off any or all of other paraphernalia. As you might suppose, this is all included in the general term *multimedia.*

One warning: you will rarely be paid to experiment, to "play," especially when all the equipment is so expensive. Thus, you must experiment a little at a time, modestly, until you have developed something that might really catch the imagination of a producer or client. A large and gaudy collection of hardware from which emanate garish visuals and brash reverberations may very well be far less creative than something on a much smaller scale. Quantity or volume of sight and sound may very well be far less enticing than sensitive arrangements on fewer instruments. Remember, a good string ensemble does not make poorer music than a larger symphony!

Gradually, and to your vast delight, you will find that you will be able to learn the new audio-visual orchestra, and, having learned it and having learned how to create with it, three satisfactions will emerge. They are, in order of importance: your own joy, the pleasure and satisfaction of your client (or producer), and the burgeoning of your finances.

There is really no limit to the subjects you can write about and get paid for in the audio-visual media. You can indeed "talk of many things—of shoes and ships and sealing wax—of cabbages and kings." There are many people who want to persuade many more millions of people about one thing or another and are willing to invest money in the effort. There are many purposes to be achieved among many millions of people, not just once, but year after year after year; this means that each year new ways of saying these things have to be devised and new ways of exhibiting them have to be developed.

There is a great deal of opportunity for people to write for the various audio-visual media. These are mass media because of the large numbers of people in the audiences. They are also, in a real sense, a kind of mass media in terms of the numbers of people who can make a living at working in them. As in most other kinds of endeavor, there are lots of jobs for lots of people, but probably more truly than in other walks of life, there is always room at the top.

Basic Definitions

Story idea or
Story outline: This is a very brief outline, as its name implies, of the idea or thread of a story with the most prominent relationships between the major subject and the most important elements affecting it.

Synopsis: This is a fairly detailed summary, in prose fiction form, of a whole fiction story. It is almost always a stage of the development of a fiction film script.

Treatment: For a non-theatrical film, a treatment may be as short as a few pages or a score or more. Its major function is to present what might otherwise be a kind of synopsis, except that it includes *all* the cinematic thought that can be brought to bear at this stage of preparation. Full indications of visual treatment and full indications of sounds and music (or, at least, the types that will enhance the cinematic presentation) will be stated.

Screenplay: For a fictional film there is very little difference, if any, between a complete treatment and a screenplay. The excerpts from *Fifty-Seventh Street* (chapter 2), for example, are from a screenplay, but I have discussed them as though they were also detailed treatment.

Shooting Script: *A Film About Film Editing* (chapter 2) is a shooting script of a special kind: it was written *from* the finished film. A shooting script, compared to a screenplay, is fully developed in terms of the planned picture and sound editing. It is usually prepared by the director, and then it becomes very much like the prompt book of the theatre director.

Mostly Audio Terms

On mike: Spoken directly into the microphone to give the acoustic of proximity.

Off mike: Spoken far from the microphone or turned away from it to give the acoustic of distance.

Live sound: *1*) Sound with brilliance increased by resonance.
2) Recorded "live" in contrast with previously recorded ("canned") sound or music.

Dead sound:	Sound that "dies" immediately because there is no resonance at all.
Fade out:	1) To diminish the volume of the sound until it disappears. 2) To fade the brightness of the picture until it becomes totally black.
Fade in:	1) To increase the volume of sound until it is at normal level. 2) To increase the brightness of the picture from black until it is of normal brightness.
Mix or Dissolve:	1) To fade out one sound while at the same time fading in another. They are mixed transitionally. 2) To fade out one picture while at the same time fading in another.
Sync sound:	Sound recorded synchronously with picture, as with dialogue or machinery.
Wild sound:	Sound recorded without picture.
Indigenous sound:	The sound normally heard in the location of the photographed action, as waves at the beach, street noises at a sidewalk café, etc.
Voice over:	Sound that is not sync, such as narration.
Sneak in:	To fade in sound indiscernibly while picture or other sounds are going on, as to sneak in music under conversation.
Segue:	(pron. SEH-gway) An Italian word used as noun or verb to mean "mix" music or other sounds, on into the next.
Attacca:	Also Italian, meaning that music must continue immediately, without pause. Used as an imperative verb.

Visual Terms

Opticals or Optical Effects:	Anything done optically to the picture to manipulate the image, e.g., dissolves, fades, spins, wipes, multiple images, and so on.
Super:	Verb or noun. Lettering, such as titles or sub-titles, appearing as though printed on top of the image.
Image:	1) The picture seen on the screen. 2) Each of the pictures seen on a strip of motion picture film.
Frame:	1) The outline of the image. Also used as a verb: to "frame" the image means to select a camera position so that the proper or desired composition is "framed." 2) Each of the images on the strip of motion picture film.
Swish-pan or Blur-pan:	A pan in which the movement of the camera happens so swiftly that the clearly defined images at the beginning and end of the pan are separated by a movement that blurs the scene covered by the camera movement.

Some Common Abbreviations

M.P.:   Motion Pictures

pic, pix: picture, pictures

FX: effects

Sd.:   Sound

Index